CW01642372

ENGLISH IN A UNIVERSITY EDUCATION

By the same author:

Imaginings
Selected Poems
Bringing Everything Home

Flesh Wounds
A Play of Passion
Nothing Larger Than Life
Worlds Apart
A Little Athens
Jennifer
The Gold in Father's Heart
Even If They Fail
Getting it Wrong with Uncle Tom
Going Off the Rails
English for Maturity
English for the Rejected
The Secret Places
The Exploring Word
Children's Writing
English in Australia Now
Education, Nihilism and Survival
English for Meaning
Education and Philosophical Anthropology
The Quest for Love
Human Hope and the Death Instinct
Sex and Dehumanisation
Dylan Thomas: the Code of Night
Gustav Mahler and the Courage to Be
Sylvia Plath: Poetry and Existence
Lost Bearings in English Poetry
Evolution and the Humanities
The Novel and Authenticity
Images of Woman in Literature
The Skeleton in the Wardrobe: the Fantasies of C. S.Lewis
Edith Wharton and the Unsatisfactory Man
Where D.H. Lawrence Was Wrong About Woman
Charles Dickens and the Image of Woman
Creativity and Popular Culture
Tolstoy, Woman and Death
Wuthering Heights: a Drama of Being
A Study of George MacDonald and the Image of Woman
Nonsense Against Sorrow: a Study of Lewis Carroll's 'Alice' Books

ENGLISH IN A UNIVERSITY EDUCATION

DAVID HOLBROOK

Emeritus Fellow
Downing College, Cambridge

Cappella Archive

Cappella Archive : 2006

© 2006 David Holbrook
All Rights Reserved

Cover illustration of Downing College
courtesy of Professor Barry Everitt

No part of this publication may be reproduced or stored in a retrieval system, nor transmitted in any form or by any means — digital scanning, mechanical, photocopying, recording, or by any other media — without prior permission of the copyright owner.

British Library Cataloguing-in-Publication Data
A catalogue record for this book is
available from the British Library

ISBN 1-902918-35-5

Cappella Archive : Foley Terrace : Great Malvern
Printed and bound by Aspect Design Ltd., Great Malvern

Contents

Introduction 1
An Existentialist Approach 18
Differences from F.R Leavis 53
What is English in Practice? 72
English in Practice: Poetry 88
English in Practice: the Novel 152
Relationships, Learning, and Society 168
An English Syllabus 179
Epilogue 217
Bibliography 221
Index 229

For those who have been my students.

ACKNOWLEDGEMENTS

Some of the discussions of poems here were given as lectures for the Faculty of English at the University of Cambridge. Other material was given in lectures when the author was Hooker Distinguished Visiting Professor at the University of MacMaster, Hamilton, Ontario. A copy of this text was given to the English Faculty at Cambridge in response to an invitation for contributions to a consideration of the future of English studies in the university. The passage about Enobarbus's description of Cleopatra's barge was published in a symposium on English at the university in *Universities Quarterly* in autumn 1986.

The author wishes to express his gratitude to the Leverhulme Foundation for a grant during the period of this book's composition.

INTRODUCTION

As I cycle in to my college to work, there are workmen in safety hats pouring concrete, newspaper fly-sheets announcing some dreadful episode of war, derelicts already drinking cider from bottles on the benches of Parker's Piece, businessmen parking their cars. The citizens I pass are paying, one way or another, for me and my twenty students to spend the morning reading sonnets from Shakespeare, or discussing a novel by Dickens. My university, like others, is being urged by a utilitarian government to examine its effectiveness and in practice this inclination is experienced as a tendency to reduce the Humanities though the sciences are suffering too. How can we justify long periods of attention to literary fiction in such a world? How could I justify my activities to the politicians and the public or, perhaps more important, to myself?

At the moment of writing, I have written to the Secretary of the University Grants Committee, protesting against the pronouncements of the government, about the need to make education more accountable to the needs of society as they envisage it, suggesting that we were now faced with decisions on such matters being made by people who are not really equipped to understand them. He has replied sourly, telling me that he wishes he could hear that my faculty, the English Faculty, could agree upon its objectives — and he tells me that I idealise my subject. So, it seems a good time to take stock, and to try to redefine the discipline.

It is common knowledge that there was a crisis in the Cambridge English Faculty at the end of the seventies, over questions of teaching linguistics and literary theory. Whatever the facts of that matter, this was but one aspect of a general crisis. At one university I am told the Faculty almost came to delete Shakespeare from the syllabus altogether, while I have met senior lecturers who have given up, so much have they found themselves harrassed by Marxists and feminists who sought to use English studies for other purposes than the study of works as art, as literature. What I propose to do here is no more than a restatement of a traditional position, though I shall in fact invoke very radical new approaches to the nature of human nature and to the nature of knowledge. For at the root of any attempt to redefine English, I believe, must be an adequate definition of what kind of mode of knowing 'English' is. And at the same time, this redefinition must not be merely theoretical, as will emerge. It must take account of the intentional and creative elements of an Arts subject, such as help to transform the student as a being. In the end this comes down to teaching the reading of books as works of art, rather than literary theory.

There is a need for a discipline which is phenomenological in that it studies the mind-experience of the human being in whole terms. It adheres to the recognition of the 'I', and the exercise of consciousness by the whole being, to perceive and to make sense of his or her world. Only by finding such a discipline can a Humanities subject like English establish confidence in itself.

In much thinking about education in our time the lesson offered by Ernst Cassirer has not been learnt. There is a crisis in man's knowledge of himself. Research goes on by psychologists and educational philosophers: but the 'modern theory of man has lost its intellectual center':

> Can we be content with counting up in a merely empirical manner the different impulses we find in human nature? For a really scientific insight these impulses would have to be classified and systematized . . . we must suppose them to have a definite structure — and one of the first and most important tasks of our psychology and theory of culture is to discover this structure. In the complicated wheelwork of human life we must find the hidden driving force which sets the whole mechanism of our thought and will in motion. The principal aim of all these theories was to prove the unity and homogeneity of human nature. But if we examine the explanations which these theories were designed to give, the unity of human nature appears extremely doubtful . . . we acquired instead a complete anarchy of thought . . . Theologians, scientists, politicians, sociologists, biologists, psychologists, ethnologists, economists all approached the problem from their own viewpoints . . . within the special fields there was no generally accepted scientific principle. *An Essay on Man*, pp.20-21

Cassirer quotes Max Scheler, who declared that the ever-growing multiplicity of the particular sciences that are engaged in the study of men has much more confused and obscured our concept of man (*Die Stellung de Menschen im Kosmos*, Darmstad, Reichl,1928, p.13f). Cassirer goes on:

> Psychology, ethnology, anthropology and history have amassed an astoundingly rich and constantly increasing body of facts . . . we appear, nevertheless, not yet to have found a method for the mastery and organization of this material. Unless we succeed in finding a clue of Ariadne to lead us out of this labyrinth, we can have no real insight into the general character of human culture; we shall remain lost in a mass of disconnected and disintegrated data which seem to lack all conceptual unity. *An Essay on Man*, p.22

Cassirer's solution was to find man as the animal symbolicum: there is a 'new characteristic which appears to be the distinctive mark of human life' — a 'qualitative change' in 'the functional circle of many'. Man no longer lives in a merely physical universe: 'he lives in a symbolic universe':

> Language, myth, art, and religion are parts of this universe. *Ibid*. p.25

In the post-Kantian philosophy of Cassirer and his follower Susanne Langer, as in the work of Martin Buber, and Michael Polanyi, there has been further explanation of this new dimension in perspectives. Perhaps we may summarise it as the discovery of consciousness for you cannot find the symbolic universe in which man lives, unless you recognise consciousness (as some psychologists cannot). One of Cassirer's points was that we cannot discover the nature of men in the same way that we can detect the nature of physical things. Physical things may be discussed in terms of their objective properties, but man may be defined only in terms of his own consciousness.

Actually he starts from biology, and quotes Johannes von Uexküll who pointed out that every living organism has a world of its own, because it has an experience of its own. With man there is a qualitative difference — there is a symbolic system between the receptor system and the effector system: man is the animal symbolicum and it is impossible to understand him unless this achievement, of a culture, is taken into account.

Not only do we have to take the subject's experience, his consciousness and his symbolic system into account: the very idea of knowing is altered:

> For it is only in our immediate intercourse with human beings that we have insight into the character of man.

Knowledge of human nature cannot be gained except through a constant co-operation of the subjects in mutual interrogation and reply:

> Truth is not an empirical object; it must be understood as the outgrowth of a social act.

When we are discussing human experience in English studies in a novel or poem, we are engaged in the critical exploration of truth, in this way of 'constant co-operation in mutual interrogation and reply'.

Susanne Langer developed Cassirer's argument further. She sees the need for symbolization as a basic need in man:

> The symbol-making function is one of man's primary activities, like eating, looking and moving about. It is the fundamental process of the mind, and goes on all the time. *Philosophy in a New Key*, p.41

So, here we have a kind of philosophy which takes off from Kant's fourth question, 'What is man?' and finds man in a new dimension, as the creature who has an extra dimension of experience, culture, and is the symbolising creature whose poetic functions are at the basis of his thought and effectiveness. In English it is just those functions which we nourish.

In a society dominated not only by science and technology, but also by a mechanistic concept of life and man based on reductionism, it seems (even to some philosophers) that questions about entities which have no referent and cannot be found and measured or validated in any empirical way are not 'real': the way we talk about them is no more than 'emotive noises'. What we know from literature, from art, is that there are genuine realities and problems which are real and demand modes of thinking by which they can be explored. There is love: there is the mystery of death: there are the problems of suffering to which we respond, even if we are not believers, as in listening to a Bach mass: there is the problem of why we are here at all, and why there are snakes and whales and men — which Darwinian theory has certainly not solved. There are, that is, problems of existence: and it is legitimate to explore these by art, and through the philosophy of being.

Of course, it is important to be realistic and we in education must satisfy 'the demands' of society, industry and the 'real world'. Our conservative politicians talk a lot nowadays about education needing to be concerned with 'social needs' by which they mean the community has to pay for education, and so education should concern itself with preparing young people to be effective in the world. The economic system, the realists declare, is what makes the money, even to pay for the arts.

But since Blake and Dickens we can recognise this view as inadequate because there is another, primary reality to be considered — the reality of the human spirit and the need for fulfilment of being and for meaning. Without consciousness and culture, as education trains these, our life would have no significance. It is also true to say, as I argued in *English for Maturity* in 1961, that in fact the most effective way to bring children to effective literacy and the capacity to deal with reality is by training the imagination.

It is imagination that makes us human. Martin Buber, in an essay on 'distance and relation' discusses that which distinguishes men from the animals, a special act of 'making present' between men, in which 'at such a moment something can come into being which cannot be built up in any other way':

> It rests on a capacity possessed to some extent by everyone, which may be described as 'imagining' the real, I mean the capacity to hold before one's soul a reality arising at this moment but not able to be directly experienced. Applied to intercourse between men, 'imagining' the real means that I imagine to myself what another man is at this very moment wishing, feeling, per-

> ceiving, thinking, and not as a detached content, but in his very reality, that is, as a living process in this man. Distance and Relation in *The Knowledge of Man*, p. 70

The social and political importance of this kind of faculty should be plain. But we attend to it because it is here, in 'intersubjectivity' where we apply ourselves to those (tragic) problems urged upon us by the recognition of our 'being-unto-death'.

Bernard Beronzi once criticised the late F.R. Leavis for trying to make English a 'religious' subject. There was some justification for this allegation, since Leavis obviously believed English studies have a beneficial influence, through which the study of great literature would refine an individual and make for a trained sensibility and intelligence which could rescue our civilisation. In the end, Leavis seemed to despair of education ever bringing about a redemption of society. This, however, as I shall argue, arose even because of his idealism, and the lack of psychological realism in his concepts of what reading can do for human nature.

On the other hand, we cannot surely deny that insofar as the Humanities are upheld in schools and universities they help sustain the meanings of a civilisation? While English may not be a substitute for religion, it is a discipline concerned with meaning. As I pointed out in *Lost Bearings in English Poetry*, 1979, many modern writers have been troubled by the question suggested by Michael Polanyi in *Meaning* (written with Harry Prosch and published by Chicago University Press, 1975) that the world of positivistic science seems to cancel out all meanings:

> We think the world is absurd because it seems to us that there is no point to what transpires in it, i.e., that there is no end or aim or purpose to the whole business. It seems to us that there is no meaning to the universe — except possibly the subjective meanings that man tries to import into it. But, in the end, the universe cancels these out. Man thus sees himself as a little boy who continually repairs and rebuilds his sandcastles at the edge of the sea, only to see the waves continually washing them away. *Meaning*, p.162

The attempt to create meaning in culture thus seems only a gesture of defiance against the meaninglessness of the universe of randomly colliding atoms.

Positivism has extended its influence into philosophy and so into the realm of what we believe to be 'true'. In science, nothing can be said to exist which is not susceptible to measurements: only measurements are real. So, in philosophy, every statement must be verifiable: all those questions which belong to being are non-questions, because they escape such validation.

The language of poetry belongs to the non-questions, in this view: it becomes a vehicle of what I.A. Richards called 'pseudo-statements'. Poetry comes to seem more tale-telling, at least invention and entertainment, at most obscurity and untruth: and this means not only the craft of making verses, says Marjorie Grene, but 'the whole work of the imagination, myth and metaphor, dream and prophesy'. (*Approaches to Philosophical Biology*, p.51). Yet, as we know from (say) *King Lear*, there are problems of being, and literature enables us to understand them and grapple with them in a 'whole' way, encompassing both inner and outer reality.

Here the work of Michael Polanyi provides a valuable antidote to the limitations of the 'objective' paradigm. Polanyi insists that thinking is done by men and women who live in bodies, and the springs of their thinking are ineffable: they can never ultimately be found, or made explicit. The 'leap of the imagination' is a crucial element here. The subjective life is as much involved in science as in anything else: science is scientists as men doing something, trying to make sense of their experience. Personal participation and imagination are as involved in science as well as in the Arts. All scientific findings are contingent and have to be continually upheld, shared and recreated: there is no 'objective' knowledge which we could write down if we had a blackboard big enough. So. there is no call to regard scientific truths as realities and the subjects of the Humanities non-real, or to do with values that are in some way separate from facts, so that the Humanities are left only dealing with fancies.

Here we enter upon a whole profound philosophical argument, with which the existentialists have been very much concerned. It can be related to Cassirer's point: since man cannot be understood in the terms of objective science, what happens if science is the one uncontested authority in the world, and only those things defined by its mathematical laws and its measurable verifiables are allowed to be 'real'? Man and his symbolic achievements cannot be found in the world, while all those things which we most care about disappear from it. This universe thus appears to be meaningless, and man's life — a chemical accident — becomes futile and absurd.

Can we live in this world? This was the question put by Edmund Husserl in his book *The Crisis of European Sciences*.

> Can the world, and human existence in it, truthfully have a meaning if the sciences recognise as true only what is objectively established, by excluding all question of the reason or unreason of human subject matter and cultural configuration?

Science 'excludes in principle precisely the questions which man . . . finds the most burning': questions of the meaning of human existence. But there is a clue to the solution within science itself. Why are scientists interested in their work? They are fascinated by the world not because it is a chaos of chance and accident — but because it displays a fantastic degree of order. Biology especially speaks another language, other than the equiprobable language of what sequence or shape might be expected to emerge from the 'laws'. Moreover, it is clear from the interaction of scientist and world, 'there is something else in the universe other than matter in motion', as Marjorie Grene puts it: 'there is conscious mind.'

So, Polanyi declares:

> Our modern science cannot properly be understood to tell us that the world is meaningless and pointless, that it is absurd — The supposition that it is absurd is a modern myth, created imaginatively from the clues produced by a profound misunderstanding of what science and knowledge are and what they require . . . *Meaning*, p.131

The world in fact is full of meaning, and there is such order in the universe that none of our theories have yet proved capable of explaining it.

> There is too much order in the world to be explained without reference to some principle operative towards more meaningful or regular relations. A.N. Whitehead, quoted in *Meaning*, p.163

There has been a long hostility and distrust of the poetic,coming our way from science: Galileo distrusted poetry and the utilitarian Bentham called it 'push-pin'. But in truth poetry (as William Blake knew) is a serious corrective to the way in which the ideal of 'scientific objectivity', seeking wholly explicit, wholly certified, truth, 'falsifies the nature of the knower and the known, of mind and the world' as Marjorie Crene puts it.

Husserl believed that the scientific revolution betrayed the original *telos* of the movement of Greek thought dissociating the objective pursuit of the external world from the investigation of subjective reality. Poetry and the study of poetry, as disciplines of thought, are correctives to this, not least in recognising the existentialist dimension of the unique life of the 'I: the dimension of which Blake, Dickens and Lawrence were aware, the dimension of being, and upheld against the quantitative threat to this from a machine society with its utilitarian ideas.

Recognition of the unique life of the 'I' requires that we take into account the inner or subjective life. So, a related discipline in philosophical anthropology which I shall invoke here is psychoanalysis.

There is still much resistance to the insights of psychoanalysis in a positivistic age. However, I take it from E.A.Burtt, author of *The Metaphysical Foundations of Modern Science*, that philosphy must come to terms with the findings of pyschotherapists. In a book called *In Search of Philosophical Understanding* (1967) he says he is convinced that:

> . . . philosophy must come fully to terms with the psychoanalytical concept of the human mind . . . the crucial fact can no longer be ignored that behind anyone's thinking there are unconscious motives, to be taken into account beside the desire for truth.

The trouble is, of course, that there are many schools of psychoanalytical thought, and the 'model' of human nature in these changes all the time. However, whichever school of psychoanalysis we take, there is one common factor which is not always recognised as primary. As Ian D.Suttie pointed out in *The Origins of Love and Hate* (1935) in his critique of Freud, there was a great difference between Freud's theory and his practice.

Freud's theory attempted to reduce everything to a somewhat bleak functional scheme — with the Death Instinct in the background — and it seemed to Suttie to belong to hate: the practice was based on love, and contained that element of care which was not visible in the somewhat quantitative theory. But there is another dimension: psychoanalysis is a talking cure, and also a dreaming and fantasying cure. That is, as well as love, there is a creative, symbolic element: the patient gives the analyst his dreams, and the analyst has to show that he understands them, as by his interpretations. He 'hears' the meanings and orderings such as the patient can bring: or helps as mid-wife to this process — and so psychotherapy is a version of the mother-child relationship, as is teaching. It is one of those processes which involve imagination.

So Freud's great work, was thus phenomenological — it was insight into the meanings of manifestations of consciousness. Jung, of course, was also fascinated by symbols, while Melanie Klein, who analysed children, established the importance of fantasy in all mental life. And there have been important books on case-histories which show clearly the role of symbolism and creative culture in cures, such as Marion Milner's *In the Hands of the Living God*, 1969, and Marie von Naevestad's *The Colours of Rage and Love* 1978.

It was D.W.Winnicott who combined psychoanalysis with paediatrics, who finally brought culture to the centre of the psychoanalytical model. Freud, he believed, never found the 'place' for culture. Freud tended to think of 'cure' in terms of the 'release' of instincts. But Winnicott found that it was useless talking like this to psychotic patients who wanted to know what life was about: like Raskolnikov in *Crime and Punishment* they needed first to find out whether they were human, and what was the point of life.

Winnicott traces the origins of culture to the child's first symbol. He calls this the 'transitional object'—-the cuddly rag, like Linus's blanket in 'Peanuts': it symbolises the child's possession of the mother. He needs it, with its feel and smell, when he is alone in the dark. So, it belongs to that strange area between mother and infant and between self and world, in its beginnings. It manifests both union and separateness — it goes with developing inner resources that enable the child to be alone, and it unites him to the mother and so to all other human beings. It stands for the 'other' and so is his first metaphor.

All these characteristics remain in the child's culture as it develops: his language both enables him to commune with himself and to know himself: but also links him with all other human beings who have used that language. It is important to note that the emergence of the self as between mother and infant is an imaginative act and also an act of creative reflection: the child sees himself emerging in the mother's eyes and responds: 'being for' is thus the basis of a capacity to perceive the world as real and meaningful. Exposure to a creative culture, which is an extension of the mother's original responsiveness in play, is thus the basis of an effective capacity to perceive the world in a meaningful way.

As Winnicottt says, as we possess the capacity to symbolise, we employ it on those two questions, about the nature of being human, and the question of the point of life. This last links Winnicott's kind of psychoanalytical thinking with that of the existentialists and *Daseinsanalysis* based on phenomenology. This branch of psychotherapy has been influenced by the philosophy of Martin Heidegger. Man is a questioning being, the only being for whom Being is in question. But man is also continually being-unto-death, and so he is daunted and haunted by the perplexity as to whether his life has any meaning before he is swept away into nothingness. He can try to establish a sense of meaning by 'little nameless acts of kindness and of love': or by domestic tasks, like baking a pie or mending a wardrobe: or he can create art — trying to make sense of his life by symbolism. Perhaps (as I try to argue over Mahler's last symphonies), all he can achieve, if he is an agnostic, is a sense of gratitude for having existed.

Thus, these subjective yearnings are the primary need of a patient: he needs first to find whether there is any point in his existence: he needs to feel the *Dasein* — the sense of 'being there', of having been meaningfully 'there' in the world: and in our world, of course, as when people are deprived of their role by unemployment, this is not easy.

Thus, the discipline of Psychotherapy, in which doctors sit hour after hour helping human beings to find their sense of identity, we find *symbolic meaning* is at the centre of the picture: culture is primary, and the sense of humanness and role in the world is foremost. The implication is that Poetry, the Arts and the Humanities are not fringe benefits, but provide for a primary need.

The disciplines which I have been invoking overlap, and there is a great deal more to say. There is an urgent need to bring into our thinking the perspectives of phenomenology, the study of the phenomena of consciousness, which requires us to develop a psychology which is not limited to the paradigms of Behaviourist or associationist psychology, but which finds the dynamics of which Coleridge was aware — that our perception of the world is an active process, and that 'meaning is an intention of the mind'. With phenomenology we may associate existentialism, which sees dangers in the abstractions and limitations of modern thought, and attends to the whole experience of being. As Kierkegaard said, 'What is abstract thought? It is thought without the thinker.' We need to restore the recognition of the unique experiencing being, who has only the one life and the one consciousness. Again. this is a lesson which we can recognise in William Blake, Charles Dickens (cf. *Hard Times*) and D.H. Lawrence.

We may find help in science too: in philosophical biology there is a new recognition of the special nature of living things — finding them as experiencing beings with 'centricity' and finding in man the additional dimension of culture — and of love. Man has a 'special way of being' as Martin Buber puts it, and this is derived from relationship: man lives in a 'mansion of consciousness' and can be aware of before and after, and of other places in space, because of the capacity to 'be at a distance': this power of consciousness is created by love. The great phenomenon of man is his 'connection with an otherness' — our special 'category of being' is a product of love.

All these disciplines speak a very different language from the reductionist, 'objective', mechanistic approach to man which dominates our thinking. Discourse on them meets with hostility still in Britain, and some ridicule, but they are disciplines which have great authority in Europe, and are beginning to be understood here and in America (where Northwestern University Press and Basic Books have done some superb pioneering work).

The important thing about this kind of 'philosophical anthropology' is that it not only vindicates a Humanities subject like English, but makes it clear that in such a subject we are concerned with the very basis of human consciousness — with what makes us man and woman, and so it underpins the traditional way in which we have been working anyway.

In reading Shakespeare, for example, we enter into, we experience, the consideration of the relationship between the individual consciousness and the claims of the social order. We are also drawn more deeply into knowledge of ourselves: insofar as we can be like Macbeth deeply divided against ourselves: or like Lear, self-deceiving and tyrannical: or like Antony and Cleopatra, irresponsible, cruel, playful, contemptuous of paltry normal life but capable of magnificent devotion to passion.

Given we are all capable of being like these, how can we believe that it is possible for man to be governed well: and how possible is it for us to find meaning and values to live for — in being-unto-death? In Shakespeare, Pope, Melville's *Moby Dick*, in the poetry of Emily Dickinson and Gerard Manley Hopkins, and in D.H. Lawrence, we find intelligence struggling with the question of man's relationship with Nature. Man is the creature who can conceive the possibility of a will to urge 'nature's germens split at once' — and so, we are engaged with the urgent question — is it possible for man to avoid destroying his world? There is no need to underline the special immediacy of that problem, but with Macbeth we are taken into the experience of the possibility of giving ourselves over to evil (demonology), and in such a wholly-engaged way that it is impossible for us to escape recognition of the dangers. We have to 'live' them.

I continue to be amazed to find how much pain students have to experience, if they are to find literature satisfying — identifying with the painful experiences of the ill-treated child David Copperfield; the final desperation and misery of Faustus; the disillusioned unhappiness of Dorothea Brooke (Mrs Casaubon) and the forfeiture of his life-hopes by Dr Lydgate in *Middlemarch*; the 'terrible' sonnets of Hopkins in his wrestling with God; and Matthew Arnold's sense of the sea of faith withdrawing from the world in *Dover Beach*, to say nothing of the agony of bewilderment at the end of *King Lear*. Yet we emerge from these literary experiences with a kind of elation, because we know we have confronted some of the worst possibilities with which life could present us — and we have been inspired by the courage and effort with which these experiences have been faced. These are experiences which belong to the *Dasein* in the face of being-unto-death, as literature can bring them to us, in symbolic form.

I was surprised, when I went back into teaching English at Downing College, in 1982, to find that the kind of gravity with which I had become accustomed to tackle the subject in adult education was felt to be a barrier, not least to the chances of the students. One could, it seemed, confront the examinations in English literature without exposing oneself to any deep involvement in meaning or even emotional response. One student, I remember, protested that he wasn't going to allow himself to be moved by *King Lear* — why should it have any effect on him? It was fiction, he pronounced scathingily.

Of course, it is true that there is problem with undergraduates, that they have comparatively little experience of life, and, being young, are insouciant and light-hearted about many of the problems of life. In a sense, they couldn't afford to be wracked by tragedy and by works which deal with frustration and disappointment. On the other hand, unless they are moved by the works of the literary imagination, they cannot be said to have begun to experience the disciplines of a Humanities subject. No doubt the growth of the present tendency, to substitute clever theoretical analysis, as in literary theory, for the sensitive reading of actual works, has to do with this inclination, in today's world, to avoid the human substance at the heart of good literature.

My case for *gravitas* may be substantiated by drawing on the obserservations of those who report on the serious confrontations of the consulting-room in psychotherapy. Here a most valuable book in *Existential Psychotherapy*, by Irvin D.Yalom. This was published in 1980 by Basic Books, and provides a useful sequel to the important landmark edited by Rollo May and others in 1958, *Existence — a new Dimension in Psychiatry*, also published by Basic Books. This symposium had a profound effect on psychotherapy in America, by bringing to the attention of the discipline the philosophical movement which inspired the 'continental' existentialist therapists. Those who worked in this area, as Yalom points out, tended to become overwhelmed in the 60s and 70s by a wide range of movements which seized on 'self-expression' and various forms of self-improvement and the seeking of 'freedom' which often generated doubts among the leaders. However, Yalom performs an important task in taking up the theme, to introduce some disciplined and studied attention to the existentialist movement in psychotherapy. And in doing so, he makes on the one hand a profound critique of modern Western society, and offers at the same time stance which we can make use of in the Humanities and English. He says,

> "If we can brush away or 'bracket' the everyday world, if we reflect deeply upon our 'situation' in the world, upon our existence, our boundaries, our possibilities, if we arrive at the ground that underlies all other ground, we invariably confront the givens of existence, the 'deep structures' which I shall henceforth refer to as 'ultimate concerns'." p.8

His book deals with four ultimate concerns: death, freedom, isolation and meaninglessness. He asserts that the fundamental problem with all of us is that we are aware of our mortality. There is in us a core existential conflict between the awareness of the inevitability of death and the wish to continue to be. Where our our symbolic creativity is concerned, we are all concerned with the need to construct meanings in our lives which can endure beyond our death. Under the heading of freedom Yalom is thus concerned with the clash between our confrontation with groundlessness and our wish for ground and structure. Beneath us there is no ground — nothing, a void, an abyss. Yalom stresses our existential isolation: each of us enters existence alone — and must depart from it alone. We must each of us construct our own meaning in life. Yet can a meaning of one's own creation be strong enough to bear one's life.

Yalom emphasises the value of great literature: 'the great novelist', he says, 'however his personality may be split among many characters, is ultimately self-revelatory', and so requires us to confront the problems of existence that impel his art.

In the end, says Yalom, the therapist's goal is what he calls engagement: he declares that we are all today affected by what he calls the 'galactic view' — the sense of the vast expanses and movements of the universe, in the light of which the individual's choices and actions seem insignificant.

> Engagement is the therapeutic answer to meaninglessness regardless of the latter's source. Wholehearted engagement in any of the infinite army of life's activities not only disarms the view but enhances the possibility of one's completing the patterning of the events of one's life in some coherent fashion. To find a home, to care about other individuals, about ideas or projects, to search, to create, to build —— these, and all other forms of engagement, are twice rewarding: they are intrinsically enriching, and they alleviate the dysphoria that stems from being bombarded with the unassembled brute data of existence.

The desire to engage life is always there in the patient, says Yalom: the therapistst's preoccupation is with the removing of obstacles in the patient's way.

> What, for example, prevents the patient from loving another invidual? Why is there so little satisfaction from relationship with others? What are the parataxic distortions that systematically poison his or her relationships? What blocks the patient from finding work that is commensurate with his or her talents or finding pleasurable aspects of current work? Why has the patient neglected his or her creative or religious or self-transcendent strivings?

From this, we can see the difference between the aim of therapy and those of the teacher in the Humanities. We are not concerned with removing barriers to self-fulfilment in this way: but we are concerned with providing sources of meaning, taking it for granted that the 'desire to engage life' is always there. We too are concerned with promoting 'engagement', and the final sentences of Yalom's book apply to us, too: 'the question of meaning in life is, as the Buddha taught, not edifying. One must immerse oneself in the river of life and let the question drift away.'

AN EXISTENTIALIST APPROACH

I want if possible to cut across present debate about the nature of English studies by suggesting what I call an existentialist approach to English — a concern to pursue the discipline as having to do with the nature of being. This approach is based on philosophical anthropology and the various disciplines indicated above.

First, I should like to try to say what a university is, or should be. Here I would like to invoke a view which comes itself from philosophical anthropology. A substantial definition was offered not many decades ago by a distinguished university philosopher who himself narrowly avoided being destroyed by the Nazis, Karl Jaspers. Jaspers, just after escaping by the skin of his teeth, attempted to define a university, and its value to society, in his book *The Idea of the University* (Peter Owen. 1960)

> Society wants the university because it feels that the pure service of truth somewhere within its orbit serves its own interests. p.132

It is essentially this belief — tacitly held — that justifies the huge annual expenditure on the universities in our country today: the implicit feeling that, as Jaspers declares the university is meant to function as the intellectual conscience of an era. (p.132)

Of course, the university is also devoted to practical ends, training young men and women to work in industry, commerce, the professions, politics and education. But it is also important to regard the university as a place where 'Value judgements and practical action are suspended in favour of the ideal or pure truth.' This does not mean, however, that a university can be neutral. 'A life away from the arena of practical affairs is meaningful only if sustained by a passion for learning and understanding', for there are serious dangers of corruption in detachment:

> Suspension of value judgements may degenerate into mere neutralist indifference; suspension of practical activity, into laziness: intellectual caution, into neurotic fear of any challenge to enfeebled energies. (p.133)

We need to recognise that the idea of a university is Greek in origin and is part of Western tradition. Learning belongs essentially to the original *telos* of Greek civilisation, a point which Edmund Husserl makes in *The Crisis of European Sciences*. The crisis with which Husserl was concerned may be seen to be related to Ernst Cassirer's diagnosis of an intellectual dilemma: the failure of modern science to find man's existence and the 'subjective' realm: devotion to the 'objective' science has been very successful, practically, but it has concentrated on the realities which can be measured and are 'out there'.

The realities of man's experience and all that is to be known by the *Geisteswissenschaften*, or ways of understanding the 'spirit' and the inward life, have been neglected, so that today's world is in awe of the truths and technologies found and devised by science, but equally feels that life has no meaning, because science has been silent about the meaning of life, and does not concern itself with the *Menschentum*.

There is a parallel crisis, in our culture, where there has also been a loss of meaning as we have seen. Here, the relationship between the university and culture at large is of great significance.

As Jaspers says, we cannot define this existential role of the university in a few sentences, but we can define it indirectly. This function, difficult though it is to define, is yet crucial in our lives: there are many issues in and around the university:

> . . . but these must not be allowed to obscure the all-important one: the ideal of the university which is the very life-blood of higher education. This ideal cannot be reduced to a few simple statements (but) . . . we are deeply committed to this ideal which has given meaning to our life . . . we know that truth, striving all around us to be seen and recognized, will live or perish with our ability to realize the ideal of the university in its ever-changing forms. (p.146)

These are the concluding sentences of his book, and in them we can catch the grateful note of one who has experienced the most menacing voice of barbarism — and survived.

Newman's famous conception of the university perhaps smacked a little of a finishing school for a Victorian English gentleman. But the best of his *The Idea of a University* displayed a case for liberal education which has been revived and strengthened, in the kind of way F.R. Leavis suggests in his *Education and the University*. Newman said: 'A university education gives a man a clear conscious view of his own opinions and judgements, a truth in developing them, an eloquence in expressing them and a force in urging them.' The similarity between Newman's concern for the university as having to do with truth and Jaspers' definition of a university as intellectual conscience is pointed out in the English edition, in the Preface of *The Idea of the University*, by Professor O. Zangwill. As Zangwill points out, Jaspers came to philosophy through medicine and especially psychiatry, where his influence is still fertile. And he has been influential as a proponent of existentialism which (Zangwill reports) has not really penetrated English philosophy as it has penetrated philosophy on the continent.

Jaspers' existential bias does not lead him to a rejection of technology: he sees technology as a new and vital element in our culture. He does not: want technology relegated to marginal institutions: it should have a central place in the university structure. This in itself may help technology to achieve a genuine relationship with the Humanities.

As Zangwill says, 'It is throughout upon the moral values of the university that Professor Jaspers dwells'. The University, as he sees it, is an instution characterised simply by loyalty to the idea of truth, no matter how awkward its intellectual or social consequences.(p.11)

Jaspers, indeed, begins:

> The University is a community of scholars and students engaged in the task of seeking truth. (p.15)

The university derives its autonomy from an 'imperishable idea of supernational, world-wide character, academic freedom.'
'Academic freedom is a privilege', Jaspers declares. It entails the 'obligation to teach truth, in defiance of anyone outside or inside the university who wishes to curtail it. But this depends upon very subtle and tenuous articles of faith, passion, ideals and convictions:

and it depends, of course, of what kind of definition of truth you uphold. This means that debate must always be open. We must uphold the 'human right that man must be allowed somewhere to pursue truth unconditionally and for its own sake.' (p.19) There is nothing anti-scientific in this. The idealism of science itself must be borne in mind. It is 'to seek for truth without limit and at any price'. The emphasis on freedom is related to the need to realise potentialities:

> Without this determination to drive him on (man) could never climb to those levels of insight of which he is capable. (p.20)

The university, says Jaspers, is the corporate realization of man's basic determination to know. There may be polarities and conflicts, but the unity of knowledge survives nonetheless. Despite diversity in subjects, scholars remain united by the *Wissenschaften*. The translator of Jaspers' book uses the phrase 'common scientific outlook' but tells us in a footnote that throughout the book both the sciences that the *Geisteswissenschaften* are equal in importance, as Jaspers would certainly agree. The goal is also understanding, and this requires the involvement of the whole man (p.21). For the truth of the subjective world is as important as an object of investigation, as it is in (say) Music, English, Theology and the various disciplines we may class under the heading 'philosophical anthropology'.

Jaspers then goes on to examine the intellectual life: science and scholarship are 'meaningful only insofar as they are part of a comprehensive intellectual life.'

He goes on to place scientific endeavour in the wider context of faith and ideas:

> Spirit (*Geist*) human existence, and responsive reason make up the all-inclusive context of our lives. Spirit is the potentiality and power of ideas. Human existence in its fullest sense signifies our serious and unconditional commitment to the search for transcendence. Responsive reason is the mind open to the intrinsic meaning of things.
>
> Spirit lives and moves wherever our striving for clarity is a striving for fullness of insight . (p.44)

In the wake of Jaspers' definition of science this enables us to take into account the kind of idealism and faith that sustains science. As Michael Polanyi argues, despite the tendency to regard science as 'objective', it is nothing of the kind. It is an intellectual edifice which is raised from the subjective life of each scientist, whose intuitive gifts and commitment impel his quest — while the whole edifice itself is impelled by passion and involvement. Jaspers goes on:

> 'spirit is the power of creative intuitions: without imagination science remains sterile. Such imagination enables us to see what is essential and real, to understand from within, that which lies below the surface, and to make this available '. (p.44)

The same is surely true of the humanities, that we must judge work in terms of the 'power of creative intuition', and that there, too, 'imagination enables us to see what is essential and real.' Culture, says Jaspers, is an acquired state: like Husserl, he traces the historical antecedents back to the Greek idea: 'The liberal arts study the spirit: (*Geist*, mind), of man . . . All of university life depends upon the nature of people participating in it.' Jaspers implies what Michael Polanyi has said: we spend our lives in service to ideals we can never hope to realise. The university stands between the state and the ideal derived from Greek civilisation:*

> As a publicly endowed institution the university belongs to the state as a privately endowed institution it is, certainly, part of a given national scene. In either case, it is the expression of a whole people. Seeking truth and the improvement of mankind, the university seems to stand for man's humanity par excellence. Humanities is part of its very fabric, no matter how often and how deeply that term has changed its meaning. (p.45)

Those who work for the university 'serve all mankind solely through the medium of intellectual creativity.' The purpose of

*As Edmund Husserl says in his *Crisis* (1970: see Bibliography), 'Spiritual Europe has a birthplace. It is the ancient Greek nation in the seventh and eighth centuries BC. Here there arises a new sort of attitude of individuals towards their surrounding world.' (p.276ff)

English studies must surely be seen within this kind of overall existentialist view of the university as a human institution?

Accepting Jasper's view of the university then, let me go on to try to develop a concept of English studies within the university, a philosophy of English based on the recognition of man as the animal symbolicum, as the animal to whom culture is a primary need and the basis of all his thinking and his acts, his effectiveness. In this perspective English is one of those subjects (like music, dance, drama, painting) which deals with a primary need and a primary dynamic of human life, in the symbolic quest for meaning and truth.

It is this kind of meaning and truth we talk about, whether we discuss a passage from *King Lear* or *What Malsie Knew* or *Four Quartets*. It is true that what we say should be supported and controlled by what we can show is in the text: but discussion of what Leavis called the 'upshot' of a work may lead us into all kinds of spheres, from the study of demonology, to the problem of whether life can have any meaning at all (as, say, over some 'black' modern drama). English is a phenomenological subject, which has to do with the nature and phenomena of consciousness: and in that it attends to experience as such, it deals not only with 'what is', but must concern itself with potentialities of being, and so it is an existentialist subject — not least because it alters us as we make our explorations.

English studies, I believe, have a clear existential function.

Existentialism is the endeavour to understand man by cutting beneath the cleavage between subject and object which has bedevilled western thought and science since shortly after the Renaissance. On this Rollo May quotes Ludwig Binswanger, who calls this cleavage, 'the cancer of all psychology up to now . . . the cancer of the doctrine of subject object cleavage of the world'. The 'whole' response to literature as experience, such as F.R. Leavis always emphasised, has a clear value in healing this cleavage. But of course there were earlier attempts to develop ways of understanding human beings which we might now call existentialist — Socrates in his dialogues, St. Augustine in his depth-psychological analysis of the self, Pascal's struggle to find a place for 'the heart's reasons which the reason knows not of'. But the main thrust of existentialism began last century with Kierkegaard's protest against the reigning rationalism of his day. 'Truth exists' he declared, 'only as the individual produces it in action'.

He protested against the rationalists and idealists who, like Hegel, would see man only as a subject. But he also fought against the tendency to treat men as an object to be calculated as the utilitarians calculated, and controlled thus (which is the impulse castigated in Dickens' *Hard Times*): so, existentialism is a protest against the whole tendency in our era to make human beings into anonymous robots to fit the vast industrial and political collectivisms of our day. This is of course the theme of Leavis's edition of *Mill on Bentham and Coleridge* (1950), and it was a theme in *Culture and Environment* (1933) which he wrote with Denys Thompson.

Rollo May elaborates usefully here, on the concept of 'reason', in relation to existentialism (*Existence — a New Dimension in Psychiatry*, 1958). He distinguishes between 'reason' as the term was used in the seventeenth century and the Enlightenment, and 'technical reason' today. Spinoza and the other thinkers of the seventeenth and eighteenth century had a confidence that reason could comprehend all problems. But their concept of reason included the capacity to transcend the immediate situation, to grasp the whole, and such functions as intuition, insight, poetic perception were not excluded. One concept also included ethics: reason in the enlightenment also meant justice. Much that was irrational was included in reason. May quotes Freud's phrase, 'ecstatic reason'.

But by the end of the nineteenth century this ecstatic quality had been lost. Reason had become 'technical reason' — reason married to techniques, as all adjunct to technical industrial progress, split off from emotion and will — 'reason, indeed, as opposed to existence': the kind of reason which Kierkegaard and Nietzsche attacked.

These saw that it was a delusion that reality could be comprehended in an abstract, detached way. They were however not antirational. We must not only study a person's experience as such, they held, but study the man who is doing the experiencing. They insist that 'Reality or Being is not the object of cognitive experience, but is rather "existence", is Reality as immediately experienced, with the accent on the inner, personal character of man's immediate experience'. (Tillich)

Existentialism, one must also emphasise, not least to those who share Leavis's views of 'philosophy', does not set out to be a comprehensive philosophy, nor a way of life. It is an endeavour to grasp the whole of reality in a more total way. It accepts man as always becoming and includes his intentionality — the way in which, in his life-time, lie is always bringing something into being. Rollo May quotes Pascal:

> When I consider the brief span of my life, swallowed up in the eternity before and behind it, the small space that I fill, or even see, engulfed in the infinite immensity of spaces which I know not, and which know not me, I am afraid, and wonder to see myself here rather than there; for there is no reason why I should be here rather than there, now rather than then . . . (*Pensées*, 1946, p.87)

This is an expression of the contingency of human life, *Geworfenheit*, or 'thrownness', experienced in the realm of unique being.

Existentialism set out to cure our inadequate thought about man. But it is not only a question of thought, because there is a sense in which we come to be what we think of ourselves. The neurotic personality of the late nineteenth century, as Freud found, was one suffering from fragmentation and division against itself — repression of instinctual drives, blocking off of awareness, loss of autonomy, weakness and passivity of the ego, together with other symptoms which result from the fragmentation.

Kierkegaard analysed in *The Sickness Unto Death* the depression and despair which results from self-estrangement. Nietzsche, in his early work, speaks of how the soul of man had 'gone stale', and there was a 'smell of failure': man had lost faith in himself. Blocked impulses were turning to resentment, self-hatred, hostility and aggression.

May also points out other forms of fragmentation: the division of public from private life (as in Ibsen's *The Doll's House*): the separation of art from life (as in academic life — a division which Leavis sought to heal); the separation of religion from weekday existence (see the work of R.H.Tawney); the denial that one was ever a child, or has the child's irrationality and lack of control (which Freud was to unravel).

In Victorian life, in which these divisions and fragmentations were rife, there was also a compartmentalization which had to do with the industrial system. As Marx and Nietzsche pointed out, the industrial system with its reduction of relationship to money terms had a depersonalising and dehumanising effect upon man and his relationship with others. As reason came to be linked with mechanics, reason came to be simply a new kind of technique.

Knowledge, too, followed a process of compartmentalization. May quotes Cassirer, who in his *Essay on Man*, discusses how there are, in the advancing sciences, many separate collections of masses of empirical evidence about man: each science of man takes its own viewpoint, so that (as Max Scheler said) 'the ever-growing multiplicity of the particular sciences that are engaged in the study of men has much more confused and obscured than elucidated our concept of man'. The clue to the problem is to find man as the animal symbolicum — the creature with a cultural dynamic, seeking meaning.

Disintegration and compartmentalization were the condition of the sensibility, even before civilisation collapsed altogether in the 14-18 war, and has teetered from one state of collapse to another ever since. Nietzsche said 'we live in a period of atoms, of atomic chaos' and out of this chaos he saw hideous possibilities, including 'the terrible apparition . . . the Nation state' and a time when 'the day after tomorrow all hunting time, (that is, time for the hunt for happiness)may have come to an end altogether . . . '

But whatever the social problems, the fundamental problem was that man, who has the power to be conscious of his existence, should block off this consciousness and fail to live up to the responsibility. Kierkegaard and Nietzsche saw that something was radically wrong in man's relationship to himself. 'This is Europe's true predicament,' declared Nietzsche, 'together with the fear of man we have lost the love of man, confidence in man, indeed, the will to man'.

English studies, as a Humanities subject, need to be thought of in the light of this crisis.

Philosophical anthropology, especially the existentialist tradition, has opened up areas of discipline which are of immediate relevance to English studies. Freud himself initiated a particular kind of attempt to understand symbols, and other forms of meaning (like body language) which require a phenomenological approach. The whole dimension of subjective knowledge has been opened up. And here, too, we now need to consider the uniqueness of each being, in his being-unto-death — a corollary to that quest for meaning in existence which is at the centre of the existentialist approach.

Roger Poole's delineation of Leavis as an existentialist literary critic (of which more later) makes it clear why we should pay attention to these subjective disciplines, in trying to find a way forward for English studies. So, here, for the moment, I propose to follow Rollo May further on Kierkegaard, Freud and Nietzsche, in his account of the origins of the existentialist movement in psychology.

Kierkegaard's two most important psychological works are *The Concept of Anxiety* and *The Sickness Unto Death* (see *The Meaning of Anxiety*, Rollo May, 1950). Kierkegaard's analysis of selfconsciousness, inner conflicts, loss of the self and psychosomatic problems antedate Freud by half a century. Kierkegaard declared that he was not a philosopher, and he did not set out to be a psychologist.

He sought to understand, to uncover, to disclose human existence. His theme was,'How can you become an individual?' The individual, he considered, was being swallowed up in man's thought about himself by Hegel's vast logical 'absolute whole', and in society by the increasing objectification of the person in industrial life. The dying religion of the time offered no support for the moral and spiritual life. Europe was sick, because of a want of passion and commitment. He declared, 'away from Speculation, away from the System!' (a cry which Husserl echoed with his 'Back to the things themselves!' — meaning 'back to consciousness itself', and which Leavis in turn echoes, in his dogged refusal to go in for intellectual schemes and abstractions, and to stick to 'life' in its concrete reality).

Every question, Kierkegaard declared, was a 'question for the single one', that is, for the alive and aware individual. If we don't start with the human being there, we could well be so overwhelmed by the collective, by the 'social idea' (as D.H. Lawrence called it) that we become robots, whose life, deprived of uniqueness and meaning, must end in emptiness and self-destructive despair. This diagnosis of our crisis is echoed by Lawrence, Gabriel Marcel — and of course by Leavis again.

In our era, 'truth' has been equated with the 'objective' truth of Science, Kierkegaard emphasised 'truth as relationship'. This is not to deny the existence of objective truths, but to emphasise that truth is only truth to persons — a view which is the basis of Polanyi's philosophy, as in *Personal Knowledge*. In 'Concluding Unscientific Postscript' Kierkegaard wrote:

> When the question of truth is raised in an objective manner, reflection is directed objectively to the truth, as an object to which the knower is related. Reflection is not focussed upon the relationship, however, but upon the question of whether it is the truth to which the knower is related. If only the object to which he is related is the truth, the subject is accounted to be in the truth. When the question of the truth is raised subjectively, reflection is directed subjectively to the nature of the individual's relationship; if only the mode of this relationship is in the truth, the individual is in the truth, even if he should happen to be thus related to what is not true.

Roger Poole, relating Kierkegaard's thought to Husserl, quotes another passage:

> For an objective reflection the truth becomes an object, something objective, and thought must be pointed away from the subject. For a subjective reflection the truth becomes a matter of appropriation, of inwardness, of subjectivity, and thought must probe more deeply into the subject and his subjectivity. (*Towards Deep Subjectivity*, p.97)

Kierkegaard, says Poole, erects a philosophy of subjectivity which takes a definite and explicit presupposition as its starting point: this is, that the individual thinker is the ultimate ethical (and religious) reality and that the whole of objectivity has finally to be judged and evaluated by him. Certainly, the only reality that exists for an existing individual is his own ethical reality.

This kind of thinking, as Rollo May makes clear, has had a profound effect on psychology. Here is the fountainhead of the emphasis on existential thought on truth as inwardness, or, as Heidegger puts it, truth as freedom. (See 'On the essence of truth' in *Existence and Being*.) In science, even, the participation of the observer must now be seen as part of the equation. The subject, man, can never be separated from the object he observes.

As I have tried to argue in *Lost Bearings in English Poetry*, in this we have a clue to how we may escape from the disease of the effects of 'objectivity' on our consciousness. Kierkegaard's emphasis releases us from bondage to the dogma that truth can be understood only in terms of external objects. It opens up the recognition that inner subjective reality must be examined in its own right, even though it contradicts external 'fact' — as when (as May points out) Freud found that his patients had crippling memories of (sexual) events which had never taken place.

Kierkegaard's emphasis here is not to be confused with subjectivism or idealism. He opens up the subjective world without losing objectivity. But this view does challenge the assumption, predominant in science (as in Psychology) that the less we are involved in a given situation, the more closely we can observe the truth. In the study of children's behaviour, for instance, a very important element is the participation of the observing adult, who needs to take his or her responses into account, as part of the reality in question.

This applies to English teaching, where it is impossible to separate the involvement of the teacher. A very considerable personal element of intersubjectivity is present, even in the straightforward 'reading' of texts: since all creative texts involve the emotions and deep responses to symbolism and unconscious themes, the complex of intersubjectivity cannot be excluded. The student is often 'giving' and the tutor 'receiving' or 'reflecting', and there must be confidence and trust on both sides — a degree of emotional bond without which learning is impossible. An existentialist approach makes this a reality which must be recognised and encountered. Moreover, many literary works themselves explore the question of throwing subjective meaning over reality — as for example, in Thomas Hardy's poem *Boterel Castle* or his *After a Journey*. It is easier to see what one is doing, if one employs the kind of existentialist emphasis found in Kierkegaard, to one's work in English.

Of course, disruptive emotions disturb one's relationship with reality: one of Freud's most important findings was that a man's whole relationship with the world could be wrecked by deep unconscious feelings. But such problems cannot be solved by detachment and abstraction. As Rollo May says, 'when we are dealing with human beings, no truth has reality by itself; it is always dependent upon the reality of the immediate relationship' .

A further concept from Kierkegaard is that of commitment. Truth becomes reality only insofar as the individual produces it in action, we cannot even see a particular truth until we already have some commitment to it. It is possible for a patient in therapy to talk for ever, but never to feel and experience his problems. So, it is possible to talk about literature in English, and never feel or 'possess' the work in question.*

The problem in English is always to discuss works while still retaining the capacity to respond adequately to them: here Leavis's emphasis on always returning to the work is invaluable, as is the emphasis made throughout the *Scrutiny* following on attention to the text of the work of art. The exploration of human truth inevitably requires passion and commitment, and this in turn requires the recognition of suffering and despair — which means, ultimately, trying to confront: the *Dasein* problem, of exerting meaning against nothingness. Nietzsche (1844-1900) lived four decades later than Kierkegaard. (He never in fact read the Danish writer.) Nietzsche was not anti-rational, and neither was he a 'philosopher of feeling'. He attacked mere reason — the arid, fragmented rationalism of his day. And he sought by reflection to find the reality which underlies both reason and unreason. Like

*Leavis is absolutely right when he says, 'You can't take over the appreciation of a poem, and unappreciated, the poem isn't 'there', *Education and the University*, p.68

Kierkegaard and Freud, he began with himself, and from a great intensity of self-consciousness. The worst problem of the world of functional, mechanistic and 'objective' thinking of our era is the loss of self: the loss of a strong sense of being, of the consciousness of the 'I'*

Kierkegaard wrote, 'the more consciousness, the more self', and Freud, 'where Id was, there ego shall be' as an explanation of his goal in therapy. Kierkegaard and Nietzsche both knew the deepest agonies of intense self-consciousness, of dread, despair (and isolation).

Nietzsche held that every truth faced one with the question, 'Can one love it?' 'All truths are bloody truths for me and error is cowardice.' The failure of modern man to commit himself in this way to his own integrity seemed to Nietzsche to represent loss of faith in his own dignity. This he associated with the decline of central traditions which gave a basis for values in Western civilisation, the Hebrew-Christian and the humanistic, with its roots in Ancient Greece. Religion had become weak: so, Nietzsche declared 'God is dead': the debilitated forms of religion had to be allowed to die.

Both Kierkegaard and Nietzsche were radically devoted to the nobility of man and sought ways in which his dignity and humanity could be restored. Nietzsche's 'will to power' implied the self-realisation of the individual in the widest sense, and this principle has been a theme in all Rollo May's writings. It is unfortunate in the history of existentialism that Kierkegaard's concept of commitment has been interpreted so widely in terms of Sartre's kind of commitment which is too often to violent and iconoclastic causes—-as in much fashionable culture, while Nietzsche's work has been associated with Nazism. The existentialist attention to self-fulfilment is much more compatible with a free democratic society.

Properly, as May insists, Nietzsche's will to power is an ontological category, an inseparable aspect of being. It does not mean aggression or competitive striving: it is the individual affirm-

*Jaspers, as May points out, believes that the forces of conformity, and collectivism in our time menace a serious loss of individual consciousness in modern man. This feeling may be found in Leavis's work on culture and society. It is also a theme in Gabriel Marcel's philosophy of being.

ing his existence and his potentialities as a being in his own right. It is the courage to be. The word 'power' is used by Nietzsche in the classical sense of *potentia*, or *dynamis*. This positive principle in Nietzsche has been an important influence in psychotherapy, as we may see in the work of Victor Frankl and Abraham Maslow(see *New Knowledge in Human Values*, ed. Maslow) Rollo May's position is also developed from this: he quotes Kaufmann, summarising Nietzsche: 'Man's task is simple: he should cease letting his "existence" be a "thoughtless accident".'

This is today called *Existenz-philosophie*.

> Man's fundamental problem, is to achieve true 'existence' instead of letting his life be no more than just another accident. In *The Gay Science* Nietzsche hits on a formulation which brings out the essential paradox of any distinction between self and true self: 'What does your conscience say? — You shall become what you are'. Nietzsche maintains this conception until the end, and the full title of his last work is *Ecce Homo, Wie man wird, was man ist* — how one becomes what one is. Walter A. Kaufmann, *Nietzsche*, pp. 133-134

This bringing one's potentialities to birth in action is the central dynamic and need of life: and, if we accept this view, this surely must be at the centre of any humanities subject?

There are also profound political implications. Happiness, power, possessions — none of these constitute an adequate goal in life. 'Not for pleasure does man strive, but for power' (that is, realisation of *potentia*).Happiness is not absence of pain, but 'the most alive feeling of power' and joy is a 'plus-feeling of power'.

The values of human life never come about automatically. The human being can lose his own being by his own choices (and there are many instances in literature, from Faustus and Macbeth to Anna Karenina). Affirming one's own being creates the values of life — a statement that Dickens, Blake and D.H. Lawrence, as Leavis presents them, would have endorsed.

> Individuality, worth and dignity are not *gegeben*, i.e. given us as data by nature, but *aufgegeben* . . i.e. given or assigned to us as a task which we ourselves must solve. Kaufmann, *ibid*, p.136

This view was developed by Paul Tillich in his *The Courage To Be*: if we do not exert the courage to be human, we lose our own being.

May relates some of Nietzsche's analysis of the spiritual sickness of our time, to Freud's diagnosis. 'Bad conscience', said Nietzsche, 'is nothing other than the instinct of freedom forced to become latent, driven underground, and forced to vent its energy upon itself.' Nietzsche's work seems to have had a considerable influence on Freud: Freud said of him that Nietzsche 'had a more penetrating knowledge of himself than any other man who ever lived or was ever likely to live'.

But Freud tended to try to link psychoanalysis to 'technical reason', to organic, functional medicine, with serious consequences (see Jan Foudraine, *Not Made of Wood*, chapter 17, an excellent critique of Freud's 'organic' approach.) There was a danger that psychoanalysis itself might contribute to the alienation of man from himself, insofar as it became a new technique for calculation and control of unconscious life and the emotions (such problems in Freudian psychoanalysis are discussed at length by Harry Guntrip in his historical surveys).

The existential movement in psychotherapy is a crucial departure from this Freudian approach, with its weight of theory and its quantitative models. It stands for basing psychotherapy on an understanding of what makes man the human being, and it employs Freud's best (phenomenological) insights into meanings and modes of consciousness, to concern itself with the fulfilment of being. It follows Kierkegaard and Nietzsche, in placing the insights of 'subjective' psychology on an ontological basis, namely, the study of man as the being who has these particular problems.

I believe that in the light of these disciplines we need to put English studies on an ontological basis, too. Later I shall discuss the implications further and try to show what I mean in practice. But in this Introduction I hope I have shown that our thinking about English studies is inevitably part of a crisis — the crisis to which Kierkegaard, Nietzsche, Freud, and later Edmund Husserl gave their attention — and to the urgent need to restore attention to being and to meaning.

Here, perhaps, it will help to pursue some of the philosophical problems further, since because of the paradigms that dominate in our intellectual traditions, there is little common understanding of the nature of the kind of knowledge one is dealing with, in a subject like English. Many of the failures of confidence in the subject one detects nowadays arise, I believe, from a failure to understand both what kind of knowing we are dealing with and how it is acquired and fostered.

I would like to refer here to a useful essay by a woman philosopher who has writen on existentialist thinkers, Dr Margaret Weldhen. Dr.Weldhen worked for a time at the Education Department of the University of Bath, and has written also on Jaspers.

Dr.Weldhen's paper was 'Living Inside or Outside the Text: two versions of English Studies', published in *The Use of English*, Vol.37, No.2, Spring 1986. She believes that we need to look more into the problem of the kind of knowledge or experience that lies at the heart of literature, and quotes a student: 'I get nothing from a tutorial that I could not get from a book'. This reveals, she suggests, how little understanding there is, as to what kind of knowledge or experience lies at the heart of literature.

Of course, she agrees, we need to get a sense of 'literature, life and thought' and of the historical landscapes — 'putting up sign posts'. But there is another dimension: that of experiencing works and through them the minds and sensibilities of authors: meeting another being through the sharing of an act of consciousness. She quotes a sentence from an article of my own: 'Ours is a phenomenological subject as well as an encyclopaedic one.' Works of art have to be experienced as well as known about.

Margaret Weldhen quotes H.P.Rickman (*Understanding and the Human Studies*, 1967) on the need to distinguish between sciences and the Arts as Humanities. We need to recognise 'what is specifically human in the human studies'. He suggests that 'the subjective, the qualitative and the interpretative' should be seen as different disciplines from the 'quantitative, the behaviouristic and the positivistic'. He accepts the distinction between the 'human world' and the 'natural world' and accepts Cassirer's notion that what distinguishes man is his capacity for symbolic activity. In his thinking the symbol is seen as one of the 'main vehicles of meaning' and viewed as requiring 'interpretation' to bring about 'understanding'.

And here Margaret Weldhen writes what I believe to be a most useful paragraph.

> What exactly is the process by which we come to carry out acts of 'interpretation', and so to 'understand'? Attempting to answer such a difficult question I would agree with the phenomenologists that 'how we come to understand' anything is really part of our commonsense, everyday experience. We are 'thrown into' (to use Heidegger's phrase) a world which is constructed of a web of already existing meanings embedded in language. In order to move about and survive in this social world we learn to interpret people's speech, gestures, actions. To 'read between the lines' is something we do all the time. So 'understanding' human action, speech, gestures, is something we just 'pick up', as it were, as we live. It is very much a part of our 'lived experience'. But to interpret speech, gestures, poems, novels, works of art, we have to 'get inside' these various forms of expression. The 'meaning' will actually be the experience and will not be 'reducible' to any prepositional form.

F.R. Leavis, of course, was continually making the same emphasis.

So, in this view of English as a universities subject, we seek 'a way of understanding the deep places of experience and the necessity of a worthwhile life' a quotation from Malcolm Bradbury. The word 'worthwhile' is perhaps elusive: what certainly is necessary to us is a sense that we can pursue a sense of meaning that has validity and is not threatened easily. One may see that this was (for example) the impulse behind D.H. Lawrence in writing *Sons and Lovers*. We are drawn into that existential exploration as we read it, and share the author's consciousness. For instance he makes his hero say to his mother, Mrs.Morel:

> 'Never mind, little,' he murmured, 'So long as you don't feel life's paltry and a miserable business, the rest doesn't matter, happiness or unhappiness.'

The whole of Lawrence's work, one might say, was directed

towards finding a meaning in existence which could overcome his dread of his mother's life being paltry and miserable: his own sense of the validity of his being seemed related to this issue. I believe we can trace the origins of many a literary work to such an ontological need — a need to find meaning at the deepest level of being (and, of course, in talking like this we are invoking the insights of psychoanalysis, taking into account the unconscious as well as the consciousness.)

Because of the increased professionalism of university English, however, another version of English studies has gained ground, and one often finds students expressing a restless desire for 'something else', as if there could be 'a literary science' and a view of the nature of the text which reduces it to the status of phenomena. It is, perhaps we could say, phenomenalist rather than phenomenological: tending to look at the subject by particulate analysis rather in terms of consciousness and its modes.

In literature this approach concentrates on how the phenomena 'work'. The English expert must be able to conduct analysis, develop theory, make hypotheses, find 'laws', deconstruct and examine text, as part of a whole range of forms, structures and artefacts, often taking in moreover a catholic range in culture at large including clothes, hairstyles and advertisements to novels, to be examined by semiology, as the empirical anthropologist might approach them.

In this there is an implicit denial that some cultural artefacts represent more of an achievement than others, and so the canon which we hope embodies the best that is thought and known in this sphere is undercut and challenged.

This might be a valuable challenge to us to restate our values. But the truth is that the onslaught on the canon goes with the attempt to make theory rather than the experience of art predominant. Margaret Weldhen quotes C.J.F.Ball:

> Literature is strongly resistant to theory. . . it accommodates all theories while failing to provide an adequate test for them. Untestable theories cannot be shown to be right either.

J.F. Ball, writing in the *T.L.S.*(6 Feb 1981) on *Modern Literary Theory — its place in Teaching*.

The tendency is for literary theorists to draw back from the kind of emphasis Wordsworth makes in the *Preface to the Lyrical Ballads*, where he speaks of 'a man speaking to men'. Margaret Weldhen points out that for Barthes, the very 'being' or 'essence' of literature lies in the system of signs — how words are related to other words within the signification system. Language does not represent a 'reality' said to be existing in the 'world', for it is language itself that creates the 'reality'. One task of structuralist criticism is not to 're-constitute the message' but only the 'system'. Literary criticism itself is not the analysis of content but the organisation of literary forms. Since language 'constructs' the world, then we all move, including the author, within a 'self-contained world of language' a 'significant-world'. We can look 'through' language into a 'real world' beyond: language is the reality, for the theoretician.

Perhaps there is a valuable reminder that language is not the real world.

But on our part we need to emphasise that a poem, play or novel is not a closed world, but is open in that it relates to a reality beyond itself. 'Art is truth as well as form' as Iris Murdoch has said, 'it is representational as well as autonomous'. The 'moral humanists' says Dr Weldhen emphasise that through the experience of literature one is enabled to see the world with new eyes, never doubting the relationship between words and 'life' or 'reality'.

This is in contradistinction to the structuralists who tend to believe that the relationship between words constitutes the field of literature. For them, content tends to dissolve into form. For the moral humanists there is a fusion of content and form in the experience or the embodied meaning.

Margaret Weldhen goes on to try to classify two kinds of approach, to the kind of knowing a discipline like English deals with.

The appreciative understanding of art involves the whole person, and so there can be no impersonal tests, observation or experiment on any scientific parallel. The reader is involved as a person in his experience of a work of art, and his judgement must be based on that. The judgements of art are valued judgements, based on 'the common pursuit': we seek standards on the basis of 'seems good to A, seems good to B, seems good to C on further reflection', by the collocation of naturalistic descriptions.* But such responses and value judgements are not in any way testable: they can only be contingent.

(Polanyi argues, of course, that in fact scientific 'facts' are contingent in the same way — upheld by the community of scientists, until some radical disproof comes along — though they may even continue to be upheld after that.)

Attempts at critical theory which do not accept this element of response can gesture towards scientific explanation: they can be something you can find in a book, and so the tutorial seems dispensable. Critical theory could be 'knowledge about', factual knowledge of theories concerning the structuring or patterning of words, codes, systems of signs and semiological interpretation.

If English were based on this kind of knowledge, the subject could become one which is, or seems, to have been created by those who profess it, as are philosophy, history, and science. Such a subject exists in the professionals' books. But our subject does not exist in literary critical works or in literary libraries. As John Bayley has pointed out, in English we do not own the matter of our subject: we did not create English literature, and it perpetually eludes us, requiring our disciplined service to it.

At a time when there is a loss of confidence in English, obviously there is a great temptation to make it seem otherwise. We could make our English seem 'a proper discipline', we could make it amenable to 'functional procedures and outcomes'. The atmosphere of a 'practical' society with an emphasis on 'realistic effectiveness' seems to lend this validity. But we would forfeit the essential task — of 'bringing actual works alive'. And (as Margaret Weldhen goes on to argue) the subject would then come to be at the mercy of vagaries of fashion and fragmentation as in French intellectual theories, and of the political sects and movements involved (as with Lacan): we find this fragmentation seriously affecting 'Feminist' studies.

The predominance of literary theory could also generate what she calls a 'scepticism of the word'.

*See John Wisdom, *Philosophy and Psychoanalysis* (1952), especially his discussion of Waddington's Ethics.

> By this is meant that words are not seen as mind's grasp of reality — the 'word' and the 'real' are not seen as totally fused, giving us access to an intelligible world.

— and perhaps by that last word but one she invokes the whole of Wordsworth's effort, including *The Prelude*, to throw meaning into life and the world by language.

To take the argument further beyond the scope of Margaret Weldhen's useful paper we may turn to Michael Polanyi's work. lie discusses the tendency in our world to move towards self-immolation of the mind, from scepticism. The scientific outlook has produced a mechanical model of man in a universe which is matter in motion, operating only by chance and necessity. In this universe there is no place for the passionate commitment of the knower, and so none for science itself. Scientific scepticism thus undermines the basis of science. This predicament moves over into the Humanities and threatens us, as when we are told there can be no values because 'we are only DNA making more DNA' — an absurd application of reductionism to our biological reality.

Out of his perplexity about this, Polanyi moved towards a quite different concept of human knowledge. It begins from the fact that we can know more than we can tell. How do we know a face? We cannot say. The same is true in biology and other sciences. it is true of English, as when we teach students 'practical criticism': we rely on 'the pupil's' intelligent cooperation for catching the meaning of the demonstration'. All such disciplines depend upon a shaping or integrating activity of 'subsidiary' modes — of the nature of which we are ignorant. Polanyi calls this tacit knowing. Of course, from tacit knowing we develop logical and analytical thought.

But Polanyi valuably extended our awareness of what knowing depends upon. In *The Tacit Dimension* he discusses subception, a kind of awareness of which we are not aware (as when we know a face). We also know that we can have skills in which we combine and coordinate muscular acts which we cannot identify, or know how we coordinate them (as when we learn to ride a bicycle). In his book *Personal Knowledge*, Polanyi develops his theory from a wide range of scientific experiments and philosophical enquiries which have revealed how we rely on unknowing knowing, even to develop our most explicit theories.

One important concept here is that of indwelling, a form of empathy — the way we know ourselves into the subjects of attention, and live in thought patterns as instruments of knowing. This is the proper way of knowing man and the humanities: and the clue to that 'other' way of knowing which is the essence of our subject.

It is a condition, often, of knowing something that we do not examine explicitly the details of the first stage of our knowing.

Polanyi here uses the terms from anatomy, *proximal* and *distal*. We attend from the first to the second. We do not attend to the particulars of the first stage of knowing: we don't know what we are doing — we simply rely on them. But in relying on the integration of the particulars, we interiorise them, and so become aware of their bearing on the comprehensive entity which they constitute.

So, in the analysis of a text, we try to judge its overall effect upon us. Then we go back to it, to try to justify our response. This can be done in two ways. As Polanyi says

> The meticulous dismembering of a text . . . can supply material for a deeper understanding of it. *The Tacit Dimension*, p.19.

But there is also a danger, that 'an unbridled lucidity can destroy our understanding of complex matters' ('By concentrating on his fingers a pianist can temporarily paralyze his movement'). So, analysis of a text can kill its appreciation, if done the wrong way, as we know — as students sometimes ironically reveal, by talking about 'doing a prac. crit.'

In science, Polanyi suggests, if it is true that all knowledge is rooted in tacit knowledge, then it is personal and so no more than scientists trying to make sense of their world — so, the ideal of strict objectivity is false. Even in science, the ideal of formalizing knowledge to the exclusion of tacit knowing will be self-defeating. And this has radical implications for science, especially for biology.

But for us in the humanities the implications are profound. We make a serious mistake if we try to make our subject 'objective' or 'scientific' in that positivistic way. Our goal is not explanation, in the cause-and-effect way: or the establishing of laws on the deductive principle: or even the postulation of hypotheses. Our goal is *understanding*, and this is to be achieved by interiorization, by possessing works in a whole way, discussing their 'upshot', and the insights they yield.

It is also necessary to emphasise a number of aspects of this process made clear by Polanyi. Much of what happens will not be and cannot be implicitly known to us and will be 'ineffable'. Much of it will depend on *intersubjectivity* and *creative reflection* — that is, in the teaching situation there is something of the parent child relationship and each gives to the other art a form of 'love'.

In all these processes such indefinable dynamics as 'the leap of the imagination' are essential. while we shall understand the processes much better if we examine our theories of perception which recognise the positive activity in the way our consciousness knows the world (as in Coleridge, who spoke of 'growledge': and in Wordsworth).We must speak as Polanyi speaks, of 'the creative thrust of the imagination' in knowing.

So to return to English as a Humanities subject. Literature is art: reading is an art: teaching is an art. If we take (say) students' writing, even academic essays: the improvement of their work is no mere question of sharp analysis of their arguments (though that is sometimes called for) — but much more a question of our capacity to receive their work, and to compare the whole impact of a work on their consciousness, with its impact on ours. Only once this has been achieved can we go back to the particulars, and try to argue the case, in terms of our grasp on the whole 'and what it tells us of life'. It is even sometimes evident that it is not necessary for us to understand everything they say: it is enough for us to be a 'scratching post' for their own self-discovery. The air that some university lecturers give of knowing everything (cf. the Faculty lecture list) is actually inimical to the proper response to literature, which requires openness and sometimes awe: certainly respect.

It is no mere jargon only to call the study of literature an 'ontological' act. In teaching it belongs to our existential concern with the student's development, rather than with the promotion of some theoretical structure, or sectarian cause, or political cause or world revolution.

It is, in the widest sense, the pursuit of freedom, as by the pursuit of truth (*Quaerere Verum*) — of knowing in that way. As Polanyi puts it (discussing the scientist):

> All his existential choices are made in response to a potential discovery; they consist in sensing and following a gradient of understanding which will lead to the expansion of his mental existence. Every step is an effort to meet an immediate necessity; his freedom is continuous service. p.81

This 'gradient' began in Ancient Greece, and we are within the same *telos*: only now we have to seek to interpret more the explanation of the subjective realm. And even in marking students' essays we shall not only seem aspiring, but be doing better if we see our work in a larger perspective, like that of Polanyi — devoted to 'the cosmic emergence of meaning': 'they need a purpose which bears on eternity'. p. 92

The purpose of our endeavour in universities cannot be satisfied in mere utilitarian terms of supplying 'society' with 'technicians': nor in constructing theoretical structures which are detached from 'life'. Our students will respond best if we relate their efforts to the primary need, to find meaning in existence, not least in the investigation of consciousness and what it means to be civilised.

While I was beginning my work at Downing I was interested to read a series of articles in the *Times Literary Supplement* (10 December 1982) on 'professing literature'. It was useful to me in preparing the present work to use those articles as a foil. I felt they would help me to hold off an impulse to work my way through literary theory and come out the other side. I had enough to do to invoke the philosophers whose work I summarise in *Further Studies in Philosophical Anthropology*. I believe they helped to suggest I was on a more profitable track.

The articles certainly confirmed my sense that there was a crisis: as George Watson said, 'literary studies . . . have lost their nerve because they have lost their sense of purpose'. Paul de Man quoted one Professor Walton Jackson Bate, writing in the Harvard Alumni bulletin *Harvard Magazine*, who declared that literary studies had become bankrupt. 'Their increased professionalism,' wrote de

Man, 'and specialization have failed, he claims, to rescue the humanities at a time when they are said to be in the weakest state they ever suffered — bent on a self-destructive course.'

Bate apparently sees the increasing concentration on literary theory as the main cause for this decline.

> It culminates in the final catastrophe of the poststructuralist era, the invasion of departments of English by French influence that advocate 'a nihilistic view of literature, of human communication, and of life itself.'

De Man says that Professor Bate's response is to appeal to the adminstrative officers of the universities to deny tenure to teachers who concentrate on theory. This seems surely a solution which smacks of lack of confidence, for surely if the approaches Bate condemns are so inadequate, they could be exposed in proper open debate? But this, of course, requires that we develop a fully adequate sense of what our discipline is.

After discussing Professor Bate's angry rejection of the new theorising, Paul de Man commended an 'experiment' which seems to him very radical. He reports that Reuben Brewer, also of Harvard, conducted literature classes, and insisted that his students were 'not to say anything that could not be supported by a specific use of language that actually occurred in the text'. Moreover:

> they were to start out from the bafflement that such singular turns of tone, phrase and figure were bound to produce in readers attentive enough to notice them and honest enough not to hide their own non-understanding behind the screen of received ideas that often passes, in literary instruction, for humanistic knowledge.

This, de Man declares, had 'far-reaching didactic consequences'. It seems to me we have come full circle — for this is just what I have always done in teaching since 1948 — and what I try to do in literary criticism. My seminars are conducted on this principle — students being guided back to the text, to substantiate their comments. I can well believe that 'students, what they lost in generality, they more than made up for in precision and in the closer proximity of their writings to the original mode'. But I find it hard to understand de Man when he proclaims that 'English should be taught as a rhetoric and a Poetic prior to being taught as a hermeneutics and a history' — even though he doesn't say what this means. In grappling with (say) a poem by Wyatt, we are, in dwelling on the 'voice', rhythm and meaning, surely, 'doing' poetics and what the Americans call 'rhetoric', meaning the study of form and structure, while also learning about the exploration of human experience (which is what I take hermeneutics to mean) and also exploring history?

Again, having recommended the 'real discipline' it seems to me, he falls away to theorise about it, and to imply there must be 'something else' which is the universal gesture made by those serving a discipline about which they are uncertain and unconfident.

Réné Wellek, in his contribution to the *TLS* symposium begins by referring to Geoffrey Strickland, and his comment that the teaching of literature has generated in some a 'terror of constructive feeling'. He discusses the fashionable anti-intellectualism, on the other hand, of Susan Sontag, who demands an 'erotics of art' and Barthes who demands *jouissance*, '*le plaisir du texte*'.

Wellek also refers to the antipathy to 'elitism', which he attributes to the uncertain feeling that taste is only subjective and relative. He mentions those who have commended everything 'kitsch', colportage, trash, *Trivialliteratur*, 'camp' (Susan Sontag), 'lovely commonplaces' and 'obscene black anti-verse' (Leslie Fiedler, who else?).

Wellek traces the history of English in American universities, to the triumph of theory and its continental influences. Leavis's kind of ('extreme') empiricism can no longer be kept up. But the proliferation of theories has led to 'neglect of the older necessary and possibly more elementary tasks: the contact with texts, the concern for history'. The student only loses if he is not, in reading, at the cutting edge of his profession; indeed, what is there, if there is not reading?

> The lopsidedness becomes particularly damaging when he is taught that all literature is about literature, is only words about words, with no relation to reality, reducing thus his life-engage-

> ment to an elaborate game with words. It leads to nihilism and cynicism.

The effect of this could be ultimately the destruction of scholarship. However, as Wellek insists, a great deal of positive work goes on, and criticism may have sharpened it. But even so, in America, what used to be called the 'general educated public' seems to have dwindled to a vanishing point. There is a vast gulf between minority culture and mass culture. The professions must resist the trend towards further trivialisation here 'without any illusions of reversing it'. All we can do is to 'rescue' literary history, scholarship and theory for future generations.

Wellek's is a sad, decent, conservative, and sound contribution: but, again, he fails to put before us the essential discipline which English is — though his ancient exchange with Leavis* should surely have impressed the nature of it on him for once and all. What is it that has made Leavis's 'empiricism' 'extreme' or outmoded?

Iain McGilchrist in his contribution made the important point that literature, that art, engages faculties which transcend the analytic. Response in English depends upon a faculty for which we no longer nave a name:

> Perhaps it could be called judgement, which comes from within . . . I don't think this makes the understanding and illuminating of literature a 'softer' or easier business: on the contrary, it makes it possibly the hardest and most demanding of all intellectual studies.

McGilchrist sees the proliferation of methodologies as belonging to what he calls the 'number-plate solution': in licensing cars, when we run out of one letter, we add another. The limited field of English means that this kind of solution proliferates.

Literature is 'oblique', in that it draws its meaning ultimately from everything that lies outside of itself. And it is full of paradox: it does not lend itself to analytic reductivism, so cannot be compared with the sciences.

**Scrutiny*, vol. V, pp. 375-85 and VI, 60-70, 105-6

Indeed, while the impulse of the scientist is to impose human will on the world, the specialist in English cannot aspire to make himself invulnerable:

> Literature simply cannot be understood without abandoning the attempt to render oneself invulnerable; nor should we pretend to resolve mysteries which are not functions of our ignorance, but of the nature of art itself. Such mysteries are irreducible.

This is well said, and accords with much that Michael Polanyi says about all knowing and knowledge, not least that in science (and McGilchrist refers to the mysteries which are admitted today in science too). But much of the analytical, theoretical and 'other disciplines' activity in English departments belongs to the impulse to become 'invulnerable', and this conveys around to students and other senior staff a daunting feeling of being afraid to admit the mysteries and perplexities, in all humility.

Iain McGilchrist suggests some kind of retreat from the worst effects of 'professionalism' and he hints at the need for a new direction:

> The pressure to keep writing (whether or not one has anything urgent to say), and above all to say something different enough to be heard above the competitive din, has set novelty before truth as the criterion of acceptibility. Indeed to speak about truth at all has become deeply suspect..

Fashions in English, he says, tend to come from scientific world pictures long abandoned by science. He suggests, and I agree, that we might accelerate developments in our thinking by seeking a sense of the implications for the arts of living in a 'non-mechanist' world, and towards this end turning away from the analytical dualist tradition of western Europe, to learn from cultures distinct from our own. However, it is perhaps worth saying that even within western Europe, on the continent, there are areas of philosophy (existentialism, phenomenology, philosophical anthropology) which are trying to do exactly what McGilchrist recommends. And I believe that it is in this direction that the future lies, for English, as I have suggested, for I am convinced that the crisis in university English, like the crisis in school English, is a philosophical one. As Polanyi says, the assumptions of positivism in the end cut the ground away beneath science itself, because science is rooted in a passionate concern to pursue truth: a model of man and the universe which accepts nothing as real unless it is 'objective' cannot allow this passion to exist. Similarly, an 'English' which flies away from its own true disciplines, as a subject discipline, to substitutes, or to establish something 'else', something which seems as respectable as the sciences, eventually ends up deconstructing itself, or sinking into cynicism or nihilism.

'Where is the essential discipline?' was the question that came into my mind, as I heard the late Raymond Williams address the Doughty (literary) Society at Downing in 1982. His talk became another of the articles published in the *Times Literary Supplement* symposium. It is clear from Raymond Williams's earlier work, as in *Reading and Criticism*, that he knows, like Leavis, that if the poem isn't 'possessed', it isn't 'there' at all. So it is all the more surprising that he can propose an English course analogous to the natural sciences.

He declares that he would like to see things being done in a diversity of ways. There was a time, for about half a century, when 'courses in English literature had an apparent and at times effective coherence. The central disciplines were literary criticism, literary history, literary scholarship, with some variation of order.' These constructed and specialised unities have now broken down, 'though they are still often fiercely defended: at times as if they were ideal essences.'

Williams does not agree with those who wish to substitute 'something else' for English — 'linguistic philosophy, cultural sociology, media studies'. These are not substitutes, he agrees. The major writing still has to be studied. But he believes it can best be done through new kinds of active collaboration 'with other disciplines, other cultures, and other kinds of work'. it is not simply a matter of 'joint' courses, it is a condition of collaboration. He believes here that the Natural Sciences Tripos at Cambridge provides a creative example. 'This requires an assembly of courses in up to six sciences in the first two years, and even then third-year specialization to a single science only from a demonstrated level of achievement.'

I cannot believe that the content of any science is inherently less than the content of any of the humanities; each is in any case much too large to be 'covered' by any degree course. May it then not be that what matters is to get, in each case, the beginnings of some real knowledge and some real skills, directly taught by those who are primarily concerned with them, and to get them not only in one relatively isolated area but in those cognate areas?

There are hints in Williams's article that he is thinking of linguistics, and he refers to: cultural sociology, and experimental psychology, especially in their accounts of effective sets of identities and of dynamically shifting subjects and objects of address. Here I believe we need to ask what Williams means by 'real knowledge and real skills': in his deference to experimental psychology and the Natural Sciences Tripos, as well is his reference to 'the content of any of the humanities' he seems to me to be selling the whole problem down the river: that is, capitulating to a view of the 'content' of English as if it were the same kind of thing as the 'content' of the Sciences.

A great deal in the Natural Sciences is indeed given to the acquisition of what may be called 'content': the acquiring of knowledge of facts. There is some 'content' and 'fact' in English — knowledge of dates, editions, historical occasions, quartos and folios, whether Keats met Coleridge, and whether Wyatt had an affair with Anne Boleyn. But the essential labour in English is not to acquire facts, while 'content' is *possession* — possession in terms of the art coming 'alive' for one. In possession we imply the creative impact of the work upon us, in terms of enlarging our sympathy, our understanding of human issues, our sense of the potentialities of being, our sense of meaning and values (as the focus of moral choices).

When we read *Mansfield Park* or *The Awkward Age* and argue about them, we are inevitably arguing about existential issues, and at depth this is concerned with 'what in ourselves, at the level of the deepest level of being, we really want' — in relation to life-tasks, and all the other complex issues of life. The developing of this kind of play of intelligence, this kind of awareness, this kind of pre-

occupation with meaning and possibilities is not at all like acquiring the 'content' of a science. To make this emphasis is not to be anti-science: the sciences do lead students to problems of meaning and value and much in science, like the training of recognition, is analogous to our kind of work.
As a scientific professor said in a letter to *The Times* (10 Jan. 1983):

> Microbiology, for example, like any other study in depth of the living world, can certainly lead the enquirer to an appreciation of intrinsic beauty, logic, hidden patterns of meaning and challenges to pure intellect, no less so than the humanities. To write of knowing 'only' microbiology is, also, a trivial semantic trap implying that a knowledge of a science must cut out all other types of knowledge. The 'material for thought and conversation' which Dr.Scruton urges us to seek by education is no less to be found in any of the natural sciences than in the Greek or mathematics which he recommends . . . All of us need to defend those humane values, in the widest sense, in education, against the current political attack on them. (Eric Barnard, writing from the Imperial College of Science and Technology, Department of Biochemistry).

It is very important for us not to be hostile to science (as Leavis often was). And it is also necessary to look at the possibilities of interdisciplinary studies, not least over the philosophy of science, and its impact on English. But in our subject something very different from anything like the Natural Science Tripos is primary — and it is crucial to make sure that we understand that the kind of thinking we deal in is recognised in its own right. Too often today we are so daunted by the authority of a reductionist 'objective' science that we may feel apologetic for disciplines which ('merely'?) attend to life and consciousness. Yet there are valid criticisms within science itself, of kinds of biology which fail to find 'the category of life', including that kind of autonomy in living creature to which some philosophers of biology give the name 'centricity', and even organisms as 'living beings'.

Here Raymond Williams's emphasis seems disastrous, not least in his deference to 'experimental psychology'. Surely a mind trained in English ought to be able to make fundamental criticisms of the models and assumptions of experimental psychology — not least because, within the discipline itself, there are complaints that it has failed seriously to yield results? (See Erwin Straus, *The Primary World of Senses*, 1963). In some philosophical analyses of experimental psychology, it has been pointed out that this discipline has singularly failed to understand the very phenomena it sets out to examine, indeed, often, cannot find it.

Finally, perhaps I may introduce here a reference to what seemed to me a very telling rejection of the whole movement in theoretical criticism, by Tzvetan Todorov in a review article in the *Times Literary Supplement* of 4 October 1985.

Todorov's argument was powerful and succinct. He pointed out that in American criticism, until roughly about 1968, the essential preoccupation was 'What does this text mean?'. Critics held one common conviction, which was that 'the most important thing to do was to determine as accurately as possible what the text was trying to say.' There were of course, problems, of attending to an author's motivation, or to the rules of the genre to which the work belonged. Structuralism did not make fundamental changes to the process, in calling attention to the internal construction of literary works. It was with post-structuralism that the question 'What does this work mean?' came to be challenged: indeed, it was asserted to be irrelevant. One kind of post-structuralism — deconstructionism — made the question about what a text meant obsolete by invariably furnishing the answer 'Nothing'. The second kind, which some call 'pragmatism' renders the question pointless by answering 'Anything'.

The assertions of the theorists tended to make the traditional pattern of reading untenable: 'There is no such thing as an outside-of-the-text', 'I don't believe that anything like perception exists', the text 'produces a structure of infinite referal in which there are only traces'. The commentary always consists in showing that the text under study always contains contradictions, and that its avowed intentions are undermined by the way it actually works. There is therefore, as one commentator puts it, 'an insurmountable obstacle in the way of any reading or understanding.'

Deconstruction is thus the extension of scepticism to consider knowledge and judgement, truth and justice, to be impossible. Whatever track a reader follows through a poem. he arrives at blank contradictions: Todorov suggests that this is why this kind of theory has been such a success in academic institutions—-'all one need do is to apply the formula to new material and one comes up with an "original" exegesis'. With 'pragmatism' it is the reader who gives the text meaning: it means nothing in itself. 'Interpreters do not decode poems: they make them'. This process relieves the critical student of literature of the obligation to be right, and demands only that he be 'interesting'.

Todorov also relates these theoretical developments to Marxism. Marxism relates literary works to the world, but this relationship is a specific one. The book is a product of the world, and is of necessity 'historical' — a product of its class and time. The Marxist impulse is to turn certain concepts — 'liberalism', 'humanism', 'individualism' — into dirty words. Any quest for value is reduced to the defence of a particular group's interests: 'good' is defined as what contributes to the 'socialist transformation of society', and all is subject to social and historical determinism.

Both the post-structuralist theorists and the Marxists have a common aim — which is the rejection of humanism — that is, the rejection of the attempt to ground science and ethics in reason. We could perhaps add that both represent a rejection of that whole telos of the pursuit of truth in Ancient Greek society. The whole trend of these 'new' movements is anti-humanist. And, as Todorov says, it is impossible to defend human rights out of one side of your mouth, while deconstructing the idea of humanity out of the other.

Todorov suggests that it is urgent that the 'relationship between literature and the world must be recognised, and both must be related to values.' lie is reviewing a new book by Robert Scholes, *Textual Power: Literary Theory and the Teaching of English*, and he quotes him as saying:

> We will have to restore the judgemental dimension to criticism, not in the trivial sense of ranking literary texts, but in the more serious sense of questioning the values proferred by the texts we study.

Todorov hopes that the whole unfortunate episode of contemporary criticism may be rapidly forgotten. 'The question "What does this text mean?" is a relevant one and we must try to answer it.' That is right. Even as the new interest in literary theory came to Cambridge, it was already *passé*, as Roger Poole has indicated. But a new task develops even from Todorov's recommendation: to answer that kind of question we need a new extension of exploration — which is that to which I have been pointing, in turning to philosophical anthropology, for every such question involves us in examining our 'model' of human nature, and our concepts of knowledge. Todorov's conclusions are close to those of Geoffrey Strickland, which I have discussed elsewhere, in reviewing his *Structuralism or Criticism?**

During the period of development about which Todorov writes, I have been engaged in the exploration of quite a different area of philosophical thought, about man, consciousness and culture. In this sphere, which I call by its general title of philosophical anthropology, I have found no clash between (say) the findings of psychotherapists and philosophical biologists, and the traditional practice of the teaching of English. There seems no call, in the light of (say) existentialist psychotherapy or *Daseins* analysis, to question our fundamental assumptions, about the importance of attention to creative art, or its value to the human sensibility. It is thus startling to find, as in reading the above-mentioned earlier symposium on teaching English, that established methods which we have long practised are now regarded as strikingly new.

Todorov, of course, has written a book on Bahktin, who seeks to emphasise that literature represents the meeting of consciousnesses and seems to me to be saying the same kind of thing as Leavis, in a more tormented form, his style a consequence of his appalling isolation.

**New Universities Quarterly*, Autumn 1981, Volume 35, No.4, P.507.

DIFFERENCES FROM F.R. LEAVIS

I hoped as Director of English Studies at Downing College to carry on as best I could the best kind of work in F.R. Leavis's tradition. At the same time it must be clear that I feel a different philosophical basis is necessary to underpin English studies. 'This is clearly a critical time.' Thus Leavis in his Preface to *Education and the University* (1943). That book was full of hope: alas, in his later books the hopes seemed to have been dashed. His early book was full of idealism. 'Such prepotency as this country may hope for in the English-speaking world of the future must lie in the cultural realm' he said in the same Preface, and demanded a 'focus of the finer life of cultural tradition'. The university that made an effort to be this would have a chance of becoming 'if not the Athens of the English-speaking world, the unmistakable main focus of the Athenian function it had done so much to confirm to this country' (P.11).

Towards this goal, Leavis defined 'critical analysis and the training of sensibility' later in his book. This was in the attempt to correct the 'futilities, misdirections and wastes commonly incident to academic literary study'. Leavis used to tell us that much of his book was 'bluff' and while there is much that was good and seminal in it, there also seems some confusion. With its pages on T.S.Eliot and its end-piece made out of *How to Teach Reading — a Primer for Ezra Pound*, it seems now something of a hotch-potch. Characteristically, too, there is much devoted to contention, to denunciations and scathing dismissal. Yet, of course, there was also much in it that was original and constructive.

Leavis wanted a 'discipline of sensibility and intelligence'. His aim was 'to deal in doctrine, theory, and general terms as little as possible.' But he did give a brief outline of his assumptions (pp.18ff). He believed we still have a positive cultural tradition — but we must surely now be more doubtful of this because of the huge new influence of television, and the subsequent collapse of reading as a habit or discipline (which D.S.Brewer has called a 'disaster'*).

*See *The Cambridge Review*, Autumn 1982.

Leavis believed that we could, in 'attempting at an ancient university an experiment in liberal education, count on a sufficient measure of agreement, overt and implicit, about essential values, to make it unnecessary to discuss ultimate sanctions, or provide a philosophy, before starting to work . . . and I believe further that what is unnecessary is best avoided.'

As will be apparent from what I have written elsewhere (as in *The Leavises*, ed. Denys Thompson, C.U.P. 1985), I believe that it was a shortcoming on Leavis's part not to work out the 'ultimate sanctions' thoroughly.

Today except for a few traditional embodiments like the traditional A level literature examination and the Tripos at best, we cannot confidently claim that we 'still have a positive cultural tradition' and we cannot 'count on a sufficient measure of agreement . . . about essential values'. It is even more necessary to provide a philosophy, to underpin English.

Leavis, at this point in his essay, reflects upon 'Humanism' and tries to distinguish his own approach from that of the Humanism of Irving Babbitt, which seeks by way of Confucius, Buddha, Socrates and Erasmus to establish a definition. Leavis reiterates the phrase 'ancient English university'—-a gesture that seems today difficult to endorse without uneasiness as does his insistence upon 'the relation of humane culture to religion, and the place of religion in civilisation', as a proper study within English.

I find Leavis vague and evasive at this point, where he is trying to define what a humanistic education in English really implies:

> The aim is to keep as close as possible to the concrete, and to deal with general considerations in terms related as immediately as possible to practice

'Given', he goes on 'the measure of actual and tacit agreement about ends that can, be counted on for working purposes.' But supposing they cannot be?

Leavis goes on to talk about the 'drift' of contemporary society, and how it is 'against those forms of liberal thinking which seem most essential to its welfare' (a quote from *The Experimental College*, Alexander Meiklejohn, p.138). Society, Leavis believes, has incurred a progressive debility of consciousness, and seems to have lost 'intelligence, memory and moral purpose'. Statesmen and other leaders have proved inadequate to their tasks. The general drift has been technocratic, and the predominant view, that all that matters is the smooth running of the machinery is over-simple: what needs to be avoided is both the breakdown of the machinery on the one hand, and its triumph — 'a final surrender to it of the human spirit'. Leavis is here also relying on *Thoughts After Flexner* by Brooks Otis, an American writer.

> Here, in this work, we have the function that is preeminently the university's; if the work is not done there it will not be done anywhere. (Leavis, p.24)

Is it the task of the university to train what Leavis calls the 'central intelligence' to tackle such problems? Is it the task of the university to produce the 'educated man' (and woman) — the man of humane culture who is equipped to be intelligent and responsible about the problems of contemporary civilisation? Should the university be a 'focus of humane consciousness, a centre where, faced with the specialisations and distractions in which human ends lose themselves, intelligence, bringing to bear a mature sense of values, should apply itself to the problems of civilisation?'

Surely it should: but, as Leavis admits, 'contemplation of the idea doesn't conduce to satisfaction with the actual'. The assumed beneficial influence of the mixed Cambridge system doesn't really generate cross-disciplinary intercourse. And I have heard it argued that Leavis's kind of emphasis on the need for the English Faculty to see itself as saving the world implied, in all that *Scrutiny* movement, a failure to acknowledge the intrinsic value of the other disciplines. Today, the argument is now advanced that sociology, anthropology, politics and other such studies have become the proper specialisms to deal with questions of 'culture and environment'. Then of course there are one's doubts about what goes on. For instance, a supervisor recently wrote on a student's essay in my own college:

> You had better think how to condense this essay for the purposes of the examination. I suggest that you adopt the structure of this

> essay and produce numbered points under each heading: once you have done this you should be able to memorise the argument.

A good deal of work for English examinations is still a parrot-like training to 'unload against the clock'. But insofar as we do try to strive to offer a real education through English, can we confidently say what is the connection between, say, reading Marvell's *Dialogue between the Body and the Soul* or Arnold's *Dover Beach* — and the development of the sensibility of the student we are working with?

Leavis, I believe, tended to simplify the problem, conceiving of his work, in the Arnoldian tradition, in terms of a moral or idealising crusade: and then, in the outcome, as so often with moral crusades, becoming disappointed and despairing because the world resisted redemption as it always does. Leavis did seem to become disillusioned in his later works.

In the Arnoldian tradition, Leavis clung to the idea of refinement of sensibility, and the exercise of intelligence, in a whole way, in literature. Quite properly, he insisted on literature at best as a form of thought about human experience and possibilities. But he was unrealistic in supposing that by teaching students and promoting good university English departments, it was possible to redeem our civilisation. The frustration of his idealism in this sphere no doubt generated his later deep despair (as, for instance, in his later exchanges with Ian Robinson in *The Human World*).*

Behind this frustration lies, I believe, a false conception, as has already been hinted at, in the 'model' of human nature Leavis used, and his sense of what good culture could do for man. Culture does not directly affect us like good health food. Though undoubtedly it has a moral effect, so that one's response to a really great work can be a 'moral teething' (to use a phrase from *Wuthering Heights*), a mere work of culture cannot affect the whole of one's psychic tissue more than a little, any more than an author can 'shed his sickness in books' (as D.H. Lawrence put

*See 'Believing In the University', *The Human World*, nos.15-16, 1974, p.98

it). It is a study of the insights of psychoanalysis which has impressed upon me the intractability of the psychic tissue — of the stubbornness of our composition as human beings.

Of course, culture can contribute to inner resources, and this is very evident in teaching young children. In a most marvellous way, they seize gratefully upon any cultural offering, using in to enrich their powers. Thus, if you read a poem by Blake or Li Po to a class of young children, you will find them using the rhythms and modes of these poets in their own writing, to explore and give organisation to their own experience. But all this happens at the level of symbolisation, from the unconscious to the conscious level: and it is a question of contributing to the search for meaning. In this there are many unseen factors — one of which is the personality of the teacher *in loco parentis*. Human beings are flexible, not to say malleable, at various stages of growth. Infants and juniors look up and expect to be fed and changed: adolescents revolt, in order to develop their own values. Young parents become very flexible, when their children are new and young. But for most adults change in the self requires the matrix of a close relationship, as psychotherapists have discovered (involving transference).

There is a great deal to investigate about the way symbolism can affect personality, and there are some fascinating papers by psychoanalysts such as Melanie Klein, Hannah Segal, Marion Milner, Marie von Naevestad, and D.W.Winnicott. One finds in case histories that patients will employ symbols which emerge from the talking cure processes of therapy, to work on deep psychic problems. This illuminated in a remarkable way in two books in particular, which I have already mentioned: Marion Milner's *In the Hands of the Living God* and Marie von Naevestad's *The Colours of Rage and Love*. But in both it is obvious that to really modify one's inner world and its relation to outer reality, by cultural effort, takes years of energetic application and engagement, the support of a close therapist, and a profound gravity of application.

So, while to seek to 'improve' people morally by literature is impossible, as we know from reports on therapy done in the context of a close personal relationship, where progress is slow and painful, to offer individuals sustenance for their quest for meaning is always valuable, as a contribution to their moral life. In the wider sphere, all one can do is to offer demonstrations of one's own search for truth, as in literary criticism, and to engage with the philosophical issues, to try to shift the intellectual climate. Leavis did both, and achieved enormous success with education and the realm of culture. But he could not succeed as he hoped, even in making a little Athens of any one university English department, even by his powerful influence on his pupils, and certainly not in transforming the world as he wanted to.

The reason was that, despite the hundreds who were personally trained by him, these could not become a dominant reading public, or really predominate in the field of literary and cultural ideas, though they did have a considerable influence in the schools and universities. Certainly, Leavis did achieve one major task, which was to help make the study of literature a serious discipline.* But the way in which the school of 'Downing English' has not continued to be a central influence has something to do with the lack of recognition in Leavis that in his work, and among the minority he established through *Scrutiny*, there was emerging a philosophical position. This philosophical position has not been consolidated. Leavis himself also turned against philosophy. He felt that he must stick by his insistence that a literary critic should avoid abstractions, and always demonstrate his discipline in 'whole' terms.

The influence of his work as it persists in 'A' level syllabuses and certainly in many university syllabuses, as at Cambridge, marks a great achievement of response to the text. But when it came to discuss the 'upshot' of the text, he had moved into more general grounds, of psychology and philosophy, but yet refused discourse. He failed to note that, in making any literary judgement, one inevitably adopts a philosophical anthropology, and must be prepared to argue the case for it, if Socratic dialogue is to be sustained as the process of finding truth. So, though Leavis told us his stance was 'This is so, is it not?', this only applied to the actual literary judgement, and not to the implications in it about psychology and philosophy.

*See the essay by the present author in *The Leavises*, ed. Denys Thompson, Cambridge University Press, 1984.

Despite his occasional pertinent references to Polanyi, Marjorie Grene and even F.J.J. Buytendijk, Leavis seemed not to recognise that literary studies, that 'English', inevitably involves us in considerations which belong to psychology and philosophy, yet it is interesting to note that he quite clearly recognised that this extension was necessary, in *Education and the University*, in his 'Sketch for an English School' even if later he refused to pursue the implications.

No-one, he says, would suppose that a 'literary education' would be satisfactory by itself.

> One of the virtues of literary studies is that they lead constantly outside themselves, and, on the other hand, while it is necessary that they should be controlled by a concern for the essential discipline, such a concern, if it is adequate, counts on associated work in other fields. p.35

This, indeed, is the basis of a proper 'liberal' education: something better than the former Classical Greats syllabus at Oxford is, however, necessary, in this broader approach.

Later, the concern for the proper discipline led Leavis to reject 'Philosophy', even when it demanded the examination of the norms implicitly invoked in critical discrimination (as in his controversy with Réné Wellek). But in his earlier sketch he postulates an intelligence trained in English which will be able to deal with issues in any Humanities subject better than those trained deal in those subjects:

> Some critics will still insist that the proposed scheme cannot produce the properly trained man, the man properly trained in anything; that it might be said to aim explicitly at the production of the amateur. The reply must be: Call him what you like; we want to produce a mind that knows what precision and specialist knowledge are, is aware of the words not in its own possession that are necessary, has a maturity of outlook such as the study of history ought to produce but even the general historian by profession doesn't always exhibit, and has been trained in a kind of thinking, a scrupulously sensitive yet enterprising use of intelligence, that is of its nature not specialised but cannot be expected

> without special training — a mind, energetic and resourceful, that will apply itself to the problems of civilization, and eagerly continue to improve its equipment and explore fresh approaches. . . p.59

One detects in Leavis's adjectives here that intense idealism of which I have spoken: did he ever find a mind, trained by himself, which matched up to the goal? As far as I know, every mind he found or trained was eventually discovered to be treacherous, or feeble, or 'unintelligent', in the end. And his own account of the actual processes of passing the Tripos seem to verge on the cynical and expedient:

> 'These are my three (or four) "questions", with one to spare, in case of bad luck'.p.50

But in his outline for 'a piece of work' (in this instance on the seventeenth century) Leavis shows that English must inevitably involve itself in a position. As it turned out (as Roger Poole made clear*) this was an anti-Cartesian Position, and an existentialist one.

He sought to promote 'the prospecting and ranging mind', by stimulating '"extra-literary" reading', declaring:

> So much in his intellectual after-life may depend upon the start a man gets and the habits he forms at the university.

So, Leavis proposes 'a specially accessible library' containing 'a number of copies of certain books e.g. 'the best of Christopher Dawson, *Middletown*, Ian D. Suttie's *The Origins of Love and Hate*, and such works of sociology, anthropology, history, political thought, and so on'. p.61

The drawing up and revision of this list, he declares, 'would be valuable experience for the seniors concerned'. Indeed it would: and one may say of the proposed list that it had not been sufficiently thought out—-both in terms of what it contained, and what it represented. It has the limitations of that rather

---

**Life Versus Death in the Later Criticism of F.R. Leavis, Renaissance and Modern Studies*, Vol. XVI, 1972 later reprinted in *Universities Quarterly*.

narrow interest in sociology, politics and history which the choice of books for review in *Scrutiny* represents. But the most significant item is perhaps Ian D. Suttie's critique of Freud:* obviously, prompted by Harding, Leavis saw that one essential area of concern was the model of man which we adopt. (Suttie's book was one which prompted the present author to write *Human Hope and the Death Instinct*.) It is quite clear from these pages that Leavis recognises that the movement out from English into philosophical anthropology is inevitable and necessary, and that the crisis in which we are engaged is an intellectual one, as well as one requiring English to attend to 'whole experience'.

Above we have seen Leavis emphasising the need to be 'concrete', by which he implies that the kind of English studies he wishes to foster would attend to the 'whole' possession of literary works of art, rather than statements of 'doctrine'. That is a valuable emphasis: but it needs to be extended — for students need to know also why they are attending to these works, and what the implications are, both of the works, and of what they are doing. What they are doing is to participate in an imaginative act which should change them and develop their sense of the meaning of existence. It should generate in them a philosophical position which also suggests a way of life. Leavis's view of this process is too much limited to the Arnoldian. The choices students made in literary discrimination he believed would transfer directly to choices in life. As I have suggested, this is too moralistic — and sentimental — a view, in the psychoanalytical sense. To develop it, I believe we should adopt a more Nietzschean view, such as I have outlined in my earlier chapter, from Rollo May's historical account of the developments in philosophical anthropology which led to the existentialist movement in psychotherapy, in *Existence — A New Dimension in Psychiatry* (1958).

As Roger Poole sought to show in his useful article, Leavis was an existentialist in his emphasis on 'whole experience' and 'life' — and on those meanings and values by which life may be lived and experience found valuable. He championed unique individual

*Ian D.Suttie's *The Origins of Love and Hate* has, I am delighted to see, been re-issued by Free Association Press, 1989.

'being', like Dickens, Blake and Lawrence. The trouble was that lie so feared and hated philosophy, as a naive substitution of rational abstractions for life, that he refused to develop the philosophical basis of his own position. Yet he would have surely understood the position of the sociologist existentialist, Feuerbach, who declared, 'Do not wish to be a philosopher in contrast to being a man . . . do not think as a thinker . . . think as a living, real being, Think in Existence.' (Quoted by Paul Tillich, 'Existential Philosophy' in *The Journal of the History of Ideas*, 5:1, 44-70 1949).

This kind of emphasis is surely what Leavis meant by his term 'concrete' discussed above. Existentialism, as a branch of philosophical anthropology, has always been a reaction against intellectualism, desiring instead to attend to vitality and immediate experience: to 'life' in Leavis's sense.

Where Leavis was wrong was in attributing the evils of the contemporary culture and sensibility to the machine and to science, and the need to serve the machinery of a materialistic, functional society. It is true that there has been a hostility to poetry to be found in science, from Galileo to Bentham and beyond (and Leavis reacted strongly against the attempts of those like I.A. Richards who tried to give a 'scientific' explanation of the value of poetry, as in *Principles of Literary Criticism and Science and Poetry*). There are philosophies of existence which relate to the industrial technological world, in the wake of Jeremy Bentham and utilitarianism, and we may even trace these attitudes to the emergence of a new faith in science and the scientific manipulation of the world, which flowered in the seventeenth century. (Leavis's 'project' for the student on the seventeenth century was intended to prompt the philosophical investigation of the metaphysical assumptions of modern science.)

However, it is not the science that is the problem, but the attitude to man which emerged from it. It is the functional or utilitarian concept of human nature which is the problem, along with the concept it has promoted of what knowledge is, and what truth is. Truth and the real have tended to become conceived in terms of scientific fact, where there must be verifiable referents.

Under this paradigm, love, the good, and the beautiful, the sense of man's tragic predicament, such issues and concepts and modes of engaging with them are relegated to the condition of nonsense and comment on them has come to seem mere emotional noises. What is real in the world is mere matter-in-motion 'molecules and atoms', while life and man are drawn into this mechanistic reduction. Even in biology what is real is the non-living — the primary characteristics of living creatures are not found in the paradigm, and we seriously fail to find 'the category of life'.

The success of the scientific revolution was actually achieved by a certain trick of mind, by which a philosopher-mathematician like Réné Descartes could divide the world into *Res Cogitans* and *Res Extensa*: the mind, all pure subjectivity on the one hand, and all the real material of the universe on the other ('objective reality'): with no connection between them but the pineal gland! Leavis saw that he had to be an anti-Cartesian, to try to heal this division: but he misconstrued the philosophical problem and supposed that the whole scientific revolution and development of technology itself had to be opposed. The truth is, of course, that even in science the limitations of 'objectivity' are becoming obvious, while the problem is also one of making technical power the servant of man's being, a need which is becoming obvious in a world-wide way, as through the growth of ecology movement and peace movements. We do not want to regress from scientific progress: what we do need is a better science and a better metaphysic (and Ethics) to direct it, and for this we need to rediscover the perspectives in which unique being and the subjective life can be found and recognised as realities.

Further problems in this realm of philosophical discourse as they affect the teaching of English at the university may be examined by taking up some arguments put forward by F.R. Leavis in a late essay, 'Justifying One's Valuation of Blake', published in *The Human World*.* Leavis is trying to say that Blake's art works in an ineffable way: where his poetry seems greatest, it operates upon us very much in the way such a poem as T.S. Eliot's *Marina* works upon us. We could not even perhaps say what it is 'about'. It is impossible to put the 'message' or 'upshot' of a poem like Blake's *Tyger* or *The Sun-flower* in 'other' words. Leavis rejects those

**The Human World* No.7, May 1972, P.42

treatises on Blake which attempt to offer a 'philosophy' deduced from the poetry: 'Blake is peculiarly exposed to falsifying expectations and wrongheaded cults that (philosophy) may very well encourage.' Yet Leavis himself takes up a philosophical position: 'Blake used the names of Newton and Locke' out of an 'insistence on human creativity—-the creativity of life'. He 'insisted in an age of Lockean commonsense', that perception was not passive, and that there was a 'continuity from the inherent creativity of perception to the creativity, trained and conscious, of the artist.' Moreover, Blake's position, 'implies a conception of human creativity that is at the same time a conception of human responsibility; and one aspect of Blake's living importance is that he compels us to realise fully and clearly what 'human responsibility' means. I believe that Leavis tends at this point to begin to make up a philosophy of his own, out of some reading he has done around Blake.

Leavis picks up terms from Blake and Blake criticism, such as 'selfhood' and 'identity', and, mingling them with some phrases from D.H. Lawrence, he devises a highly tendentious position, which he uses to resist the attitudes of humanism. Leavis believed that the worst sin was to be 'enclosed in the ego': this debarred individuals from 'tragic experience'. The hubris of the humanist position consists in believing that one does 'belong to oneself' — and Leavis's insistence, which is really religious, is that one does not 'belong to oneself':

> The 'self-hood' is that which asserts itself and seeks to possess from within its self-enclosure. The 'identity' is the individual being as the disinterested focus of life; it was 'identity' that Lawrence's Tom Brangwen 'knew he did not belong to himself'. Blake was voicing the same recognition when he said of his paintings and designs, 'though I call them mine, I know that they are not mine.'

Leavis here has in mind two aspects of the creative process. One is the feeling some writers have recorded that when they are being truly creative they feel as if they are 'taken over' by some other power, which writes 'through' them. But Leavis also seems to believe that human creativity in general, our intentionality, is a manifestation of deference to a reality in the cosmos outside ourselves, to which we must feel a profound responsibility. To seek to manipulate 'life' for our ego-bound purposes is an offence to this greater responsibility. Here in the background we may detect the Iong emphasis in *Scrutiny* and the 'Culture and Environment' movement, on the dangers of man feeling that he has a right to exploit the resources of the world, and to manipulate life for the purposes of exerting his sense of a god-like power over matter.

Most people would want to use the word 'God' for the power to which we ought to defer, but Leavis cannot do this. At the same time he is influenced by philosophers like Michael Polanyi and Marjorie Grene who have been resisting the position taken up by a mechanistic, positivistic science, which tends to be unable to find 'the category of life'. What Leavis failed to recognise was the complex difficulties of finding one's way among the philosophical positions here.

He sees that Blake is an ally, in the attempt to find a philosophical position from which it is possible to find 'life'. He says that Blake was a 'great psychologist': but in this he asserts that he imposes 'an anti-positivist, or anti-pseudo-scientific, sense on the word "psychology".'

A great deal more needed to be said here, however. It will not do to equate 'positivist' with 'pseudo-scientific'. Leavis was probably thinking of I.A. Richard's attempts to explain the effect of poetry in terms of the gratification of 'appetancies', which does surely represent a false application of organistic concepts to the realm of consciousness. But positivism is a respectable scientific position — it only becomes false if it is extrapolated to suppose that it can include the whole of reality, both inner and outer. It is appropriate for a scientist to declare that he will take account only of those things which can be measured or seen, for certain purposes. It is only when he declares that, because he has adopted this position, those things which cannot be measured or seen, like love, or consciousness or existential insecurity, do not exist at all. It is perfectly proper for a scientist to develop a theory from the measurement of phenomena, to apply to things in general, even living organisms. But where lie comes into conflict with a thinker like Blake is when he implicitly denies that 'life' only exists in terms of individual unique beings, each with a once-in-a-lifetime experience of his life-world, in which alone his valid existence is.

What Leavis needed here was a much more thought-out critique of modern Western science to apply, and to use in his rejection of the effects of utilitarianism. He obviously has in mind the kind of objection Dickens made, through Sissy Jupe, to the mathematical way of looking at human existence, which derives from the utilitarian 'calculus' as Leavis called it. Leavis is really resisting the kind of 'blasphemy' to which Kierkegaard objected, when man's existence and life are subjected to the disciplines of an 'objective' natural science. Leavis is championing the reality of the unique being's 'thisness'.

Leavis however, should have been aware that he was making in this essay an existentialist statement: referring to a book on Blake's Humanism, he says:

> 'what the author intends by it is to emphasise (rightly) the characteristic of Blake's thought expressed in his insistence that Man, concretely ' there' only in the individual human being and governed by his knowledge that he doesn't belong to himself, is responsible for determining what his responsibility is. That is indistinguishable from determining what he himself is in relation to what he ought to be (according to the *ahnung*, the divination, he at the same time develops, tests and sharpens).

Leavis was very evasive about what he meant by this word *ahnung* (which should be spelt *Ahnung*). It means 'inkling' and seems to indicate a feeling a man has, that there is some kind of obligation upon him, coming from the cosmos, pressing upon him a sense of obligation, to use the life that has been given to him, to serve higher purposes that are not his to determine, but for him to seek to understand and follow.

But at once, we may sense difficulties. For while Leavis approves of the general idea that Blake possessed, that man was fallen Adam, and our task is to redeem him, Leavis goes on to reject Blake's ideas about how this is to be achieved: he falls, says Leavis, into 'wordy and boring unreality'. How, then do we recognise when our *Ahnung*-promptings are 'true', and when they are 'boring' or 'unreal' Leavis declares that 'the creative' agents of human insight and wisdom must 'resist' the 'promptings of religious and metaphysical thought' whenever they 'incite to the presentation of the unimaginable'. This seems to be the kind of objection Leavis makes to Eliot's exploration of the possibilities of another world, in *Four Quartets*, and it sounds too terribly like an echo of Mr. Gradgrind's, 'You are not to imagine!' In any case, how do we decide what is the true insight from our creative powers, our *Ahnung* — and what is false, because it comes from our religious or metaphysical promptings? Leavis mentions Lawrence, and here we encounter an acute question. For Lawrence, like Blake, had his own promptings — and many of these were certainly unreal (and could be boring) — as in his enthusiasm for sodomy (as in *The Rainbow* and *Lady Chatterley's Lover*), for domination over woman by a man capable of murder (as in *The Plumed Serpent*) and other demented fantasies. When was Lawrence prompted by genuine insights into the relationship between man and woman, and when was he acting out in fantasy extremely dangerous false solutions, in terms of putting woman under control because she was so dangerous? And how do we judge?

Answers can only be explored, by careful examination of the nature of true and false solutions, in the inner life, such as we may find in psychoanalytical discourse. This, of course, was not an area of exploration of consciousness that appealed to Leavis. But what Leavis does see is that we belong to an era, and that this era imposes upon us its particular philosophy of existence. In its concepts of what knowledge is, and thus of what the world is, it imposes limitations upon us, and Blake was one of those who was concerned to throw these limitations off. Here he quotes Marjorie Grene's famous passage, about the need to throw off the Newtonian cosmology and the Newtonian method. Literary studies, in English, Leavis sees belong to this impetus. Human creativity has fallen into a fallen condition, because of the effects of 'Newton's sleep'. Leavis even sees that a new kind of philosophical biology is necessary:

> For Blake, the enemy of Locke and Newton, might have inspired Marjorie Grene's account of our need, and brings a good deal

> more than endorsement to the wisdom of Michael Polanyi, the scientist-philosopher whose pupil Marjorie Grene was. Few educated persons will dispute the reasonableness of the assumption that there was once a time when there was, in the world of Nature, no life. Life emerged, and no scientist or philosopher has been able to explain how, or by what causation — apart from the persistent offer to explain it away. Though we have to recognise that Darwin's life testifies to the existence of intelligence and purpose, his theory of evolution offered to dispense with the need for those words.

Indirectly, in this essay, Leavis is making out a case for inter-disciplinary studies, and for that combination of attention to psychology, epistemology, sociology, history, and philosophy which he made in a paragraph in *Education and the University*. Blake represents a challenge to being, or rather on behalf of being, against the whole tendency of our era to deny being implicitly. This bears upon the nature of our thought, and the way it brings down upon us a mechanistic universe in which intelligence and purpose do not seem at home, do not seem to exist. We need to restore not only a sense of being at home in the universe, against a sense of alienation, but also of being capable of intentionality, of creative perception and creative engagement with the universe — while at the same time feeling our deepest sense of responsibility, to life, and to our own capacities to know: for we are the only knowers of the universe.

> Essential or Blakean responsibility manifests itself in the full accepting recognition that the directing *Ahnung* implicit in life and the *nisus* that had led to the achieving of mind and anticipatory apprehension and initiative are to be thought of as, in the world we know (Los's world), pre-eminently represented by humanity. They are, as Blake conceives it, human responsibility.

Leavis quotes Collingwood: the human world entails of its very nature the recognition that (in Collingwood's words) 'it must ultimately depend for its existence on something other than itself.'

Leavis does not sufficiently spell out what it is he means, by these explorations into metaphysics, and the philosophy of being. What he does convey to us is the sense that Polanyi conveys, that there is much that lies beyond the grasp of our minds, and that there are mysterious aspects of our existence to which we need to be respectfully deferential. But what Leavis fails to make clear is that what Blake was concerned about was the 'mind-forged manacles' — that our state of being fallen Man is very much a matter of being imprisoned in inadequate concepts of 'life', or the universe, and of ourselves, by which some of the more significant aspects of our existence are excluded.

It was valuable for Leavis to insist that 'It is because he was a great artist that (Blake) matters'. His essay makes it clear that, if we begin with (say) Blake's *Tyger*, we are taken, inevitably, into profound philosophical issues — using the word 'philosophical', that is, to indicate problems of the philosophy of being. Blake's Tyger, Leavis says, indicates the problem of 'energy'. But Leavis does not say, as he should have done, that there are two problems indicated by the symbolism of the poem. There is the problem of destructiveness 'out there' — there are cruel and terrible things in the world, and these pose questions of the nature of the dynamics which brought them into being.

But the terror evoked by *The Tyger* is also a terror of aspects of the inner life: that kind of destructiveness is within us,too. The imagery in *The Tyger* seems to derive from echoes of the apocalyptic images in Macbeth's famous soliloquy, in which he sees Pity, like a naked new-born babe, striding the blast, evoking a universal compassion. So, when the stars see the creation of the tiger, they throw down their spears in a shower of cosmic pity. How is it possible for there to exist in the universe, such creative, redemptive entities as the Lamb, and such destructive, if beautiful, terrors as the Tiger? How do we come to terms with the co-existence of these forces? And in coming to terms with them do we not have to accept the mysterious, terrifying, appalling and dark capacities we know there to be, in our inner world, as well as love and creativity?

From reading a poem like *The Tyger*, thus, we move out into profound questions of the nature of existence, and the nature of nature. Who made the world? How did it come into being? How do we even think about the nature of the world and being? What meaning do these things have? Leavis resists the translation of these problems into explicit 'philosophy' and 'psychology', but here he was wrong. We can both explore them explicitly, and admit their ineffable quality. We can both respond to poems, recognising that we shall never fully plumb their depths, and discuss the implications for a philosophy of being and an exploration of the inner life. And while we must face the problem that our existence does depend upon 'something other than itself' — that there are mysteries, that there may be a need to recognise some 'innovative principle' in the universe, and some organising 'intelligence' which has 'achieved' the higher forms, we do not — as Leavis seems to suggest — have to accept some new dogma, such as Leavis's insistence that Human reality, the human condition to which art belongs, is inescapably a matter of individual human beings in their relationship with one another, the only conceivable way in which Man could be 'there'.

For some there will be 'ultimate ends' and another kind of reality altogether, such as Eliot finds in *Four Quartets* (but which Leavis will not allow him). It is true that poetry is 'heuristic' and that it is 'concerned with discovery, or new realization — with apprehensions and intuitions that of their nature can't be stated'. But those related explorations which can be stated may be pursued alongside the poem — just as, in reading *Marina*, we may discuss the meaning of femininity (as indicated by the reference to a 'daughter'), symbolism of the sea and shore, and the echoes through the fog, even when we could never put *Marina* into 'our own words'. Unfortunately, Leavis became increasingly dogmatic and exclusive: yet he should have known, from his own reading of Polanyi, that all we can have is open Socratic dialogue, allowing any kind of commentary, in the hope that out of the exchanges will come new insights and apprehensions of truth. 'English' studies are an important contribution to that pursuit of truth, and no-one has done more to define them as such than Leavis. But in his distrust of 'philosophy', his peculiar narrow view of 'psychology', his rejection of science as 'pseudo-science', his distrust of science and hostility to it, he was not serving learning in a sufficiently disinterested way. He was seeking to create a dogmatic position, even amid philosophies which of their very nature abhor dogmatism. Attending to Blake, as to every creative artist, should generate openness in us, and attention to the new and undiscovered. While there is a philosophical position to be established, from philosophical anthropology, it is by way of indicating that many of our modes of thought (like 'Newton's sleep') are limiting and confining: our aim must be to move into wider dimensions, and thereby find out more of truth.

In this we need to move beyond Leavis, not seeking, as he did, to establish a position from which to establish authority and control, but to open out again the kind of questions the ancient Greeks pursued, at the beginning of our era in seeking the truth both about outer and inner reality.

WHAT IS ENGLISH IN PRACTICE?

McGilchrist (above) rightly detected, in his *T.L.S.* contribution, behind current uncertainty is the fact that English exists within a higher education system which is predominantly based on the philosophies of the scientific revolution, on positivism, reductionism, mechanistic materialism, and its essential denial of 'life', consciousness, being and mystery. No wonder Leavis found himself at the heart of a philosophical anti-Cartesian, anti-utilitarian debate!

Now, it seems to me, two steps need to be taken to 'rescue' English. First, we need to insist that what we are doing in our normal day-to-day work on poetry, drama and novels is a real discipline: getting students to read and to be articulate about their reading, while we try to exemplify good reading in our own work. My demonstrations of attentive reading, however, should make it plain that as soon as one opens a book or opens one's mouth in English one is moving into philosophical anthropology; and so there is a new need to extend the context of the subject into the wider field of the Humanities.

Let me try to demonstrate what is involved in this discipline, taking an ordinary everyday example of the kind of thing one might do in supervision.

Here is an exercise, comparing a passage from North's *Plutarch*, with what Shakespeare made of it:

> A. 'Therefore, when she was sent unto by divers letters, both from Antonius himselfe and also from his frends, she made so light of it, and mocked Antonius so much, that she disdained to set forward otherwise, but to take her barge in the river of Cydnus; the poope whereof was of gold, the sailes of purple, and the owers of silver, which kept stroke in rowing after the sounde of the musicke of flutes, howboyes, citherns, violls and such other instruments as they played upon in the barge. And now for the person of her selfe, she was layed under a pavilion of cloth of gold of tissue, apparelled and attired like the goddesse Venus, commonly drawen in picture: and hard by her, on either hand of

her, pretie faire boyes apparelled as painters doe set forth god Cupid, with little fannes in their hands, with the which they fanned wind upon her. Her ladies and gentlewomen also, the fairest of them were apparelled like the nymphes Nereides (which are the mermaides of the waters) and like the Graces; some steering the helme, others tending the tackle and ropes of the barge, out of the which there came a wonderfull passing sweete savour of perfumes, that perfumed the wharfes side, pestered with innumerable multitudes of people. Some of them followed the barge all alongest the rivers side; others also ranne out of the citie to see her coming in. So that in thend, there ranne such multitudes of people one after another to see her, that Antonius was left post alone in the market-place, in his Imperiall seate, to geve audience; and there went a rumour in the peoples mouths, that the goddess Venus was come to play with the god Bacchus, for the generall good of all Asia. When Cleopatra landed, Antonius sent to invite her to supper to him. But she sent him word againe, he should doe better rather to come and suppe to her. Antonius therefore, to show himself curteous unto her at her arrivall, was contented to obey her, and went to supper to her: where he found such passing sumptuous fare, that no tongue can expresse it.'

B.

ENOBARBUS: I will tell you,
The barge she sat in, like a burnish'd throne
Burnt on the water: the poop was beaten gold,
Purple the sails; and so perfumed that
The winds were love-sick with them
The oars were silver,
Which to the tune of flutes kept stroke, and made
The water which they beat, to follow faster
As amorous of their strokes. For her own person,
It beggar'd all description, she did lie
In her pavilion, cloth of gold, of tissue,
O'er-picturing that Venus, where we see
The fancy out-work Nature. On each side her,

Stood pretty dimpled boys, like smiling Cupids,
With divers colour'd fans whose wind did seem
To glow the delicate cheeks which they did cool,
And what they undid did.

AGRIPPA: Oh rare for Antony!

ENOBARBUS: Her gentlewomen, like the Nereides,
So many mermaids tended her i'th' eyes,
And made their bends adornings. At the helm,
A seeming mermaid steers: the silken tackle
Swell with the touches of those flower-soft hands
That yarely frame the office. From the barge
A strange invisible perfume hits the sense
Of the adjacent wharfs. The city cast
Her people out upon her; and Antony
Enthron'd i' th' market-place, did sit alone,
Whistling to th' air: which but for vacancy,
Had gone to gaze on Cleopatra too,
And made a gap in Nature.

AGRIPPA: Rare Egyptian!

ENOBARBUS: Upon her landing, Antony sent to her
Invited her to supper; she replied,
It should be better, he became her guest:
Which she entreated, our courteous Antony,
Whom ne'er the word of no woman heard speak,
Being barber's ten times o'er, goes to the feast:
And for his ordinary, pays his heart,
For what his eyes eat only.

AGRIPPA: Royal wench:
She made great Caesar lay his sword to bed,
He plough'd her, and she cropp'd.

ENOBARBUS: I saw her once
Hop forty paces through the public street,
And having lost her breath, she spoke, and panted,
That she did make defect, perfection,
And breathless power breathe forth.

It might seem a long way from two legendary descriptions of an Egyptian queen and today's news, but it is not. As we expand out of the Shakespearean lines into the themes of the play as a whole, we find ourselves into perplexed questions of our own nature, and whether there can ever be an adequate form of rule, or international *modus vivendi* in the world: whether human nature is capable of being adequately governed. We begin, however, with the words on the page.

Shakespeare adds to North's account the phrase:

'like a burnished throne'

Burnt . . .

The repeated word 'burn', and the hot glow of *burnished* are critical — for the image becomes in his lines one of consuming passion, and a pride of display that both catches up men to work (creating images of panoply and power) and exhausts them. (Later, in the sea battle, all the marine pride is brought to nothing, because of the waywardness and fickleness of passion):

beaten-purple . . . perfumed . . . love-sick . . .

Behind these words lie a pervading sense of a certain kind of sensual intensity which is ennervating (Antony's heart is a fan to cool a gipsy's lust) and ultimately deathly (because the touch of death is like a lover's pinch that hurts and is desired). The water is amorous of the strokes of the oars: and from this sensuousness, this sensuality, arises the existence problem — as this royal couple intensify their enjoyment of ease and love, they become even more driven by appetite (her appetite increases by what it feeds on) — so that in the end it becomes sterile, an empty aspiration which, in its infertility, seems to lead inevitably towards death. The images of the Nile, which turns either into corruption or fertility, deepens this theme throughout the play.

Of course, we have in Enobarbus' speech the presence of the consciousness of the man, the character: admiring, out of character, a display which is quite foreign to his down-to-earth soldier sensibility. We also have a seen picture, presented to our imagination — and in terms which mean we cannot but admire it. Her aspiration — even Antony's death and her death—-even her delusions about Antony — are admireable. We cannot but respond to their impulse to live a larger-than-life existence, to bestride the ocean, and to enjoy delights that are dolphin-like, that show their backs above the element they live in. There is a meaning in that vitality itself.

So, we are already in a complex of enigmas. And we are intensely present at the scene. Compare North's prose; 'the sailes of purple, and the owers of silver, which kept stroke in rowing after the sounde of the music of flutes . . .'

Purple the sails; and so perfumed that
The winds were love-sick
With them: the oars were silver,
Which to the tune of flutes kept stroke, and made
The water which they beat, to follow faster
As amorous of their strokes.

The transformation is masterly. The heavy perfume making the winds (normally a source of fresh air) love-sick (which we associate with closed rooms and droopiness) make the passion in the background stifling, self-defeating, exhausting, even paralysing.

Shakespeare picks up the phrase 'which kept stroke' and hears in it, in his intensity of imaginative realization, a rhythm, the movement of the oars. 'Flutes kept stroke' sounds like oars on a stroke, rattling the rowlocks: the comma gives the pause at the end of the stroke, 'and made' the beginning of the power stroke, while the line break gives the 'feel' of the oar under pressure in the water. But the water is 'following faster' as of clinging to the blades: so, again, we have a feeling of cloying, of an energetic act leading to bafflement — as exhausted love often does, when desire outlives performance, or love is so heavy that it cannot be transmuted into physical form: and below it all (as throughout the play) is a hint of slightly sadistic desperation in this (as amorous of their strokes). The water following and clinging to the oars is like a love-sick woman clinging to a man.

So, the description is about sexual passion, displayed in powerfully symbolic, majestic, form. What we do in supervision is to attend to the language, and this means deepening and extending our responsiveness — that is, in the spirit of Empson's *Seven Types* and Leavis's close analysis, exploring the many possible meanings, and selecting from them those that are relevant. That is what I take the essence of 'practical criticism' to be. Take the word 'beggared'. Perhaps it was prompted in Shakespeare by North's word 'commonly':

> apparelled and attired like the Goddesse Venus, commonly drawen in picture . . .

Shakespeare was evidently engrossed with the idea of Cleopatra as an uncommon woman, and their level of experience being above the norm ('rare for Antony'): so, while Venus may be commonly depicted in pictures, Cleopatra's attire makes all other descriptions beggarly, wretchedly common, as poor as the lowest vagrant. As we say the word, the word *beggar'd* lies behind the effects of words to come like *cloth of gold, of tissue*, so that we have a double image, in which the fabrics are torn, and the limbs show through, but instead of the fabrics being wretched, and the colours drab, or the limbs withered or filthy, the described magnificence shines above the best words can do. The effect is complex: the art o'er-pictures, soars magically above the description: at the same time a grounding of mortality underlies the whole splendour, as, indeed, it does throughout the play. And this has a moral effect, since to beggar is to make poor, while to have silver oars is absurdly an effort at conspicuous waste: so, the wide-spreading social and political effects are kept in mind (though we, too, may share Cleopatra's view that ''Tis paltry to be Caesar').

Shakespeare makes his boys 'dimpled' and 'smiling', rather than just 'pretty fair boys', and their enjoyment suggests an odd teasing effect which the queen likes to indulge in, as she indulges her curiosity with the eunuch Mardian. She is very curious about what it is like to be a man ('She wore my sword Phillipa') and what it is like for a man to have desire when lie is incapable of performing. So, behind the image of antithesis:

> With divers colour'd fans which they did cool,
> And what they undid did . . .

we have another image of self-defeating sensuality: too much perfume in an erotic atmosphere generates love-sickness: too much amorousness in the entranced water clogs the oars: the provision of pretty boys to fan her cheeks means that their attentions arouse in her a sexual curiosity which arouses passion in Cleopatra's cheeks. The masterly enactment in the language of the antithesis, 'undid

did' adds to the underlying perplexity, that there is an essential contradiction in sensuality: the more a human being seeks to intensify the assault on the senses, the more likely he is to have the opposite effect, by cloying the sense responses and ennervating the power which luxury and indulgence invite: the culminating image is one of emptiness:

> Antony . . . did sit alone,
> Whistling to th' air: which but for vacancy,
> Had gone to gaze on Cleopatra too,
> And made a gap in Nature . . .

Cleopatra's purpose is to extend the attraction of her beauty and capacity to tempt into a huge public (and so political) show: the effect is to threaten Nature itself with potential emptiness, as if even the air itself could be seduced.

Everything seems to respond to her power to evoke a potent response: her attendant women seem to evoke a tumescence even in the ropes: . . . 'the silken tackle,

> Swell with the touches of those flower-soft hands,
> That yarely frame the office'.

Shakespeare adds to North the complex sensuousness of 'silken' to 'silken tackle' with its slight alliterative texture adding to the richness, and the fascinating combination of robustness and gentleness generated by 'yarely', 'frame' with 'touches', 'flowersoft' and 'swell' — all evocative of a strong physical sexual energy latent in the beautiful scene. Because the language is a mixture of high civilisation (amorous, pavilion) and common words (yarely, did), so the relation between rare high living and ordinary life at large is emphasised implicitly.

The magnificence thus has beneath it themes which relate to the overall themes of the play: the intense, hungry sexuality of Cleopatra with a degree of desperation in it ('so perfumed that/The winds were love-sick'): the vast reverberations abroad of this ('made a gap in Nature'): the problem of mortal existence, whenever men and women try to live with their backs above the element they live in—and so the magnificence is no sham or mere gesture, but the spectacle of a real attempt to live in a way that is larger than life — with all its perils.

An hour's discussion will not exhaust the quality of this language. But once we have trained ourselves to respond fully to it we can move out to find the themes struck and developed in the rest of the play—-the theme of cloying, exhaustion and melting, for instance ('my sword, make weak by my affection . . . the crown of the earth doth melt . . . '): the theme of appearance and the human reality under it ('sometimes we see a cloud that's dragonish . . . ') and the dangers in taking appearance as the reality:

> . . .even with a thought
> The rack dislimns, and makes it indistinct
> As water is in water —

and the theme of love leading, even in its burning intensity, to death:

> A bridegroom in my death, and run into 't
> As to a lover's bed.

With this theme we may associate that of poison: if she is cold to Antony, says Cleopatra:

> From my cold heart let heaven engender hail,
> And poison it in the source . . .

This possibility of love turning to poison may in turn be associated with the alternatives in the Nile mud, of fertility and corruption. Cleopatra's love is infertile, and her baby is the asp:

> Dost thou not see my baby at my breast
> That sucks the nurse asleep . . .

And yet can we condemn the aspiration to transcend mortality:

> I am fire and air, my other elements I give to baser life . . .

So, starting with attention to the syntax ('Beggar'd all description' 'undid did'), the symbolism ('the silken tackle swell'), the texture, the movement ('flutes kept stroke'), the sound, the imagery, we enter into a state which one may call an enriched consciousness, as we read those lines. It is as if we were relating a vivid dream to a psychotherapist, and exploring its meaning — only in this case the organising power of the poetry has come from the consciousness of a creative genius who is deeply involved in his contemplation of human nature and existence.

What we follow, as we move out into the play, is thought — that mode of thinking to which Leavis draws our attention in one of his last books *Thought, Word and Creativity*. The thought — at one with a 'whole' apprehension, of emotion and inwardness, as well as abstract issues — is about many problems with which the present-day thinker about human problems must surely concern himself: not least the psychoanalyst and existentialist philosopher. What is the nature of woman, and what attitudes towards her trouble our conscious and unconscious minds (Shakespeare had a problem with woman, as we know from Lear's outbursts, Hamlet's words to his mother, Timon and *The Sonnets**)? with disturbances of the reality sense can an infatuation bring? Can one believe in the capacity of any human being to rule and act in state affairs without the possibility of catastrophic consequences of some emotional disorder at any time?

And do we want to live with a merely sane and 'normal' control over this problem? Do we prefer the cold and utilitarian Romans? Are there modes of living which celebrate greater heights that are possible in human life? Or is this always mere empty sensuality? Can there be a meaning in love — even in a love that burns itself out, in terms of the world well lost? Or do we prefer a state of affairs in which there is nothing left remarkable beneath the visiting moon?

At the end of teaching *Antony and Cleopatra* we will probably, at best, be left bewildered—-but aware that there are profound questions of 'How to live' about which we have been drawn to argue, by Shakespeare's own perplexed contemplation of man and woman. If we are fortunate, when we 'possess' the words, we will be deeply moved by the way the characters take their fate upon themselves: even in suicide

> . . . and it is great
> To do that thing that ends all other deeds
> Which shackles accidents and bolts up change:
> Which sleeps and never palates more the dug
> The beggar's nurse and Caesar's.

Even in rejecting life here Cleopatra is saying that it is better to die rather than languish in a state of merely surviving and holding on

*Discussed by the present author in *Images of Woman in Literature*, New York University Press, 1990.

to existence. And in this there is an impetus which we must surely pick up — an impulse to use our time to best advantage. What that 'advantage' may be, of course, is another existential question — but in an age of trivial distraction and false solutions it is a good one to hold before us in a Humanities discipline.

When, after a close reading, students go and weep (as they do) at a good performance of *Antony and Cleopatra*, they are sharing that exaltation, that elevated sense of being human, and that human fate matters, that the Greeks shared in those marvellous D-shaped stone theatres one can still visit in Mediterranean countries, in Turkey and Greece. Will not this sense of humanness sustain them when they themselves are overcome by fate, as we all do at times? They will certainly be able to relate this ploy to the nature of love as pursued into our own era, in *Anna Karenina*, *Women in Love*, *Daughters of the Vicar*, or *Under Western Eyes*: appearance and reality are themes which can be explored in these works, too. Students can be caught up in such themes with intense excitement. This particular ploy seems to be one which has a special appeal to young adults who are just beginning to be aware of the complexity and gravity of sexual experience and if the supervisor can use it as a 'third ground' on which to explore the related problems of consciousness it is a most valuable work for this reason.

The whole process, like the art, can never be made fully explicit or schematized — and much of what one does is simply 'played by ear'. One improvises: so do one's students. It is this that I reassure myself about sometimes when I wake up in the small hours worried about my students. It will be all right in the morning I tell myself: and it nearly always turns out to be so, because nothing would work unless the ability to share an act of consciousness through the experience of words weren't a natural capacity. It is a true form of 'meeting'. Literature depends upon there being in every potential reader a capacity to engage with the text, and a desire to make use of it:

Takyth the fruyt and let the chaffe be stylle.

The 'fruit' is that grain of meaning which can nourish our continuing efforts, at the conscious and unconscious level, to sustain an identity, a reality sense, a sense of meaningful existence, and a civilised mode of being.

Commenting on the above exercise a reader suggests that it is the kind of thing students will have done at school anyway. From recent experience, I cannot agree. It is just what students have not had enough of at school, and it demands the kind of attention we need to train in order to teach today's students to read well. Obviously, in any account of what one is doing in such a discussion session, there can be no simple account of the value of the disciplines involved. It won't do to say that such work enables students to assemble evidence and conduct an argument: that it opens their eyes to history and character: that such investigation contributes to social change. What I believe to be central here is not covered by Raymond Williams's desire that English should be more like a Natural Science subject, as if its 'content' were parallel to that of various other disciplines. At its centre is that kind of possession and understanding to which Margaret Weldhen points: we meet in an act of consciousness.

First: we must insist that the words must be read, if the students don't respond, there is nothing to talk about: this truism, seems simple enough, but it is not always grasped. The 'existence' of a literary work is actually a mystery — it is somewhere between the print on the page, and the consciousness of the reader, somewhere between memory and the sounds of a poem being read in the room. Ultimately it is intangible, like the way in which we know what music means. To adapt a phrase from Lawrence — you can't put a finger on it — nay, not even your mind.

One is concerned with adequate — with good — reading. Suppose one were conducting a cello class: the title of the project might be 'How to interpret in one's technique the meaning of Dvorak's Cello Concerto'. What would be the point of going on, if the members couldn't play the cello, or were tone deaf, or could not read music? Of course, there is something else, too — the capacity to hear the music and to talk intelligently about its meaning: but in music one cannot be spurious — either one is 'musical' or not. So ought we not to insist that English requires that people doing it can read?

The first duty of the English teacher then is to teach reading. By this word something very complex is meant, for it is obviously not enough to read and understand at the level of translation say, the capacity to make a précis or put the original into one's own words. It is necessary to be able to respond in a great many ways — to rhythm, to symbolism, to tone, to syntax, and to the special 'voice' of a writer.

What one means by 'voice' cannot be defined — though it is real enough. No-one else other than Henry James could have written 'Olive Chancellor was unmarried by every implication of her being. She was a spinster as Shelley was a lyric poet, or as the month of August is sultry.'

Somebody else however could (mind you) have written: 'Miss Birdseye . . . had no more outline than a bundle of hay. . . . ' — indeed, one could trace that kind of language — hyperbole in caricature — back through Dickens to what Shakespeare puts into Falstaff's mouth, just as one can trace Miss Birdseye back to Mrs Jellyby. But one of the fascinations of English is relishing the special unique quality of a writer's voice, and then exploring the foundation upon which it was created — to which foundation it added something of its own, as Henry James derives from Jane Austen and George Eliot, and then becomes Henry James; or Lawrence draws on Thomas Hardy and Arnold Bennett, but then finds his own essential voice. The 'voice', of course, goes with a consciousness, an intelligence, a sensibility, a stance towards the world. The originality emerges from a complex relationship between tradition and the individual talent.

So, the purpose of making such connections is not an academic question of tracing 'influences', for the picking up of voices goes with a picking up of symbolic themes, of human interests — with Henry James, the theme of authenticity, of attention to the profound moral concern with what is right for oneself, in relation to others: with Lawrence, it is the relationship between man and woman — especially over woman's destiny picking up from *The Old Wive's Tale*, *Tess* and *Jude* and developing in *The White Peacock* and with Ursula Brangwen, in *The Rainbow*. And so the capacity one develops to respond to the peculiar way a writer uses language to explore his meanings is at the same time a capacity to possess the consciousness of the artist, in his exploration of human experience.

About this there are two important things to say, both of what one does oneself, and what one does in teaching. First there is John Bayley's point, that we do not make our subject. We in English must continually defer to a created body of literature, which we serve. This does not mean it is not altered by our criticism, reappraisal or selection. But it is greater than us.

Secondly, we deal in tacit powers, in Polanyi's sense, so that we can never bring everything — the meaning and effect of poetry, its 'effects' as through rhythm and movement — into the clear light of intellectual knowledge. Response to literature relies upon subsidiary powers, and teaching even more so. In reading we 'dwell in' the work, and the teaching is a discourse about indwellings—-in which we can never know, and can only guess, the degree to which each student has made his own possession of the text. If we thought too much about the intangibility of these processes, we might well lose heart or give up: we simply have to pull ourselves together, muster what resources we can, have confidence, and go on. Against the popular view, of science and the idea of science as a cold, objective and accurate procedure, in fact a great deal of science is like this, too, as indeed Polanyi shows. But in both disciplines, to be really heuristic is to allow tacit processes to operate dynamics deep inside the body and mind of a person are at work, to enable him or her to enter into new realms of possibilities to apprehend new spheres of reality — in the case of science mainly 'objective' reality. The sphere of the English specialist is particularly the nature and scope of human consciousness.

As Polanyi points out, when a lecturer points, we do not look at his finger, but beyond, at what he is indicating. Our attention to a work also points 'beyond' — to its meaning. So, in English, we attend to the works, in that third ground between us, 'the criss-cross of utterance between us' as Leavis puts it: and it is always a risky and intangible sphere, because one can never be sure of success

It is because of this risk, and the pain it involves, I believe, that we can have so many substitutes for the real work. Just as some writers, like Arnold Bennett, cannot go on facing the trying existential issues, and so on to the something else, in dead, empty, works (as Bennett did after *The Old Wive's Tale*), so English teachers can escape the rigors of truly sharing the possession of literary works, by moving off into spheres where it may be felt that the subject can be made our own, or where it can be pinned down — as by linguistics or literary theory, academic disciplines of tracing influences and derivations, sociohistory, structuralism, etc., or attending to literature as an instrument of social change — contributing to 'the revolution' or to the liberation of women.

It is often noticeable that some people, when they come near a university which stands for 'knowledge' to them, feel there must be a theory, some verifiable 'objective' system and criterion by which to pin down the subject. In this respect universities can become anti-creative, in not being able to tolerate the ineffable aspects of an arts subject. What this really means is that we do not have an adequate philosophy to deal with such subjects: the attempt is made to pin down a subjective discipline to a positivistic frame, which cannot find the phenomena of consciousness. In English this can lead to false comforts, for they can become ways of avoiding the truly revolutionary impact of the creative use of language, which is to explore the unknown, to point to the potentialities and possibilities of experience, of human scope — and, ultimately, the awful question of whether anything can have a meaning, in the face of death — the tragic problem.

For ultimately, insofar as the literary work points 'beyond the words', it points at one's own breast (like Raskolnikov pointing to his own breast) — and brings home to one one's own tragic problem.

Having reached this point, one may, I believe, assert that English is a true humanities subject, because it thus tackles the *Dasein* problem. This word, meaning 'being there', comes from continental philosophy, and we may pick it up from where existentialist psychotherapy has been influenced by the gloomy philosophy of Martin Heidegger. We are all in a state of 'being unto death' and behind our daily life is the eternal dread of death and nothingness. one day, we shall become nothing — and, indeed, whenever we attend a funeral we have to contend with the terrible truth, and most of us for a time on such an occasion experience a kind of madness, a deep struggle with a threat of the loss of meaning. Culturally, we experience this threat in the work of Mahler, Shakespeare, the author of *Eccclesiastes*, Dostoevsky, Dickens and the Lawrence of *Odour of Chrysanthemum*. And of course in the marvellous Burial Service from Cranmer's Book of Common Prayer, now abandoned by the Church for alternative services which read (as P.D.James has declared) like a D.H.S.S. circular. What can we assert against death? What meaning triumphs over its appalling reduction of everything to absurdity? Shakespeare's *Sonnets* represent one kind of striving: 'that you shall shine more clear in these contents . . .' In such a love, a human being finds a meaning that asserts the *Dasein*, the sense of 'being there', of existing in such a way that meaning seems to be established that can never be eroded, even though

Nothing 'gainst Time's scythe can make defence . . .

In the Sonnets the ostensible aim is to persuade the young man to cheat time by having children: to erect a memorial in verse that can outlive him, but essentially to uphold a sense of the value of love that is not dissipated

With Time's injurious hand crush'd and o'erworn . . .

It may be that in the greatest works, whether we take Conrad's *Victory* or Shakespeare's *Lear*, the human attempt to establish deathless values is contemplated with irony even when being portrayed positively. But even to be disturbed by such works is to find a profounsd sense of relief, to have one's deepest problem of existence recognised. So, in defending English or making a claim for it in the syllabus, one could well invoke the work of Victor Frankl, the existentialist psychotherapist. He spoke of a characteristic kind of neurosis in the modern world, characterised by loss of interest and lack of initiative — a deep kind of apathy or acidee (to use the medieval word):

> Time and again the psychiatrist is confronted by patients who doubt that life has any meaning. These conditions I have called 'existential vacuum'.

Frankl refers to a statistical survey he made among his students. In the University of Vienna, only forty percent of the students (German, Swiss and Austrian) said they knew from their own experience the feeling of absolute insecurity. In America he found the figure for the insecure was eighty-one percent. He believed the problem was related to industrialization. (it certainly cannot have been improved by cultural changes which have come to mean that 60m. Americans are illiterate and another 60m. are 'aliterate' — which means they can read but never do.)

We know, in English, that a high degree of whole literacy including, that is, the capacity to respond to imaginative literature — is a mark of the civilised person. We know that to be so literate brings an individual into the dimensions of that whole era of humanistic achievement, that realm of consciousness, which marks the era following the *telos* of Greek civilisation, as Edmund Husserl saw it.

Whatever literature can or cannot do for us, it certainly, opens up access to meanings, through discourse and dialogue: to questions about the grounds of moral choice, the understanding and government of emotion, and our grasp of the reality of others and the world. These are its justifications as a Humanities discipline. And Matthew Arnold, despite his odd preoccupations (such as his choice of 'high seriousness' as a touchstone) was essentially right: a civilisation concerned only with coal and iron, with manufacture and material ends, is nothing — since it cannot engage with the question as to what its resources shall be directed, as to what kind of life it is to have. Insofar as it devotes itself merely to possessions, or comfort, or a 'higher standard of living' in such terms, or trivial distractions 24 hours a day made possible by satellites in space, a society cannot solve the problem of meaning.

This is not to say English is a 'religious' subject, but it does provide, at least in school and college, the kind of engagement with problems of existence such as was once provided by (say) the mystery plays, the folk-songs, Elizabethan drama and the nineteenth-century novel.

It is this kind of assumption that lies behind the exercises one sets one's students.

ENGLISH IN PRACTICE : POETRY

When I began work with undergraduates again I used terms with which I was familiar —talking about 'meeting in' the poem, and 'possessing' it. To my astonishment some students found it very difficult to grasp these concepts. Yet for me they described exactly what happened in a seminar, when a poem came to life, 'in the criss-cross of utterance between us' (to use Leavis's phrase once more).

It wouldn't perhaps have been so difficult for them, if they had been musical and were concerned with musical performance. Here, standards seem nowadays very high, and one is aware that, as students perform music, they 'become the music' and would have no difficulty in seeing how technique enables one to 'dwell in' a piece of music — and enter into another consciousness through the symbolic world that the music is.

Would they have the same difficulties with painting as they had with poetry? If I stand in a copse and paint a scene in France, I throw myself into the landscape and make it mine: if the painting is a success, the viewer will enter into the vision, the feeling about the light and heat and colour, and share something of the consciousness of the painter.

Once more, what is needed, if we are to teach poetry adequately is a grasp of the kind of knowing it represents: of the kind of experience we are dealing with. The idea of a shared act of consciousness is central to my approach. But, of course, to talk in such a way in an age dominated by mechanistic and positive concepts is unfamiliar, and perhaps this accounts for the neglect of poetry and the poor way in which it is, for the most part, taught.*

Perhaps we may add a rider to this, to suggest that a great deal of modern poetry presented in school anthologies is journalism, and does not have those qualities of symbolic content which are necessary for a sharing of consciousness through language at the deepest level.

Here I propose to 'talk to' a number of poems, showing by exam-

*Recent reports by Her Majesty's Inspectors in Schools suggest that poetry teaching today is poor.

ple the kind of thing I might do in a supervision or seminar. First, I want to convey if I can the 'ineffable' quality of such work.

We call it 'practical criticism', and I suppose we are so used to the phrase we no longer even question what it means. I believe indeed it was Coleridge who first used the phrase. But I have a feeling 'practical criticism' came back as a phrase employed in English studies as an answer to Cambridge positivism in the 20s. The impulse was to show the scientists that we in English have a discipline with a realistic or 'practical' basis. So, it may be associated with I.A. Richards's ambition to find a vindication for poetry in an organic paradigm, in terms of emphasizing its effects in terms of 'equilibrium' or whatever in the nervous system, a matter of 'appetencies' as he argues in *Science and Poetry*. There, surprisingly, he talks of the 'pseudo-statements' of poetry, a phrase which cannot but imply that poetry is not 'real'.

The value of poetry cannot be defended in such terms, because we can never observe or analyse the 'effects of poetry on the nervous system' in the way Richards hoped to do. Poetry and its effects can only be dealt with by phenomenological disciplines — that is, by disciplines that have to do with the phenomena of consciousness.

Polanyi is a valuable philosopher to invoke here, because while evidently a philosopher able to deal with the nature of thought, and a scientist, he renounces all mechanistic and particulate approaches to the explanation of thinking.

Polanyi drew attention to the origins of thought, even in its most rigorous forms, to what he called 'tacit' powers. We can never be fully and explicitly aware of all the stages of our thought: we can never fully analyse it. It is rooted in our bodily life, and it emerges from mysterious powers, some of which have been studied by scientists themselves, such as 'subception' and 'indwelling' — our capacities to rely upon shadowy and as yet unformulated thought, as when we 'sleep on' a problem, and to 'dwell in' either an intellectual theory, or a tree we are studying. There is also the 'leap of the imagination' — such as Kekulé experienced when he dreamt of snakes with their tails in their mouths, and realised this was an insight into the structure of benzine rings. Much scientific thought depends upon the imagination (and for instance in Professor Beveridge's book *The Art of Scientific Investigation* there are chapters on Intuition and Imagination).

In this, one important feature of our response which needs recognition (though we always take this for granted, too) is that any work of art is ineffable. We cannot fully ever extract or make explicit its meaning. Yet despite this we may try to investigate its meanings in a phenomenological way, by which I mean the way Freud analysed dreams, by the effort of understanding. Freud's achievement was a phenomenological one: he opened up insights into the way we 'speak better than we know', the way the whole consciousness, body and being, speaks through symbolism, about the human predicament, with its roots or origins in the infant's discovery of self and world. Our disciplines in English deal largely with tacit processes as Polanyi defined them.

Polanyi argued that the meaning points beyond the words: this comes from Polanyi's essay in *Knowing and Being*, on 'sense-giving and sense-reading'. At the beginning of his essay Polanyi points out that if I point to the clock, the audience does not look at my pointing finger. It looks at the clock. The sign I make with my finger is a pointer to the object. If we look at a face, without knowing how, we recognise a physiognomy and interpret its mood. We attend from the features to the mood.

So, in reading a poem, we examine the components, but our aim is to integrate our possession of these parts, without knowing altogether how, into the meaning of the whole. We look beyond the words at their meaning. The various bits of response may be, in Polanyi's terms, called things of which we possess a subsidiary awareness: the purpose of our skill is to integrate these and to endow them with meaning. We *attend from* the words on the page to something else which becomes its meaning. We *indwell* in the poem, and we must be careful not to let our analysis become only a kind of exteriorization which kills meaning: that it can do so (says Polanyi) confirms the sense-giving powers of indwelling.

If we switch the focus of attention back on the object as by over-intensive intellectual analysis, it may be rendered external to us.

> And as it acquires the status of externality, the object loses its

> meaning. It is well known how a word we speak can be reduced to a meaningless utterance of sounds by repeating it a number of times, attending closely to our lips and tongue and the sounds they make. p.185

I think something of this kind often happens to us, in the analysis of literature, in writing 'answers' for examinations or essays: it can even happen in seminar discussion. In doing 'practical criticism', 'I'll do a prac. crit. on that' may almost mean, 'I'll kill it'. So, one of our problems is learning to understand, while maintaining the living presence of a work and pursuing that meaning beyond the words.

We must look beyond the words, because unless we have 'possessed' the words there is nothing to talk about, but just as when I point at the clock, the meaning is not in my finger, but in the concept of time in our lives, so we need to reach out beyond the poem to the act of consciousness in the world it is.

Reading a poem, then, is an art in itself. As we practise this art, we also inevitably come across problems of being: and it is in this kind of discipline that English studies belong to the Humanities in the fullest sense of the word.

In the philosophies of Ernst Cassirer, and Michael Polanyi, with his emphasis on 'the leap of the imagination' we find a confident recognition of the poetic, as a primary mode of perceiving the world which was, of course, Coleridge's emphasis. We do not in any way need to feel inferior in our concern with poetry, to any of the other disciplines like mathematics, logic or scientific investigation which are seemingly more 'real' or 'practical'. What we deal with is a primary activity of the mind, and must be explored in its own (phenomenological) dimensions.

Let us then speak not of 'practical criticism' but 'criticism in practice': and let us extend and develop the word 'criticism' to mean 'critical reading', or a kind of reading which looks critically at itself as it is trying to be articulate about meaning: the kind of thing (say) William Empson did at best, as in his examination of poetry in *Seven Types of Ambiguity*. This kind of reading attends to all possible nuances of meaning, often by 'free association'. Often, in psychoanalytical sessions, a patient may be asked, if the symbolic meaning of a dream is still hidden, 'Freely associate about clouds' (. . . or bottles or trees, or whatever).

It is this kind of open exploration of the many possibilities of meaning, followed by an attempt to establish which of these possibilities are relevant which seems to me the proper, and central, discipline of our work: a real phenomenological discipline, which allows, indeed enjoys, the recognition that the human consciousness naturally works in this symbolising way, and is ineffably rich in its complexities and ramifications of meaning. A classical text here might be Coleridge's own *Kubla Khan*, followed by a study of John Livingstone Lowe's *The Road to Xanadu*. A study of the way the symbolism was selected and concentration would need to recognise too that the meanings of that tantalising poem have not all been brought forth, and well could be — which is what I mean by using the word 'ineffable'.

Instead of taking a whole poem with such a massive field of remembered material behind it, however, let me take one line of poetry:

> As though a rose should shut and be a bud again . . .

That line came into my head on the first of June, as I went out into the garden for the first time, the first roses just appearing. At the same moment, the last of my students were taking their last exams, sweating at their comments on poems which they knew only too well, or perhaps couldn't place, or didn't understand, or didn't like, in 'practical criticism' papers.

The study of literature (there is no need to tell an English student) is a highly artificial activity — being compelled, for instance, to 'discuss' things people don't want to discuss. Perhaps they just want to enjoy them. To anyone who really cares about literature, enjoyment is the main thing — the exercises we have to perform have their roots in this joy, in our 'love' of literature. Sometimes, in an early morning supervision, after reading a poem aloud to some young men and women, all of us being deeply moved by it, it seems that there is nothing more to say.

So, as well as being highly artificial, our response to literature is also very natural. This I have tried to show elsewhere by looking at some poems written by children: they use what we call poetic techniques quite naturally and very subtly, without one lesson in poetic structure.

But first I want to open up the most primary questions about poetry: what it is and what we can say about it.

Let me take that one line above. Why does it come into my head at all? I see a fat bud on a Scottish rose bush I planted last year. I think of the bushes suffering the severe winter, and I know how glad I am that they have survived, and are now growing so vigorously, not least because the snow has fixed extra nitrogen in the soil. The first buds coming are therefore full of meaning for me — they symbolise the renewal of life in spring and summer.

In psychological terms — terms borrowed from psychoanalysis — you could say that I identify with the roses, or, to use other terms I project over them feelings I have, about woman, about progeny, and about Nature and the world. I indwell in them. I enjoy the roses not only because of their colours and scent and the glossy new green of their leaves, not in mere 'aesthetic' pleasure in form and colour, but because they become the focus of certain imaginative dynamics. These dynamics have their roots in the earliest encounter between mother and infant, from which encounter develops the capacity to use symbols, the use of language, and to relate to the world.

It is because the budding rose is the focus of this cultural and emotional complex that it evokes in my memory the line:

As though a rose should shut and be a bud again . . .

The response within my own consciousness to this single line of poetry is so complex that it could take up half a book to exhaust the subject. This is one aspect of poetry which we may take cognisance of at once. It is the most concentrated form of language, using all the components of language to convey its meaning.

The line I am discussing emerges from my memory because of its rhythm. At first I can't remember who it is by. But then I reflect on its especial tender qualities, its sincerity and its particular mode of anthropomorphism — that is, the feeling one gets at once that it is about a human being, a young girl — and I recognise the character of John Keats. That is, I hear a voice—-the unique voice of a certain writer. As I say the line to myself I become aware that it consists of six iambic feet: it isn't an iambic pentameter; it is an Alexandrine: it must be the last line of a stanza which has Alexandrines as concluding lines.

I now realise it must be from *The Eve of St Agnes*, and so it takes its place among all the rich sensuous imagery and flavour of that poem.

It is the rhythmical shape of the line that makes it memorable: 'memorable speech' is a phrase we know and often use. For some reason we are better able to remember things if they have a rhythm, and it is clear from poems like *Sir Gawaine and the Green Knight* which belong to the oral tradition before universal writing and printing how much a formal structure and rhythmic pattern made possible the amazing feats of the public reciter in the oral tradition. I remember 'As though a rose should shut and be a bud again . . .' as I remember a melody. I am also helped by the slight alliteration, *should shut* (which does the shutting, or expresses the wish that underlies it) and be a bud again, where the repetition of the 'b's and the repeated 'a' (again) enact the yearning to reverse the natural process.

The line having, as it were, popped up into consciousness, what also comes to mind are those complex meanings which are embodied in the rhythm and texture. The subtle rhythm which is like a melody, moving up to the word shut 'As though a rose should shut . . .' and then descend again . . . 'and be a bud again'. — this melodic shape, and the alliteration, spring from an intensity of meaning: that is, they can't really be called 'technique' though they are technicalities — they can only come in the moment of creation: they can't be manipulated, 'done', or faked. They are the product of the heat of imaginative creation, which forges the words into a certain temper or form. We recognise the particular character of Keats's inscape or texture in this line as we do in lines like:

with beaded bubbles winking at the brim

or: summer hath o'er brimmed their clammy cells.

The way the consonants are used comes from a particular kind of oral intensity, an intense relish felt in the lips which generates the labials here.

I don't of course have to be looking at a rose bud when I read the poem. But if I am, I note two things about it. From experience I know that by the end of the week the mature bloom will begin to break up, fall, wither and decay. But each new bud is also a renewal which comes to the rose again and again: and here by the word *rose* I mean of course a rose bush. We say, 'I think I'll put a rose in that corner' or 'we'll have roses here'. And this use of the word, which I suppose is a form of synecdoche, using the part for the whole enables there to be ambiguity in the line.

The first meaning has that effect we often find in poetry, of evoking the opposite. As Leavis points out somewhere, if we speak of the topless towers of Ilium we see towers, and if a poet writes of the domeless courts we see domes. So when we read 'As though a rose should shut and be a bud again . . . ' what we experience is a strange double image, one of a sequence like a film of a bud unfolding run backwards, and the other of trying desperately to twist or compress a full blown rose back to its tight bud. The two images, full of a passionate energy to wish things other than they were, combine to imbue the symbol of the bud with a profound, if not tragic, poignancy.

I should at this point, I believe, put the line in its context:

XXVI

Anon his heart revives: her vespers done,
Of all its wreathed pearls her hair she frees;
Unclasps her warmed jewels one by one;
Loosens her fragrant bodice; by degrees
Her rich attire creeps rustling to her knees:
Half-hidden, like a mermaid in sea-weed,
Pensive awhile she dreams awake, and sees,
In fancy, fair St Agnes in her bed,
But dares not look behind, or all the charm is fled.

XXVII

Soon, trembling in her soft and chilly nest,
In sort of wakeful swoon, perplex'd she lay,
Until the poppied warmth of sleep oppress'd
Her soothed limbs, and soul fatigued away;
Flown, like a thought, until the morrow-day;
Blissfully haven'd both from joy and pain;
Clasp'd like a missal where swart Paynims pray;
Blinded alike from sunshine and from rain,
As though a rose should shut, and be a bud again.

XVIII

Stol'n to this paradise, and so entranced,
Porphyro gazed upon her empty dress,
And listen'd to her breathing, if it chanced
To wake into a slumberous tenderness;
Which when he heard, that minute did he bless,
And breath'd himself: then from the closet crept,
Noiseless as fear in a wide wilderness,
And over the hush'd carpet, silent, stept,
And 'tween the curtains peep'd, where, lo!
— how fast she slept.

The feeling behind the lines is that of wishing against the intrusion of time and reality that a state of innocence could be preserved (cf. 'Bright star were I as steadfast as thou art . . . '). Such a wish that things should be other than they are is one which belongs to immaturity — to childhood or to adolescence, with its idealism: the adult is obliged to recognise the poignant impossibility of such a desire. We know it can never happen, that a rose should shut again. Though some flowers do in fact shut at night, and some even if a shadow falls on them — like crocuses in a rain storm: so it is not improbable. What is impossible is for a full-blown rose to do this because it has matured too far, and is too complex a form. As Sylvia Plath put it in a poem about growth:

I am too big to go backwards . . .

If it did happen of course it would be a great mystery — so the state it describes as a simile ('As though . . . ') takes on that mystery.

The unfolding of a rose is a mystery too, as is the coming to maturity of a woman and *The Eve of St Agnes* is about just that: the creative moment of maturity in love, when the deadly world which opposes or constrains it is rejected and relinquished.

The rose is here a symbol of a young woman. So, a number of complex meanings attach themselves to her. She behaves as if she were a rose that can shut itself — so, she is very mysterious, in her flowering, and as the object of the hero's love. But woven with this is the ambiguity arising from our recognition that this return to a bud could never happen. A young woman is symbolised by a rose because she has a beautiful face and rosy cheeks: she blooms, and glows like a rose.

Her clothes are like the petals of a rose, and all her blossoming qualities belong to sexuality as the rose does: it displays *Selbstdarstellung*, that is, the manifestation of the qualities of the self on the surface: a display of unique qualities, and it is, her blossoming, an addressed phenomenon. That is, it is intended to please and delight, to convey what kind of being she has, what vitality she has, what breeding capacities, and so to attract her lover. This quality of a woman's appeal is, of course, contrary to much of today's fashionable feminist thinking, but it indicates a biological reality all the same (see Ann Ulanov, *Receiving Woman*).

The budding stage of this rose in symbolism clearly relates to virginity, and the full blossoming to maturity. The maturity however moves on in time towards blowing and decay: the rotten rose (as Hardy puts it) is ripped from the wall. In *The Winter's Tale* the flower imagery is rich with sexual ambiguity:

> . . . pale primroses
> That die unmarried ere they can behold
> Bright Phoebus in his strength
> The marigold, that goes to bed with the sun
> And with him rises weeping . . .

and, of course, so are Shakespeare's Sonnets:

> Lilies that fester smell far worse than weeds . . .

The line I am discussing pivots rhythmically and in its sound on the word 'shut': and the whole expresses the urge to retreat back to virginity: to withdraw from that sexual fruition which means ultimately blowing. For the enigma is that we all want to move on, towards fruition and fulfilment — but this merely exacerbates time, and hastens our progress towards our end — as Shakespeare's Sonnets proclaim and as Marvell's *To His Coy Mistress* recognises. As though a rose should shut actually conveys physical defensive movements as of a resistance to ravishment: the original impulse.

So, the meaning of my line is bound up with certain intense feelings about time, and about being and time; about the proximity of enjoying to taking or ravishing and the polarity between love and death. Its beauty emerges, like Mozart's melodies, from an agony about time and death: about being-unto-death, to take the term from Heidegger. If only there were some magic which could mysteriously reverse the ageing process, turning us back from maturity to virginity! Once we are born we cannot get back to that beginning, and all joy intensifies the fugitive nature of experience:

> And joy, whose hand is ever at his lips . . .

In the event, the lovers merge as if in a dream — as one does in happy sexual love: but there is sufficient reality present to make the love experience real, and so rich, in Keats. So the line moves towards a kind of gratitude for continuity, as does the whole poem, which is about the way young love will fulfil itself and take flight into the world, leaving behind the cold relies of mere duty and routine:

> And the long carpets rose along the gusty floors . . .

It is different from:

> Glut thy sorrow on a morning rose
> Or on the rainbow of the salt and wave
> Or on a wealth of globed peonies . . .

Mysteriously, in the imagination, the rose does shut and is a bud again. While 'As though' suggests it isn't possible, we have an effect which is the same as that of

> Who can hold a fire in his hand
> By thinking on the frosty Caucasus?
> Or who can wallow in December's snow
> By thinking on fantastic summer's heat?

The effect is of a tension between the delighted fantasies of the imagination and its capacities to inform the world with meaning: and the actual reality which we have to bear and come to terms with —

that is, the rose can't be put back in the bud, the woman can't be made a virgin again, and we can't retreat to the womb. It will not satisfy to reject maturity because of its dangers, because it must lead to blossoming, withering and decay: to choose 'life' is to choose the acceptance of mutability and maturity.

As though a rose should shut and be a bud again . . .

is (like gloating on the rainbow of the salt sand wave) a fancy which admits by its implication the impossibility of that visionary glimpse. In the terms of literary studies I suppose this is a conceit, a 'fancy': but, as I hope I have shown, it has a deeply serious complexity of meaning: a gravity (which is why I used the word 'tragic').

Shut is an interesting word: Sylvia Plath uses a softer word, perhaps echoing Keats, in her suicidal *Edge*:

The petals of the rose close . . .

Shut seems such an unpoetic word: but it belongs to that sinewy tough Anglo-Saxon element that is so full of muscular feeling and onomatopoeia. Shut both enacts the physical feelings of the shore, shoot, shock, group of words and also makes the sound of a closing trap or door. Again, here, it sets its hard force against the soft subject and the magic yearning, and adds that touch of almost bitter resignation to the underlying recognition that the wish is impossible. 'English must be kept up' said Keats, and he meant Shakespearean English, that sinewy quality which is not afraid to employ words like *clammy*, *plump*, and *twitter* to such effect in.*The Ode to Autumn*.

I have talked about one line of poetry, not, I hope, being merely ingenious. What I hope I have done is to indicate the special complexity of our discipline, which is a very exacting and subtle one: and I hope I have shown it to be one that attends to complex meanings.

I have to recognise besides of course that there are meanings in the line that still evade me — and that is an important component of art. We know that when we go back to the Quai Dorsay or the Tate Gallery we shall see things we never saw before, and we shall see familiar paintings in a new way.* The main purpose of criticism in practice as I see it is, indeed, in opening up these richer meanings for us, and if the primary human need is for a sense of meaning in life, this is a primary human activity, without which we become bewildered barbarians.

Now I want to demonstrate this approach in practice further, by discussing a number of poems, as I would try to discuss them in seminars and supervisions. In a seminar I produce a poem and let the students do the talking: I simply hold the fort, and try to keep order — though I have an idea where the discussion will go, and hope to demonstrate by conducting the discourse, that minds can meet in a poem, and that its universal qualities, embodied in the universal language, may be shared in a common reading. In a supervision I adopt a more didactic role, though that again cannot be successful unless the students are in the process of 'possessing' the poem.

Given that the whole meaning of a poem is ineffable, what are we doing in talking or writing about it?

When I begin to study an unfamiliar poem, I find it often rewarding to ask myself about the areas where I do not understand it. I accept that I may never be able to give an account of a difficult poem at all: I can never, in any case, with any poem, 'put it into other words': its meaning is its meaning is its meaning. A lady once asked Schumann what one of his works was about: he simply went to the piano and played it again, in answer: and as Gustav Mahler said, 'All commentary is disgusting'. But what I do need to know if I am to say anything in criticism or elucidation, is what kind of thing is being meant: and then I must try to work from the particulars towards insights into the whole meaning, which I am trying to possess.

Let me take as an example Emily Dickinson's Safe in Their Alabaster Chambers. Let me ask a general question about it. This is a good poem to use, in asking what we are doing in English, in the spirit of my chapters above. In a utilitarian age, obsessed with practical things, and practical applications of learning, what meaning does this have, and what value may be said to be found, in our attention to such a poem and its meaning?

---

*Cf. also the key sentence in *Portrait of a Lady*, where Ralph Touchett says to Isabel, 'Don't force your development too much: it's like unfolding a rose bud before it opens . . .'

Safe in their Alabaster Chambers*
Untouched by Morning and untouched by Noon.
Sleep the meek members of the Resurrection —
Rafter of satin, And Roof of stone.
Light laughs the breeze In her Castle of sunlight —
Babbles the Bee in a stolid Ear,
Pipe the Sweet Birds in ignorant cadence —
Ah, what sagacity perished here!
Grand go the Years — in the Crescent — above them —
Worlds scoop their Arcs —
And firmaments row —
Diadems — drop and Doges — surrender —
Soundless as dots — on a disc of Snow —

I placed this poem recently before some candidates for university entry at their interviews — rather unfairly, I believe now, as it is a very difficult poem. They saw it first as a comment on Christian ideals — and saw it as an ironic comment on people so encapsulated in their hope of another world that they were 'untouched' by reality, by history and change. In a way, they themselves seemed to have become cocooned, in the alabaster chambers. One student saw a row of alabaster effigies.

Only after struggling with the poem for some time did these students find that it was about the dead, and about life and death, in time and history: and about being in consciousness, and being without consciousness. In saying what it is 'about' like that, of course, I am actually summing up a great deal of work on it, in which the original experience of being encapsulated or embalmed seems an important part of possessing the poem, as it does what it says, as by the somewhat stifling air of the first stanza.

One student, I noticed, who had as yet no idea what the poem was 'about', saw that it displayed in the third stanza, a grand manner, with its references to Doges, and its spacious or cosmic perspective:

---

*This is how the poem appears in an edition I have. I gather from the Life of Emily Dickinson that one version was originally edited with stanzas 1 and 2 and another with stanzas 1 and 3. I propose to stick to 1, 2 and 3.

Grand go the years in the crescent above them
Worlds scoop their arcs — and firmaments row.

He could see that the rhythm was an important part of this gesture: its stately cadence, by contrast with the narrowness of the place where the meek are lying, perhaps conveyed by that echoed double feet:

Sleep the meek members of the resurrection

by contrast with

Rafter of satin and roof of stone.

Where the repeated initials R-S echoing R-S convey a sense of structure, the firm structure of the tomb, which holds the dead.

At this point, I try to draw out from myself an adequate reading, by attending to phrases I find it hard to understand: the fresh unusualness of certain words is here a mark of the superb originality of the art:

Rafter of satin . . . Castle of sunlight . . . Babbles . . . stolid ear . . . What sagacity . . . Diadems drop . . . Soundless as dots on a disc of Snow . . .

Now, I notice ambiguities in the Empsonian sense: that is, multiple readings that enhance the sense. Is the *stolid* ear that of one of the dead — or is it of the living? The bee is *babbling*, a sound which expresses life, but is bubblingly meaningless: certainly the ear cannot understand it. An infant babbles: so, it is a sound of primitive natural innocence, which one cannot yet understand. The ear of a dead person may be said to be stolid, because however loudly you shout at a corpse, it won't understand, and so seems stupid and dull. But, then, how much do we understand, when alive? The juxtaposition between being attentively and sensitively joyfully alive, and inertly dead, is intense.

A tension develops in the poem, between being conscious, and not being conscious. It is, of course, unresolved, and the art, as so often, is in keeping the matter unresolved. The tragic perplexity of 'in the midst of life we are in death' is held here in deeply disturbing suspension. So, as we go on through the poem, the opening word 'safe' takes on a particular vibration, or uncertainty, or ambiguity: like a loose key-stone in an arch, it threatens to give way, like the satin rafters (the roof, however, is of stone — you don't get out of the grave — so, the stifling effect of the first stanza moves on towards a feeling of the senses being closed and paralysed).

Safe in their alabaster chambers

It takes on so many meanings. There they are, fully secure in their hope of another life, having died believers. There they are, in good expensive coffins, in which even the lid is lined with satin. 'Sleep' and 'meek' even seem to combine to give 'sleek' — and we have a note of comfortable belief as in Pope's

To rest the cushion and soft dean invite . . .

Because of the image which forms with 'Rafters of Satin', in which one almost has an eye looking up at the secure coffin lid, we even get that stifling impression, which puts an ironic note into 'Safe'. They're safe all right: even if you cut the dead they don't bleed. They don't breathe. Theirs is the safety of being petrified, almost. So, they are

Untouched by morning and untouched by noon . . .

For to be safe in this way is to be insensible of the rhythms of time, insensible in the senses, the excitement and promise of morning, the gladness of mid-day. Even by the end of the first stanza, we want to get out of that kind of safety, as if we had been buried alive. But by the symbolism, what the poem is trying to do to us is to draw us out of our complacency about death, by a 'terrifying honesty', like Blake's, to see ourselves in a proper tragic perspective: a perspective that satisfies us because it presses upon us the real (existential) need for meaning: the *Dasein* problem, of recognising our 'being unto death' and our urgent need to establish some sense of meaning in our lives before we become nothing. Incidentally we may note that 'untouched' evokes being touched, and so we feel enhanced the condition of being touched by morning and noon.

The second stanza by contrast is a poem to being alive:

Light laughs the breeze in her castle of sunlight . . .

The labials enact the delight of being free in the world outside the tomb. It is a marvellous touch to make the breeze a woman (her) because she at once becomes a diaphanous dancing figure, like one of those in Botticelli's *Primavera*. The breeze spinning about the living world seems to have a substantial presence in a construction of light: the sun on the world looks like a secure structure: in the stanza is a garden, with stone sunlit walls, bees, birds singing albeit with ignorant nonchalance: how marvellous it is to be alive! And what sagacity perishes when we die!

Exactly how do we take that word *sagacity*? It means conscious intelligence, knowing the world. Note the words stolid, ignorant, sagacity: the whole poem is about being-in-the-world and being conscious of it, having learnt to know the world. throughout infancy and childhood. What a lot we know about the world — and what a great deal — that is as achievements—-dies when any group of people dies: or when one dies, when 'being in the world' comes to an end. The world which is a known world (even if we don't understand its babble, while the birds are ignorant of what they are saying or of what is happening to human beings) is a meaningful one, a structure, a complex — as a world unknown, not the subject of consciousness, is not. Behind the poem is a terror of this not-known world, world of un-touch, without the living consciousness playing upon it, without the life world: for we live in a life world, the *Lebenswelt* which is one of the key concepts in phenomenology.

Diadems drop is synedoche: the word diadem is used instead of 'crown', the headgear standing for the historical person. One after another, queens and countesses fall — their heads are cut off, they fling their jewels down in despair, or they die. *Diadem* evokes a sparkle of jewels, and perhaps we see showers of tears: at any rate the phrase evokes a perspective of beautiful women in power processing and falling, as in a Venetian splendour.

It has all the power of that remarkable phrase from Nashe which Empson analyses: 'Brightness falls from the air'. *Doges surrender* suggests the collapse of empires: epochs of empire and waste in war. The words pick up from our memory many images in paintings of doges in their opulent crowns: the special kind of crown a Doge wears echoes, visually in our minds, the diadems (dropping).

The perspective now widens even to the cosmic: firmaments row across the galaxy, like galleys, in a procession: but, to the dead, whose sagacity is extinguished, these are not seen — or heard. They might as well be spots of dust around which have formed the discs of the snow-flake.

The alabaster chamber, the satin rafters, the hopes of the resurrection, among the devout New England dead, seem to claim a significance for their lives. God cares for each one: so the Christian believes. By the time we reach the end of the poem that claimed significance has gone. They were not as important in the world as the Doge or any one of the diadem-adorned ladies — yet even these are dust and dropped away. They lie on into eternity, in which even the firmament of the heavens has shifted away: and become utterly insignificant, as insignificant as the smut in a snowflake. *Dot* and *disc*, as short words, express the insignificance of the particulate, reduce the grandeur of everything, from the castle of sunlight to the firmaments themselves, to nothingness. The last stanza is a recognition that everything is *being-unto-death*. And just as they do not hear the message of the bee, or see the sunlight, so, they do not hear any meaning in the immense cycles of history or the shifts of the universe: these are all 'soundless' (which has a terrifying echo of 'groundless' and distantly the concept of touchless). But we — we too for a moment offered a stolid ear to the bee's babbling, just as the birds offer only and ignorant cadence. So, we hear no meanings either. Soundless means that they cannot speak any meanings, cannot utter (cf the birds who babble). The small continual reassurance of sound, 'noise', which convince us that we are alive. are no longer heard by the dead: somewhere here too perhaps is the soundlessness one experiences in snow.

The poem leaves us with a perspective of total meaninglessness, in death: yet so controlled is the poem there is such delight in the vitality of the senses, in being alive, and in sagacity, that we don't feel terror. We feel resignation: we feel a relief in contemplating our predicament nakedly. So, I believe, it is a tragic poem.

So we feel directed towards the question, as to whether there is any meaning in our lives. And, however, we respond, we hear, throughout our ponderings, a ringing ambiguity and irony, echoing from that word 'safe' — for anything we summon up by way of belief threatens us with an encapsulation, against the true recognition of our plight, our mortality.

I don't surely have to labour further the value of attending to the meaning of such a very courageous poem by Emily Dickinson, in a world that threatens us with false meanings or meaninglessness on the one hand, and a lack of opportunities to pursue the problem of meaning on the other!

You might say that a poem like this by Emily Dickinson — a religious recluse writing esoteric poetry of this kind — is as far away as you could get from what Martin Buber calls 'the world of outcomes': of economic growth, or economic stagnation, the needs of the economy and the rest.* How could we justify our attention to such expressions of existential perplexity at a time when education is tending to evade such issues even in the name of the Humanities?

How do we answer that world if it challenges the time and energy we devote to such an 'obscure' poem about death? The answer may be given perhaps in some such terms as Mozart's letter to his father, which I quote in my book about Mahler:

> 'Since death (take my words literally) is the true goal of our lives, I have made myself so well acquainted during the last two years with this true and best friend of mankind that the idea of it no longer has any terrors for me, but much that is tranquil and comforting. And I thank God that he has granted me the good fortune to obtain the opportunity (you understand my meaning) of regarding death as the key to our true happiness. I never lie down in bed without considering that, young as I am, perhaps I may on the morrow be no more. Yet not one of those who know me could say I am morose or melancholy, and for this I thank my Creator daily and wish heartily that the same happiness may be given to my fellow men'.

A great deal in our civilization is manic—-belonging to what the psychoanalysts call the 'manic denial of death', with its artificial liveliness and 'attachment to things: strangely, like Mozart, we get a

*I refer the reader at this point to a question in the specimen examination paper on The Literary Representation of Women. In this question, references to a 'Gap' and an 'Abyss' in a poem by Emily Dickinson were related to themes of 'lack' and 'absence' in the writing of women poets — clearly implying that these words refer to the deprived status of women in society, rather than the predicament of the human soul *sub specie aeternitatis*. There could be no greater tendentious distortion of enquiry into poetic meaning.

great deal of satisfaction, even joy, from the contemplation of our 'being-unto-death': and the reason is, I believe, that this kind of confrontation, if it is genuine, if it displays a real capacity for 'tragic experience' (to use Leavis's phrase), impels us to 'construct something upon which to rejoice', to find some sense of the *Dasein*, the sense of 'being there', of having meaningfully existed, before we are swept away: for, at least, while we are still in consciousness we can at least reflect, with the artist, on our fate.

To feel this, in the light of philosophical anthropology is a primary need: and no civilization can go on, and certainly cannot find adequate aims or values, unless it has some sense, at the heart, of what kind of meaning in human existence may be set against death. The disastrous deficiency of such existential security in our time may be experienced at any funeral today, especially at the funerals of those who have no belief. In the face of death, many — humanists, Marxists, agnostics, unthinking people — simply go to pieces. In attaching to the reality of our predicament — as by responding to a poem like this one of Emily Dickinson, we are doing something which I suppose we may call religious, if only because it manifests a kind of seriousness or gravity which is rare in our time, but very necessary, if the deep unease of our time is to be overcome.

What I am trying to show in this chapter on poetry is that in reading and discussing poetry we are exercisig a phenomenological discipline — which is both natural and easily available to us, and yet extremely complex and ineffable.

Two aspects of consciousness are of central importance in the phenomenological discipline. One is symbolism, and the other is time. Behind the latter theme lies here the insights of Martin Heidegger, especially as they have been picked up by existentialist psychotherapy — especially the concept of being-unto-death.

The human consciousness is driven primarily by a need to find a sense of meaning in life, because we are always sinking through a film of time (as Merleau-Ponty puts it) towards death — towards nothingness.

We have to try to establish meanings which hold, even though we can do nothing to stem the flux. Out of this need emerges the impulse of intentionality: all consciousness is intentional — an aspect which mechanistic views of the mind disastrously fail to encounter. As Husserl himself put it, 'meaning is an intention of the mind'. In British psychology the mind tends to be thought of as passive (a *tabula rasa*, a bundle of sensations and associations): by contrast, in the continental view of the mind, influenced by Leibnitz, it is active — a theme of course, which fascinated Coleridge. Consciousness is always consciousness of something: a play of the mind actively upon the world — what Leavis called the living principle. our discipline, then, of reading and discussing poetry, is a phenomenological one, which must take account of symbolic meaning (essentially of metaphor), intentionality, time and being-unto-death. To illustrate I take the poem *Two in the Campagna* by Robert Browning:

I wonder do you feel to-day
As I have felt, since, hand in hand,
We sat down on the grass to stray
In spirit better through the land,
This morn of Rome and May?

For me, I touched a thought, I know,
Has tantalised me many times,
Like turns of thread the spiders throw
Mocking across our path for rhymes
To catch at and let go.

Help me to hold it: first it left
The yellowing fennel, run to seed
There, branching from the brickwork's cleft,
Some old tomb's ruin: yonder weed
Took up the floating weft.

Where one small orange cup amassed
Five beetles, — blind and green they grope
Among the honey-meal, — and last
Everywhere on the grassy slope
I traced it. Hold it fast!

The champaign with its endless fleece
Of feathery grasses everywhere!
Silence and passion, joy and peace,
An everlasting wash of air —
Rome's ghost since her decease.

Such life there, through such lengths of hours,
Such miracles performed in play,
Such primal naked forms of flowers,
Such letting Nature have her way
While Heaven looks from its towers.

How say you? Let us, O my dove,
Let us be unashamed of soul,
As earth lies bare to heaven above.
How is it under our control
To love or not to love?

I would that you were all to me,
You that are just so much, no more —
Nor yours, nor mine, — nor slave nor free!
Where does the fault lie? what the core
Of the wound, since wound must be?

I would I could adopt your will,
See with your eyes, and set my heart
Beating by yours, and drink my fill
At your soul's springs, — your part, my part
In life, for good and ill.

No. I yearn upward — touch you close,
Then stand away. I kiss your cheek,
Catch your soul's warmth, I pluck the rose
And love it more than tongue can speak —
Then the good minute goes.

Already how am I so far
Out of that minute? Must I go
Still like the thistle-ball, no bar,
Onward, wbenever light winds blow,
Fixed by no friendly star?

Just when I seemed about to learn!
Where is the thread now? Off again!
The old trick! Only I discern—
Infinite passion and the pain
Of finite hearts that yearn.

Perhaps what we notice first is the 'sakes' of the man,the way the poem goes, which embodies his particular unique 'voice' — a quality which is utterly beyond analysis. It is a record of a particular consciousness, with its modes of coming at the 'other' and the 'world'.

The first thing we notice is the light, easy flow of the spoken voice, playing over the strict verse form, which perhaps echoes Donne:

I wonder do you feel today
As I have felt, since, hand in hand,
We sat down on the grass . . .

To begin a poem 'I wonder' must surely echo

I wonder by my troth what thou and I
Did, till we lov'd . . . ?

Donne's *Songs and Sonnets* are often about identification — *Aire and Angels*, for instance, and this poem by Browning picks up this theme: one of the underlying themes of the poem is whether she feels the same as he feels. The poem belongs to that category of poetry which explores the I-Thou.

Here I will pick up a word in the last line: 'finite': 'finite hearts that yearn'. Here, in terms of my phenomenological analysis, there are two themes. One is the bounds of the self: one is in one's body and mind, in space. The other is the finite nature of one's mortality, in Time, which presses upon one the need to find a meaning in existence, before the end of that finite time. So, We have a poem with an existential theme, dealing with love in the context of being-unto-death. It is a *Dasein* poem: they are 'being there', exerting a sense of meaningful existence against a vast background which dwarfs them.

Love is a focus of meaning, and here the love between the poet and his woman is being contemplated against the long perspective of time symbolised by the relics of Rome beneath the grass of the

Campagna. Being-unto-death is exacerbated by this perspective: the self seems threatened with dissolving in:

> An everlasting wash of air

A beautiful line which conveys the sense of the wind blowing endlessly across the Campagna throughout history, and now: the evanescence of all things.

At the beginning of the poem he remembers how:

> hand in hand,
> We sat down on the grass

So, we have the two beings, the two bodies, sitting down at the remembered moment on the grass that cloaks the ruins, feeling the threat of death and dissolution into nothingness, holding hands to assert their state of being alive and in love, against the erosion of time, by that 'wash' of air:

> They sat down to think:
> to stray
> In spirit better through the land
> This morn of Rome and May.

For human beings there is one consolation for being bound in a finite body: the mind can stray, and make itself a thing of infinite space, as Hamlet knew, and as Coleridge recognised in *Frost at Midnight*. In that poem, as we shall see, he identifies with his sleeping infant, and also with the flame fluttering on the bars of the grate (see pp.124-30) .

In this state of mind there are two dangers. One is that one may experience a disturbing loss of self, in intense identification with the other. The other is that one may enter so much into subjectivity, making 'a toy of thought', that one may lose all hold on reality, and dissolve into nothingness: one may fear the forfeiture of a continuous consciousness in touch with reality. Behind this is perhaps a fear of something like going mad; or at least suffering such a regression that the identity seems likely to collapse and to be unable to come back.

In Coleridge's poem the route back to stability is by intentionality, by imagining the infant securely and creatively in touch with the real world, a wish culminating in those lovely last lines about the snow and the sun.

The disturbance in Browning's poem also has to do with 'encounter', the I-Thou. There is a degree of anguish over the question of identification: of tending to treat the other person, in intimacy, as part of oneself. This, we know from the philosophical anthropology of psychotherapy, is a universal problem. It is a problem of life. We also know this from Chaucer, as in the *Franklin's Tale*: and it raises the question we struggle with all our lives — that of mutual freedom in love: of letting 'the other' exist as an independent being. This in turn relates to 'the living principle': we need to let the world be, but find it as benign.

The beauty of those last lines of Coleridge's *Frost at Midnigh*t has a great deal to do with his discovery, by projecting himself into the child's future, wishing him a more creative relationship with the world, of the world as benign: the summer clothes the earth with greenness as the landscape at the moment of writing is being ministered to by the frost and clothed in mysterious whiteness: the juxtaposition of sun and snow symbolises the multitudinousness of our experience of the world and all its modes, while (as a student pointed out in a seminar) the images of periodicity, of gaps, (heard only in the trances of the blast, 'betwixt the tufts', the rows of icicles) go with the interstices in the thought, and enact even the way in which in the mind memories form and dissolve, in a rhythmic way (which the rhythm of the poem enacts, too).

To return to Browning: one of the seeming escapes from the finite mind and body is in that state of being-at-one with which lovers experience: it is a version of that sense of blissful union which the baby can experience with the mother — the root of what Freud called the 'oceanic experience', and which more recent observers relate to the concept of 'being for'.

But as we all know, the problem between man and woman is that while enjoying union, they also have to learn to let the other go, to find the other's being, without which there is no 'I-thou', no mutuality. There are serious dangers in over-possessiveness and the impulse to dominate — that is, to so wish the other person to be oneself, that any attempt on their part to exert their freedom is regarded as a threat, as if part of the self is revolting against one, like Alice's feet in *Alice in Wonderland*.

We can find this problem discussed, as I have said, in Chaucer

Which was the mooste fre, as thynketh your?

The Franklin's Tale, 1621-22

It is the problem symbolised in Criseyde's dream, in Chaucer's Troilus and Creseyde (Book II, line 925)

And as she slep, anon right tho hire mette
How that an egle, fethered whit as bon,
Under hir brest his longe clawes sette,
And out hire herte he rente, and that anon,
And dide his herte into hire brest to gon,
Of which she nought agross, ne nothyng smerte;
And forth he fleigh, with herte left for herte.

The premonition of love seems to be of such intense identification that one actually becomes the other: hearts are exchanged, and, the symbols suggest, the impulse to become the other is so intense that it might tear one to pieces. The eagle, feathered white as bone, even seems like death himself; yet she feels no dread ('agroos' from agreyson) or pain — the mutual becoming-the-other is deeply desired.

We can also follow it in Lawrence, who is at one moment declaring

So I hope I shall spend eternity
With my face down buried between her breasts . . .

and then rejecting what he called 'horrible merging'.

In *Manifesto* he writes a whole tormented poem on the problem, of finding his wife as another person: 'she is all not-me.'

So, here, Browning says:

I would that you were all to me,
You that are just so much, no more —
Nor yours, nor mine, — nor slave — nor free!
Where does the fault lie? What the core
Of the wound, since wound must be?

It seems as we read the poem that this 'wound' has something to do with guilt — say sexual guilt induced by the morality of the time.

'Let us be unashamed of soul' then seems to be a claim to be triumphant over morality, or repression. But the next stanza goes on:

I would I could adopt your will,
See with your eyes, and set my heart
Beating by yours, and drink my fill
At your soul's pring — your part, my part
In life, for good and ill.

So, the inevitable 'wound' seems rather something to do with being and identity. Here, surely, he is still beating at the desire that she should be him: that he should experience with her the kind of experience of union only possible between infant and mother. He wants her to be him: 'your part,my part' — which is essentially narcissistic, since the essence of it is that he wishes only to find himself in her, her part, his part.

In such a narcissistic union there would be no possibility of a meaning which could triumph over death and nothingness. Solipsism is no solution to the problem of being-unto-death: only a mutual recognition in love can generate that kind of meaning which can transcend mortality. Love can only be where there is a 'Thou' to which the 'I' can relate, in mutual freedom.

So, the inevitable 'wound' is the recognition that the total identification cannot be achieved — that indeed it belongs to infant magic and monism — and is not appropriate where there is such an intense need to find the 'thought', the sense of meaning, in love in time. The quality of the poem is in its registering of the anguish of consciousness over this, and the progress in the insights as in that 'No', which is so significantly placed:

No. I yearn upward — touch you close,
Then stand away. I kiss your cheek
Catch your soul's warmth, — I pluck the rose
And love it more than tongue can speak —
Then the good minute goes.

He still yearns for transcendence: but he lets her go. He is in touch with her: but stands away. The result is an intensifying of love, because it is more exciting and much more of a mystery to love someone who is not oneself, as Lawrence finds in *Manifesto*: this is the true discovery of 'the other':

So I put my hand out further, a little further
And I felt that which was not I . . .

It was the unknown . . .
I cannot tell you the mad, astounded rapture of its discovery . . .
New Heaven and Earth

So, the colour of her cheek, in Browning, the immediate sympathy of her soul's warmth, and the sense of taking in from her beauty, generate a feeling of love which is so strong it cannot be spoken. But, of course, there is a price to pay, not least for the realism of recognising her separate existence:

Then the good minute goes . . .

As in Marvell's famous poem, the attempt to make time stand still merely exacerbates the devouring nature of time. And so, he drifts away into the everlasting 'wash' of time:

Already how am I so far
Out of that minute? Must I go
Still like the thistle-ball, no bar,
Onward, wherever light winds blow,
Fixed by no friendly star!

Or, as Lawrence puts it, in *Song of a Man who is not Loved*,

I . . . feel a big wind blowing
Me like a gadfly into the dusk . . .
So much there is outside me, so infinitely
Small am I, what matter if minutely
I beat my way, to be lost immediately . . .
I am too
little to count in the wind that drifts me through

Browning cries:

Just when I seemed about to learn!
Where is the thread now? Off again!
The old trick! Only I discern . . .

The excellence of the poem is in the discerning, the registering, step by step, of the experience of the tormented consciousness. The poem does not begin from any generalisation or principle: nor does it advance towards one. It realises and registers the experience, and preserves the ambivalence in suspension as it goes. Whether Donne was an influence here I couldn't say, but one quality of Donne's verse belongs to this same capacity, to follow the progress of thought and feeling, in the bed, in the room, at that moment — which by the time it is written about is over, of course, since not even poets actually write their poems in the bed. A poem is a reconstruction of the experience recollected in tranquility: and it follows the remembered pattern and progress of the thought, towards resolution.

I have discussed what seems to me to be the phenomenological theme of the poem. From this approach, I see it as a search for meaning — an attempt to ponder the meaning of a moment which is full of both anguish and joy.

The search for meaning now provides a clue to the symbolism:

Where is the thread now? Off again!

The thread is the thread of consciousness (symbolised by the spider's web). The 'old trick' is that the significance always seems to elude one: just as one feels one is about to grasp the point of life, or the meaning of love, it eludes one. Yet, 'I discern', the poem is at least a record of the exploration, even if 'we missed the meaning,' and a record of the meditation.

So, if we return to the beginning of the poem, we can see that the second stanza relates the contemplation and the writing of the poem together: the attempt to 'catch at rhymes' and to 'let them go' is at one with trying to understand experience and then to let it be, to speak for itself. The kind of discipline I am trying to exemplify — the study of symbolism and meaning — often gains its satisfactions from asking awkward questions. Here, the awkward question one must ask oneself is — why the word 'mock'? The operation of consciousness in its quest for the significance, is like the spiders' webs that throw their web lines across the Campagna. These 'mock' because they speak of the moving away of time, of the processes of decay, of being unto death in the everlasting wash of air: but also of the persistent dynamics of life (and thought) in the face of this. They mock because they make it clear that, in spreading out to take in the whole perspective, his thought undertakes an impossible task: in weaving over the whole Campagna, the spiders' webs take in the whole of this historical space.

The significance eludes him, just as the spun webs seem to spin everywhere, linking everything, but are intangible and diffused.

He wants to hold a thought: an insight: a poetic achievement of meaning, which shall be caught in the 'rhymes' just as the webs link one thing with another. But what is the thought? He never reaches it: all he reaches (as we have seen) is an ambiguity, between the finite (and mortal) self, and the yearning for some infinite meaning that shall come out of the mysterious union of love, and transcend.

This itself dissolves off into the plain of feathery grasses. (Note the insubstantiality of the main images of the poem, symbolising memories and the thoughts he is grasping at: 'floating weft' 'fleece of feathery grasses', 'thistle-ball', 'the thread', the 'wash of air . . .')

The webs seem to me to symbolise the intentional consciousness, that runs with its creative perception over the scene. But, at least, it attaches itself to significant points: to real points, by the 'living principle' of significant perception: first it left

> The yellowing fennel, run to seed
> There, branching from the brickwork's cleft,
> Some old tomb's ruin; yonder weed
> Took up the floating weft,
>
> Where one small orange cup amassed
> Five beetles,—-blind and green they grope
> Among the honey-meal, — and last
> Everywhere on the grassy slope
> I traced it. Hold it fast!

I suppose I respond to these lines with such excitement because I am an amateur painter of landscapes. In painting (it is relevant to say) one doesn't ask, 'Why did I choose to paint this fennel?' It isn't necessary in order to respond to this poem 'Why mention the fennel?' 'Why mention it has run to seed?' But if we are professionally engaged as literary critics or students doing 'practical criticism', then this is our essential discipline — again to ask the awkward questions. What is the point of the fennel? What are these beetles doing here?

The yellowing fennel was there on the Campagna, and is mentioned I believe because it is a wild flower, and is yellowing — its colour contributes to a golden kind of glow (orange cup, honey-meal) with which the poem suffuses the Campagna, and is a 'primal naked form' — all this being a benign back-ground to their love: the world (despite the underlying decay and the wash of time) is felt to be benign. The five beetles are in a flower, among its pollen.

They symbolise humble living creatures, like the lovers, in the long perspectives of space and time, in the Campagna and its embodiment of history since Rome. Like the lovers, they are among the honey-meal, groping. They are blind and green, they cannot grasp the significance of their living existence any better. They just go on living: they represent 'life' — of which Leavis said it was a 'necessary word', even though one can't always define it. They are seeking joy, as the beetles the pollen.

I talked earlier of the ultimate resignation in the poem, to being separate, and to never being able to find meaning in a total union with the loved one. There is a plea for resignation of a different kind, in the middle of the poem, after a contemplation of human existence in history:

> Such life there, through such lengths of hours,
> Such miracles performed in play,
> Such primal naked forms of flowers,
> Such letting Nature have her way
> While Heaven looks from its towers.

It is a kind of holiday perspective: as if from Heaven: from a sense of detachment and freedom, it is possible to 'allow' all the manifestations of the human drama and culture ('play') because they seem like the many varieties of life, as in the wild flowers.

So, the fact that they are in love, and so tormented by it, should be seen as one of the multifarious manifestations of nature: it is nothing to be ashamed of, and it is (marvellously) beyond control: it takes on a 'life' of its own!

> How is it under our control.
> To love or not to love?

In this there is a resignation to a certain kind of freedom in resignation to joy — very much at odds of course with the conventional morality of the time: very brave.

From this, the poet goes on to explore the problem I have discussed earlier, of identification, and of being: of self and other.

How are these connected? Here I think I would use the concept of creative becoming used by Erwin Straus in an essay on *Shame as a Historiological Problem*:

> The secret that shame protects is not . . . as prudery makes the mistake of believing, one that is already in existence . . . those who are in becoming are also hidden from themselves. Their existence is first made explicit in their shared immediate becoming . . .

Browning declares that they need not be ashamed, for being in love must be seen as fate grasping them by the throat, as it were: but then comes 'shared immediate becoming' and out of this spring inevitably the problems of identity and existence with which the poem goes on to deal. The dynamics of this 'shared immediate becoming' are symbolised in the poem, by the webs, the flowers and the beetles: these belong to the same 'life', struggling to survive there and realise themselves.

I have tried to discuss complex and profound issues which this poem explores. To do so, I have taken to disciplines which belong to the attempt to understand the phenomena of consciousness. But I have also, I hope, allowed the poem to be responded to as a work of art. Its effectiveness depends upon its direct and simple voice, which follows the inflexions of intimate speech, despite a tight stanza structure — an achievement in itself. Its symbols are fresh and alive — and subtly enmeshed in a complex mood. In its poetic argument, it has the advantage of not offering any solutions, though it does offer the experience of resolution — a progress is made, towards resignation: to seeing that one's human lot is both to yearn for ultimate meaning, and yet never to find it: yet (as so often) a meaning has been constructed, which is the poem.

Possessing a poem in this way is our discipline. All I have done is to read it — reading being here an active, participating process, for I have brought a great deal to the poem. In this, it has illuminated and extended my range of experience: I have been there with the lovers; I have seen the scenes in my imagination; I have felt its awesomeness, and its effects on consciousness and attitudes to being, meaning and being-unto-death. I have experienced again the perplexing problems of freedom in love. And I experience satisfaction in the completeness of the poem, its achievement — just as I am glad when a picture is painted, when one has the feeling 'it is finished'. There is an implicit analogy between the spun webs on the Campagna, and in the attempt to catch a thought by 'rhymes' the poem as a work of art itself. And behind that again the worn away tombs and bits of brickwork on the plain. But I am delighted by its tantalising air of leaving the problem 'in the air': it is the honesty of not grasping the thought that makes the experience familiar to us.

All of which, as I hope I have shown, is difficult to explain, but, as the exercise of a discipline, is hard and exacting: central to 'English'. And as a discipline which attends to the imaginative exploration of human experience, it contributes, in English as a humanities subject, to the sympathetic understanding of human nature, to our recognition of the torment of love, to a sense of man's place in history and time, and to the groping in which we are all involved, towards a sense of meaning in life.

I shall now turn to some poems by Coleridge who, as psychologist and philosopher is an important ally in our need to vindicate our discipline (a key text here is *Mill on Bentham and Coleridge*, edited with an Introduction by F.R. Leavis). First I shall discuss his *Frost at Midnight*.

> The Frost performs its secret ministry,
> Unhelped by any wind. The owlet's cry
> Came loud — and hark, again! loud as before.
> The inmates of my cottage, all at rest,
> Have left me to that solitude, which suits
> Abstruser musings: save that at my side
> My cradled infant slumbers peacefully.
> 'Tis calm indeed! so calm, that it disturbs
> And vexes meditation with its strange
> And extreme silentness. Sea, hill, and wood,
> This populous village! Sea, and hill, and wood,
> With all the numberless goings-on of life,
> Inaudible as dreams! the thin blue flame
> Lies on my low-burnt fire, and quivers not;
> Only that film, which fluttered on the grate,
> Still flutters there, the sole unquiet thing.
> Methinks, its motion in this hush of nature

Gives it dim sympathies with me who live,
Making it a compassionable form,
Whose puny flaps and freaks the idling Spirit
By its own moods interprets, every where
Echo or mirror seeking of itself,
And makes a toy of Thought.
But o! how oft,
How oft, at school, with most believing mind,
Presageful, that I gazed upon the bars,
To watch that flattering stranger! and as oft
With unclosed lids, already had I dreamt
Of my sweet birth-place. and the old church-tower,
Whose bells. the poor man's only music, rang
From morn to evening. all the hot Fair-day,
So sweetly, that they stirred and haunted me
With a wild pleasure, falling on mine ear
Most like articulate sounds of things to come!
So gazed I, till the soothing things, I dreamt,
Lulled me to sleep, and sleep prolonged my dreams!
And so I brooded all the following morn,
Awed by the stern preceptor's face, mine eye
Fixed with mock study on my swimming book:
Save if the door half opened, and I snatched
A hasty glance, and still my heart leaped up,
For still I hoped to see the stranger's face,
Townsman, or aunt, or sister more beloved,
My play-mate when we both were clothed alike!
Dear Babe, that sleepest cradled by my side,
Whose gentle breathings, heard in this deep calm,
Fill up the interspersed vacancies
And momentary pauses of the thought!
My babe so beautiful! it thrills my heart
With tender gladness, thus to look at thee,
And think that thou shalt learn far other lore,
And in far other scenes!
For I was reared In the great city, pent 'mid cloisters dim,
And saw nought lovely but the sky and stars.

But thou, my babe! shalt wander like a breeze
By lakes and sandy shores, beneath the crags
Of ancient mountain, and beneath the clouds,
Which image in their bulk both lakes and shores
And mountain crags: so shalt thou see and hear
The lovely shapes and sounds intelligible
Of that eternal language, which thy God
Utters, who from eternity doth teach
Himself in all, and all things in himself.
Great universal Teacher! he shall mould
Thy spirit, and by giving make it ask.
Therefore all seasons shall be sweet to thee,
whether the summer clothe the general earth
With greenness, or the redbreast sit and sing
Betwixt the tufts of snow on the bare branch
Of mossy apple-tree, while the nigh thatch
Smokes in the sun-thaw; whether the eave-drops fall
Heard only in the trances of the blast,
Or if the secret ministry of frost
Shall hang them up in silent icicles,
Quietly shining to the quiet Moon.

The central fact of this poem is the presence of the sleeping infant, which draws Coleridge into a kind of state which is found in woman, at the stage of psychic parturition, and which men may experience (when it is called *couvade*).

This state was recognised among others by D. W.Winnicott, who called it 'primary maternal preoccupation'. We accept easily that a mother goes through profound physical changes, to bring a child into the world: and we recognise that there are emotional changes. The pregnant woman develops a certain kind of peaceful abstraction from the world — she gets called 'cowlike': but it is as though she is no longer interested in the things of this world.

She goes over entirely to the mystery of the new being, and identifies very profoundly with her baby. This relationship begins long before the baby is born.

Winnicott explored this very special state in an essay on *Primary Maternal Preoccupation* dated 1956. He found a very special state of the mother which deserved a name. It is especially intense for a few weeks after an infant's birth, and is such an extension of the mother's psyche that if the baby dies it shows up as a kind of schizoid illness.

It is one of the most disturbing features of human existence that our sense of identity, our consciousness, and our reality sense, depends upon our experience of this state of the mother, at a time when we are totally dependent upon her.

In a later essay, Winnicolt speaks of the 'mirror role' of the mother, and speaks of 'creative reflection'. The baby, as it were, looks into the mother's face, and into her mind, to see what kind of idea of him she has: and he becomes himself by realising his potentialities in this reflection. He sees what he might become.

At first the baby does not know it is a continuous self in a whole body, in a world over and against which it is. At first it even believes that its mother is itself, or is part of itself, an extension of itself: the mother, as the object of the need for relationship, is the subjective object. She allows the baby to believe this. And at first, the baby does not know that being fed, and bathed and clothed are all things which happen to the same baby. Gradually the mother disillusions him — that is, enables him to find the world as the world, the self as the self, and her as herself, another, the objective object.

We know about these achievements from those who have studied the problems of those who have never completed these processes — and are left in various stages of psychic disability. One of Winnicott's patients, for instance, a twin, had never found herself as a separate person: when her twin was lifted up out of the pram she could not understand why she did not rise into the air.

But what they reveal is that our capacity to deal with the world is an achievement, which has behind it strange processes of interrelationship, between one consciousness, and one body, and another consciousness and body: and in these forms of interrelationship, the imagination, play and symbolism are, as Winnicott has also shown, of great importance. Anyone who has played the game of 'gone!' with an infant will realise that the child is engaged on deep problems of self and world which are of the kind that belong to poetry and philosophy.

There are also serious dangers, because if we allow ourselves to open up the problems of the subjective life, and of close identification, such as we experienced as infants, since we are thus brought to realise that our grasp of the real depends upon subjective factors, and the evanescent dynamics of relationship, it may seem that the world itself may dissolve, in a Bishop Berkeley way. The infant, as a certain stage, may actually feel that if his mother goes into a shop, or puts out his light at night, or is not looking at him, he may cease to exist.

So, if we open up this kind of problem (as Marion Milner did, in her own psychoanalysis, when trying to take up painting, as someone brought up on science: see *On Not Being Able to Paint*) we may reach a position of being afraid that the world may cease to exist, or we may cease to exist, or in some way the relationship between self and world may be disturbed. Sometimes, of course, this can be a blessed release, as it was to Marvell when tormented, among other things, by the agony of the Civil War:

> Annihilating all that's made
> To a green thought in a green shade . . .

By the way, this is one thing that is terrible about love, and why it is often feared as being like death: so intense can mutual identification be in love, that the lover can go mad, as far as the world is concerned: the world ceases to become real for him (or for her) — and this is part of the enigma of *Antony and Cleopatra*.

We may seem by now a long way from *Frost at Midnight*, but we are not. The poem is about the effect produced upon Coleridge by the presence of the baby at a very quiet moment of solitude, when the only thing to be heard is the baby's light breathing:

> Dear Babe, that sleepest cradled by my side
> Whose gentle breathing, heard in this deep calm,
> Fill up the interspersed vacancies
> And momentary pauses of the thought . . .

One of the most disturbing things about a very young baby is one's awareness of the slightness of its breathings, and it is a common experience to be extremely worried that this breathing will stop. It is such a gentle manifestation of life, of the living spirit. And in between breaths it does stop.

In Coleridge's poem there is a kind of counterpoint between his bursts of thought, pauses of the thought, and the rhythmic light breathings of the infant. In the interstices between the thoughts there is such a silence, and vacancy that he has a dreadful feeling of going out of existence. This dreadful feeling belongs to his couvade, his male experience of 'primary maternal preoccupation', that (schizoid) extension of the identity, in identification with the sleeping child.

In the face of this dread of going out of existence he clings to the ongoings of life, and one on-going, one earnest of continuity, is the secret ministry of the frost.

That first beautiful line evokes an image of white-robed acolytes outside in the night attending to everything in a mysterious way, preparing them to be seen (as they are seen at the end of the poem, above the eave-drops)

> . . . or if the secret ministry of frost
> Shall hang them up in silent icicles
> Quietly shining to the quiet moon.

The moon is a symbol of the mother, and this last image is perhaps an image of the benign presence of the mother to whom this experience may now be properly handed over.

Secret ministry also suggests of course the magical dynamics of the life of the world. And I believe it also suggests the mysterious processes of growth to which the child belongs; as it sleeps it is growing to a human consciousness.

If we are in any situation in which our identity is not confirmed, by the presence of others responding to us, or the bustle of a community, or other goings on, we may be troubled by a feeling of restlessness and unease. Here, everyone has gone to bed, and Coleridge is experiencing solitude, except for the babe. The calm, as he contemplates it, is disturbing.

> 'Tis calm indeed! So calm, that it disturbs
> And vexes meditation with its strange
> And extreme silentness.

He casts about to think of the physical surroundings in the world: repeating the names of the larger realities:

Sea, hill and wood,
This populous village! Sea, and hill, and wood
With all the numberless goings-on of life,
Inaudible as dreams.

Since there is no evidence of them, they might as well not exist, or be dreams. The usual relationship between perception and reality seems to be dissolving. And this is due not only to the silence, but to the presence of the baby, which is drawing him into a loss of himself, by identification, and, as it were, swallowing him in its own rudimentary consciousness.

His consciousness, which is now the only continuous thread, seems to be a mere flame, perhaps in relation to the other little flame, the sleeping infant's consciousness. The two flames seem to me symbolic of the two minds, belonging (in identification) to the same fire, one thin and low, but steady, the other an even more evanescent fluttering one. He both identifies with this and finds it a 'companionable form': as if his consciousness had entered into the primitive consciousness of the sleeping baby. And if he does that — if he goes back to that stage, he will enter again the stage before the achievement of a firm reality-sense.

Then, the freaks and flaps of that one mind may be interpreted by his spirit, in various moods, in terms of echoes or mirrors of itself, and played with like a toy. Even thought itself, it seems, could go out like the puny flame: and if consciousness went out like that, what would be left?

The words echo and mirror are important, because they reveal the state of maternal preoccupation in which Coleridge has been drawn, so that he is experiencing creative reflection, in the realm of the I-Thou. In these lines it is almost as if he is beginning to cease to know who is he and who is the babe, and to fear that, if one or other puny flame goes out, or if his own consciousness is drawn into the kind of toy-play of which an infant is capable, all reality will dissolve.

Having reached this point, he goes back in memory to his own childhood. The fluttering flame, which seems so much like the fluttering consciousness of the babe (and yet has dim sympathies with me who live), is called a 'stranger' in superstitious belief. It is a sign that a stranger is to come next day.

Through the process of identification, Coleridge now regresses to his own childhood, and remembers how as a child, when he saw such signs, he seemed to hear as in the sound of the bells, a voice

> falling on mine ear
> Most like articulate sounds of things to come!

Next day, as a child, he tried to read his book, but it swam before his eyes, while he yearned for the stranger to appear — that might be some friend or relative, or his sister, with whom he was once 'clothed alike'.

It should be clear by now that the stranger is here the Babe, and that the mood of expectancy he is remembering is with him now, in his mode of wondering what it will become, being ready to creatively reflect the new being.

So, he begins now, after the initial moment of approaching loss of all sense of time and reality, to move back towards a realised future.

> Dear Babe, that sleepest cradled by my side,
> Whose gentle breathings, heard in this deep calm,
> Fill up the interspersed vacancies
> And momentary pauses of the thought!
> My babe so beautiful! it thrills my heart
> With tender gladness, thus to look at thee,
> And think that thou shalt learn for other love
> And in far other scenes.

He has turned from remembering himself in regression, and now turns to create, as it were, a good life for the babe, in gratitude. The child shall (he hopes) have a richer life than his, because he was put in the great city, and the child shall experience the Lake District: where he shall learn all those sources of wisdom that Wordsworth found there ('one impulse from a vernal wood! . . . ').

It is significant that he symbolises this creative interaction between the child and the world in images of reflection:

> and beneath the clouds,
> Which image in their bulk both lakes and shores
> And mountain crags . . .

In those lines we see the clouds echoing the forms of mountains, shores and crags: but because of the woods, lakes, sandy shores with lakes and shores repeated (as in a mirror) the clouds and mountains also reflected in the lakes.

God, he prays, will teach the child by giving to him in such a way as to make him ask about the meaning of the beauty of the world. Just as he himself is, by creative reflection, giving the child a good life, so, he hopes will God give him the power to inquire and explore, and seek out understanding of the world.

Therefore all seasons shall be sweet to thee . . .

At the beginning of the poem, as we have seen, there was a solitude and silence in which there was such a degree of sensory perception that it seemed as if the self and the world might go out of existence. By an immense act of creative reflection, and benign fathering, Coleridge has not only regained a sense of the reality of the world, but now gives an intensely 'present' world to the child: and in doing so, of course, he gives an intensely realized world to us. The world he gives is benign, and has a quality of rhythmic, seasonal continuity (like that expressed in Mahler's *Song of the Earth*):

Whether the summer clothe the general earth
In greenness, or the redbreast sit and sing
Betwixt the tufts of snow on the bare branch
Of mossy apple-tree, while the nigh thatch
Smokes in the sun-thaw . . .

There is a beautiful juxtaposition of cold and warm, bare and mossy, cold sparseness of chill gaps (as between the branch and the nigh thatch) and the smoke of the sun's unusual heat. The interstices (between the tufts) suggest one stage merging into another, and also the rhythmic pauses of the thought, and the child's regular breathing: all life is unified by this cyclic pattern — and this is reflected in the trances of the blast, and the rows of icicles.

The emptiness of the moments between thoughts, which were full of dread and loss of reality, threat of loss of consciousness, have now become beautiful ranks of phenomena, as the drops are turned into ice:

whether the eave-drops fall
Heard only in the trances of the blast
Or if the secret ministry of frost

> Shall hang them up in silent icicles
> Silently shining to the quiet moon.

The reappearance of the 'secret ministry' with its crisp sounds, suggests that the stilling of the drops, and the turning of them into serrated ornaments of night is a 'meant' process: the mysterious dynamics of Nature yield these beauties, in which our senses can delight: and the benign Mother of the heavens looks on them too and (as it were) blesses them like the moon in *The Ancient Mariner*.

The same harmony which turns the drops heard in a gale into a silent row of icicles in a frosty night will turn the infant's primitive consciousness (manifest in his quiet breathing) into an intense and creative life, experience of the world, full of rich meaning.

The poem can be understood and responded to, of course, without knowing anything about psychoanalytical studies of mother infant relationship or male couvade. But if we do know about creative reflection, we can follow more easily the poetic logic of the poem, and the act of consciousness, the record of a progressive movement of consciousness that it is, moving from a loss of self, through regression, to a view of a world full of potentialities and meaning — given to the next generation: leading out from self-absorption to a very beautiful moment of generosity, in which we too share intense sense-feelings, and the sense of joyful harmony with nature.

In its contribution to our consciousness, the achievement of the poem itself, its form, and its verbal richness (as at the end) generates a feeling of the possibility of achieving meaning. it tells us a good deal about 'what it is to be human' — and helps to explain (for example) the kind of unease and involvement we experience with a very young infant, as we are drawn into his psyche, and his need to be 'reflected'. And who, after reading those last lines, could feel that life has no point: they are, of course, at the utter other extreme from the lines in the *Dejection Ode* in which Coleridge expresses his distress, at finding when looking at the clouds in the sky.

> I see, not feel, how beautiful they are —

— a terrible experience of perception without apperception.

Frost at Midnight conveys above all the conviction that the imagination is the primary agent of human perception: and so, in the terms I have expressed, is a valuable poem for our time: because it enacts in us the power of intentionality, the giving of meaning to the world, and, in gratitude, to others.

One of the perquisites of returning as I have done, after a number of years, to teaching literature is that one finds oneself obliged to attend to poems and other works which one has previously neglected or missed: fashions alter, and students demand that you attend to something that interests them.

So, one finds oneself engaged in the kind of experience a student must often have — reading a poem for the first time, and trying to 'possess' it. This word 'possess' as I have said before seems to give my own students considerable difficulty, though it gives me none.

If you say to me 'Van Gogh' or 'Monet' I have inward images brought to mind out of memory, and I know the kind of effect these painters have on me. I would find it harder if you said Delacroix, or David Hockney, or Rothko: but I'd be all right with Picasso — and, because of personal prejudices, Berthe Morisot or Michael Andrews. Some painters I have possessed: others I have not possessed, or have taken into myself only partially. I have possessed Mozart, and can usually tell his voice when I hear it: I have possessed *Verklärte Nacht* but little else of Schoenberg and I have not possessed Harrison Birtwhistle or Stockhausen.

Again, I must emphasise, we are dealing with tacit elements. We could discuss poems by John Donne or Milton or Wyatt or Shakespeare's *Sonnets* in great detail: but even so, we could never give an adequate account of how we know that voice: what the features of the face of the voice are. I put it like that, because recognising a poet's voice is like recognising a face: it is ineffable. It cannot thus be reduced, as I believe fingerprinting can, to computer analysis, or any scientific procedure. How we recognise a face, or a voice, we can never say, and it is not a logical or linear process: it is a gestalt process, requiring something like 'a leap of the imagination' or a moment of complex perception and indwelling, in which, with Ezra Pound's hero in *The Women of Trachis* we cry:

> Splendour! It all coheres!

It is perhaps worth pointing out that while we cannot reduce recognition to scientific explanation, the tacit processes of personal knowing which we employ (you will notice that I am using the terminology of Michael Polanyi in *Personal Knowledge*) is used in science, as in crystallography, or especially in biology. Professor C.F. Pantin used to tell his students, 'Bring in any worms that sneer at you' — indicating that the detection of this particular species involved a capacity like that of recognising a face.

Here is one capacity of our phenomenological discipline, and one aspect of the art we study. In the poem we read, for pleasure or practical criticism, we attend to a consciousness: we recognise (or perhaps not) a mind — or, since bodily feelings and experiences are involved, a being-in-the-world. We possess what Hopkins called the inscape of that being: the particular, unique, characteristics of the soul of a man or woman: its 'sakes'.

What compels our attention in trying to possess a work of art like a poem is that a soul is trying to find meaning. Of course, not all art has a profound quest for meaning: a poem may be the equivalent of Percy Grainger's *Shepherds Hey*: but next door to such a lively piece will be his setting of *Shaller Brown* which is the equivalent in music of the long Australian novel *The Fortunes of Richard Mahoney* — a deeply moving expression of the tyranny of distance, and the agonies of separation and time which people have gone through, in the historical relationship between Britain and Australia.

What compels our interest, I believe: compels even our joy in art, is to possess something of a gain in meaning, of a *Dasein* kind: that is, of a sense of meaning grasped in the face of a recognition of death, and our ultimate nothingness. What is called *Daseinanalysis*, a development from existentialist psychotherapy, itself a development from psychoanalysis, very much under the impact of the gloomy philosophy of Martin Heidegger, is that beneath every human manifestation is the recognition that all our life is a question of being-unto-death, a flowing away towards nothingness: and our deepest satisfactions are in constructing something upon which to rejoice, something which holds a meaning, which speaks of the *Dasein*, the being there by which, if only temporarily and briefly, we can stem the tide.

Obviously, here, mere hedonism only exacerbates the march to death, while even the most intense ecstasy as in passion, while it may enhance meaning, also has the effect of quickening the pace of time and the menace of death:

Let us roll all our strength and all
Our sweetness up into one ball,
And tear our pleasures with rough strife
Thorough the iron gates of life:
Thus, though we cannot make our sun
Stand still, yet we will make him run. Andrew Marvell

This reiteration of a *Daseins*-analysis approach to the reading of poetry is the preamble to a poem I wish next to discuss, Coleridge's *This Lime-Tree Bower My Prison*.

Well, they are gone, and here must I remain,
This lime-tree bower my prison! I have lost
Beauties and feelings, such as would have been
Most sweet to my remembrance even when age
Had dimm'd mine eyes to blindness! They, meanwhile,
Friends, whom I never more may meet again,
On springy heath, along the hill-top edge,
Wander in gladness, and wind down, perchance,
To that still roaring dell, of which I told;
The roaring dell, o'erwooded, narrow, deep,
And only speckled by the mid-day sun;
Flings arching like a bridge; — that branchless ash,
Unsunn'd and damp, whose few poor yellow leaves
Ne'er tremble in the gale, yet tremble still,
Fann'd by the water-fall! and there my friends
Behold the dark green file of long lank weeds,
That all at once (a most fantastic sight!)
Still nod and drip beneath the dripping edge
Of the blue clay-stone.

Now, my friends emerge
Beneath the wide wide Heaven — and view again
The many-steepled tract magnificent
Of hilly fields and meadows, and the sea,
With some fair bark, perhaps, whose sails light up

The slip of smooth clear blue betwixt two Isles
Of purple shadow! Yes! they wander on
In gladness all; but thou, methinks, most glad.
My gentle-hearted Charles! for thou hast pined
And hunger'd after Nature, many a year,
In the great City pent, winning thy way
With sad yet patient soul, through evil and pain
And strange calamity! Ah slowly sink
Behind the western ridge, thou glorious Sun!
Shine in the slant beams of the sinking orb,
Ye purple heath-flowers! richlier burn, ye clouds!
Live in the yellow light, ye distant groves!
And kindle, thou blue Ocean! So my friend
Struck with deep joy may stand, as I have stood,
Silent with swimming sense; yea, gazing round
On the wide landscape, gaze till all doth seem
Less gross than bodily; and of such hues
As veil the Almighty Spirit, when yet he makes
Spirits perceive his presence.

A delight
Comes sudden on my heart, and I am glad
As I myself were there! Nor in this bower,
This little lime-tree bower, have I not mark'd
Much that has sooth'd me. Pale beneath the blaze
Hung the transparent foliage; and I watch'd
Some broad and sunny leaf, and lov'd to see
The shadow of the leaf and stem above
Dappling its sunshine! And that walnut-tree
Was richly ting'd, and a deep radiance lay
Full on the ancient ivy, which usurps
Those fronting elms, and now, with blackest mass
Makes their dark branches gleam a lighter hue
Through the late twilight: and though now the bat
Wheels silent by, and not a swallow twitters,
Yet still the solitary humble-bee
Sings in the bean-flower! Henceforth I shall know
That Nature ne'er deserts the wise and pure;

No plot so narrow, be but Nature there,
No waste so vacant, but may well employ
Each faculty of sense, and keep the heart
Awake to Love and Beauty! and sometimes
'Tis well to be bereft of promis'd good,
That we may lift the soul, and contemplate
With lively joy the joys we cannot share.
My gentle-hearted Charles! when the last rook
Beat its straight path alone the dusky air
Homewards, I blest it! deeming its black wing
(Now a dim speck, now vanishing in light)
Had cross'd the mighty Orb's dilated glory,
While thou stood'st gazing; or, when all was still,
Flew creeking o'er thy head, and had a charm
For thee, my gentle-hearted Charles, to whom
No sound is dissonant which tells of Life.

I will pick out first the lines:

Friends, whom I never more may meet again
On springy heath, along the hill-top edge,
Wander in gladness . . .

What Coleridge has experienced is a forced parting, which is like a little death. He is depressed, and thinks the worst about everything. It is really, surely, very far-fetched to say that his friends have all gone out, and he may meet them never more again! They have only left him for a few hours, and will be back for supper.

So, he is exercising his poetic licence. He has had an accident — Sarah spilled some boiling milk on his foot — and this evokes fears of what the Americans call 'happenstance': 'Ye know not the hour nor the day . . .' 'In the midst of life we are in death.'

These passages from the Liturgy and Authorised Version lie behind the poem. (It is by the way worth reflecting upon the consequences of the fact that students, readers — all of us — no longer near the old Burial Service, the Collects or Lessons for the day from the A.V., or indeed any of the magnificent language of the traditional literature of the Church which has inspired English literature since at least 1550 until (say) 1950: a certain kind of metaphysical habit of language, the natural possession of the English over centuries, is lost to us.)* The poem is clearly written in a 'religious' vein, not least because of the reference to the 'Almighty Spirit'. But I think in a more general poetic way, the Bible's way of dealing with Time, age and death lies behind lines like:

> Most sweet to my remembrance even when age
> Had dimm'd mine eyes to blindness!

Many phrases from the Authorised Version are found here: 'I will lift up mine eyes unto the hills', 'Help me Lord in my blindness', 'they that look out of the windows are darkened'; 'Remember now thy Creator': indeed, the Psalms and *Ecclesiastes* are strongly behind the tone of the language, and so behind the mood of the poem, which is about loss, separation and death — and what may be set against these. Besides the Bible, there is Shakespeare:

> When to the sessions of sweet silent thought
> I summon up remembrance of things past . . .

The tradition passes on: Keats would surely be aware of Coleridge's poem, and so his swallows reappear in the *Ode to Autumn*. Coleridge wrote:

> and though now the bat
> Wheels silent by, and not a swallow twitters,
> Yet still the solitary humble-bee
> Sings in the bean-flower. . .

(As Leavis points out somewhere, if we read about the topless towers of Ilium, or the domeless courts of proud Olympus, we see tops and domes: so, here, the swallows twitter: or, at least, have just twittered. They re-echo later in 'Twittering swallows gather in the skies' and Coleridge's bees, too, re-echo in Keats's lines.)

The poem thus belongs to a certain English mode — a metaphorical mode, with the Psalms and other Hebrew writings behind it,** in which grasshoppers and almond trees become symbols of aspects of experience and everything seen — hills, swallows, leaves,

---

*George Eliot on Caleb Garth in his difficulty of finding speech for his thought, 'he caught, as it were, snatches of diction which he associated with various points of view or states of mind; and whenever he has a feeling of awe. He was haunted by a sense of Biblical phraseology, though he could hardly have given a strict quotation'. (*Middlemarch*) CL XL

** See 'The Mediaeval Idiom in Shakespeare' by L.A. Cormican, *Scrutiny*, Vol.XVII, Nos.3 & 4, 1950.

flowers—-are redolent with a universal meaning, a tragic meaning, evocative both of mutability and death, but also of the delights of being alive that may be set against these.

This accounts for the great concentration Coleridge achieves. He 'paints a scene': but painting a scene, of course, has an existential quality. One holds something out of the flux, and gives it form. The painting of the summer flowers can be looked at in winter, and may even be enjoyed at night when the world is dark.

It will be enjoyed when the artist is dead, and what we enjoy in the Quai d'Orsay is the capacity to enter into the artist's perception of his world, the exercise of his consciousness, at that (long dead) moment, at a moment when he was excitedly engaged in perceiving it — perceiving it in an intentional way, that is a way which seizes upon it creatively, to make the artefact in the frame.

It is this intentional, creative perception that Coleridge here sets against his deeply disturbed feelings of suffering a 'little death' through the departure of his friends. There are two things to note here: one is his footnote to the line in a MS letter to Southey:

> Struck with joy's deepest calm, and gazing round
> On the wide view** may gaze till all doth seem
> Less gross than bodily.

In the poem the lines are:

> So my friend
> Struck with deep joy may stand, as I have stood,
> Silent with swimming sense, yea, gazing round
> On the wide landscape, gaze till all did seem
> Less gross than bodily . . .

We may note that some of Coleridge's most interesting poems are written around experiences of perception: in *Frost at Midnight* he fears losing his hold on his own being, in the silent night, when he is drawn, as it were, into the primal consciousness of his baby sleeping in the room: and the whole poem is a movement towards the sharp and realised sense of being-in-the-world in the last lines. In *Dejection, an Ode* he sees how beautiful the bars of light in the sky are, but does not feel how beautiful they are: perception is not matched by apperception: in the rest of the poem he explores the

* You remember I am a Berkleyan.

whole question of how we throw from our subjective life. meaning over the world. And here, in a Berkleyan way, he tries to record a feeling by which normal perception of reality can be transformed, so that it becomes all subjectivity.

and of such hues
As veil the Almighty Spirit, when yet he makes
Spirits perceive his presence.

In *Frost at Midnight* he wishes for his infant a life in which the beauties of the natural world represent the influence of his Almighty Spirit which by teaching will make the child enquire into the nature of things — into their meaning. Here, a state of excited transcendine of a beautiful sight can be like becoming a spirit capable of apprehending the presence of God — that is, of arriving at ultimate meaning.

The 'little death' of the poem is that of being robbed (by accident) of this kind of experience. He hoped that in the exciting presence of friends he loved, he would have richly meaningful experiences that would stay with him for the rest of his life as a source of meaning. What he does, in fact, is to recreate the experience as it might have been, in his imagination, where it becomes perhaps more vivid and more meaningful, than the real expedition would have been: the poem, the imagined scenes, with all their symbolism, will remain in his memory throughout his life: and, of course, since he achieved the work of art, they go out beyond his memory, into ours, with the same effect, if we possess the poem.

Well, they are gone, and here must I remain
This lime-tree bower my prison! I have lost
Beauties and feelings

The words *gone* and *lost* have obviously an undercurrent of reference to death, which deepens when we get to:

Friends, whom I never more may meet again

It is, actually, like a very young child's feelings, which is true of other poems by Coleridge: he seems, as it were, to have kept open the pathway to the child's feelings of being in existence and not-being.

If people dear to us go away, we do often feel dreary and empty: we have in a small way feelings similar to those we have when someone dies. To the infant, of course, at certain stages, it does seem to spell extinction, when the love-object leaves him, which is why children sometimes cry in the dark — they feel they may go out of existence.* One of the effects of this loss by separation is that things, the realities in the world, seem blank, as if deadened, as if meaningless. And what Coleridge mourns is the 'beauties and feelings' which are experienced in good company, which are so bound up with a significant moment that they will remain always in the memory to yield an inner reassurance of meaningful perception even when one is blind:

such as would have been
Most sweet to my remembrance even when age
Had dimm'd mine eyes to blindness!

The expectation then cuts off very vivid experiences, and the absolute loss of these makes the pleasant place (the lime-tree bower) a prison: in prison one is cut off from the meaningful activity of creative life—-that is why prison is such a terrible punishment.

To compensate he thinks of his friends, and sees them (as we see them) like a sequence in a film:

On springy heath, along the hill-top edge,
Wander in gladness, and wind down, perchance,
To that still roaring dell, of which I told;
The roaring dell . . .

But then we have something that no film could do: the roaring dell (the phrase repeated) has affinities with the underground fountains in *Kubla Khan*.

The opening word and its pause suggest resignation:

Well, they are gone . . .

and what Coleridge sees, when in his imagination his friends descend to this secret and mysterious spot, is images of reconciliation. Of living things, making do with their 'condition' — to use the

* See *Feeling and Perception in Young Children*. Len Chaloner. London. Tavistock. 1963. esp. pp.29 and Chapter VII.

word in the Sartrean sense and to thrive there. (There is, by the way, an echo of Shakespeare 'few poor yellow leaves' surely echoing *Sonnet 73*: 'Where yellow leaves, or none or few, do hang' — which indicates that the symbol is a metaphor of a human condition. And, I suggest, there are affinities with George Crabbe, whose eye was so often fixed on the courage of the weeds, which was like that of the poor — though I don't know whether Coleridge ever read Crabbe).

> The roaring dell, o'erwooded, narrow, deep,
> And only speckled by the mid-day sun;
> Where its slim trunk the ash from rock to rock
> Flings arching like a bridge . . .

Down there (in a world like a prison) even the mid-day sun only thrusts a speckle or two of light (a very beautiful image) and there the ash makes do, desperately flinging a 'slim' trunk from rock to rock trying to bridge a gap, despite its disadvantages:

> that branchless ash,
> Unsunned and damp, whose few poor yellow leaves
> N'er tremble in the gale, yet tremble still,
> Fann'd by the water-fall

The tree is at least spared the gale despite its 'branchless' loss of freedom and vitality: and it trembles in a domesticated or confined way (as he does in his lime-tree bower) fanned by the increasing water-fall and the little breeze it creates. One might say this image is one of sustaining a lesser vitality by one's inner resources in a state of deprivation. He is identifying with the ash, in its prison:

> . . . . and there my friends
> Behold the dark green file of long lank weeds,
> That all at once (a most fantastic sight!)
> Still nod and drip beneath the dripping edge
> Of the blue clay-stone.

It is a humble image, such as Wordsworth or Crabbe would focus upon, in certain states of tormented (and depressed) soul.

The verse here takes on a tactile intensity — witness the labials in 'file of long lank weeds' that picks up the labials in *yellow leaves*, *waterfall*, *tremble* and *gale*: one might say that the tongue is made to enact the poet's delight in the watery scene. There is an internal half-rhyme: *fall* and *file*: intense if shady colours (dark green file, blue clay-stone) and an image of regular shapes, suggesting order. We have intense images of this kind in the last lines of *Frost at Midnight*, where the robin is singing betwixt the tufts of snow on the bare bough, there are trances in the blast, and regular rows of icicles: these images of periodicity go with the intervals between thoughts. These regularities also, I believe, suggest a recurrence of benignity, to set against the chaos that threatens beneath the surface (as in *Kubla Khan*).

'The dark green file of long lank weeds' is an image of episodic persistance: of the fact that life goes on, nodding, and dripping all at once (a most fantastic sight!). It is fantastic because it looks as if man had made it: yet it is 'life' that made it. So, even in a state of deprivation, that makes one feel that one might go out of existence because one has lost touch with the world, one can restore the situation by going out in imagination into that world—-and find in it reassurances, even in the humblest places, beneath the edge of the blue clay-stone, that life will go on and have a meaning: this is what the images of sequence imply.

So, having found that meaning down there in the sunless water-source (cf *Kubla Khan*) his friends (he imagines) can come back to the world, in a more creative state. In the next section, lines 20-32, they are seen as free and surveying the world, full of glad images — a many steepled tract, a ship's sail lighting up:

> The slip of smooth clear blue betwixt two isles
> Of purple shadow!

The landscape offers particular solace to Charles Lamb, who during the previous year had suffered a shocking tragedy in his family: his sister had become deranged and had stabbed their mother to death.

> With sad yet patient soul, through evil and pain
> And strange calamity.

He wishes upon Charles that release from reality, in which perception leads towards something 'less gross than bodily', and near to God.

Again, as so often with Coleridge, an out-going act of gratitude gives him delight. (In *Frost at Midnight* it is wishing a creative future for his infant: in *The Ancient Mariner* it is the protagonist blessing the water-snakes; in *Dejection* it is wishing joy to the lady.)

A delight
Comes sudden to my heart, and I am glad
As I myself were there.

There follows an odd double negative:

Nor in this bower,
This little lime-tree bower, have I not mark'd
Much that has sooth'd me —

Meaning 'it would not be true to say that I have not marked much here that has soothed me'. The nor. . . not construction enacts the unwillingness to do what he proceeds to do: that is to say, it is forced upon him, to transfer the gains of the imaginary outing with his friends, to his 'prison' without having stirred from his seat:

Pale beneath the blaze
Hung the transparent foliage; and I watch'd
Some broad and sunny leaf, and lov'd to see
The shadow of the leaf and stem above
Dappling its sunshine! And that walnut-tree
Was richly ting'd and a deep radiance lay
Full on the ancient ivy, which usurps
Those fronting elms, and now, with blackest mass
Makes their dark branches gleam a lighter hue
Through the late twilight.

(I noted recently, in a *Scrutiny* analysis of *Kubla Khan*, the critic pointed out that inspiration flagged at line 12 (or whatever it was) and revived again at 22: it was as if one said that this patch of water-lilies in a Monet was not as well done as that corner all of which seems to me impertinent.)

The lines here about the lime-tree bower are not as intense as those about the weeds in the waterfall. But they have the quality of a painting (makes their dark branches gleam a lighter hue) *made possible* and enriched by, the vision of the pool. He envisaged Charles seeing the pool: now he is seeing himself, his vision made richer by the gift of metaphorical vision to his friend. But while he was contemplating his own feelings about death as the beginning of the poem, these lines are about the world, the actual imprisoning world around the lime-tree bower, in all its contrasting richness: and the richness is full of ambivalence that is, an admixture of love and hate. The ivy usurps the elms, which are *fronting*, are thrown into contrast, a *lighter hue*, by the *blackest mass* of the ivy. A bat wheels silent by, somewhat ominously: the swallows no longer twitter, but are gone leaving their echo: and only a single humble-bee sings in the bean-flower . . . The richness is sparse: but the benignity (as of the solitary humblebee) is positive enough to teach him a lesson.

Nature ne'er deserts the wise and pure . . .

Purity occurs in other Coleridge poems, such as *Dejection*. I believe we may read it as meaning 'of integrity': those who attend to ultimate and serious problems of the meaning of life will be given a sense of meaning (and joy) by Nature.

Sometimes it is a good thing to be deprived of a promised good (and, after all, we have the poem because of Coleridge's disappointment).

The final image is another menacing one, from Shakespeare again:

when the last rook
Beat its straight path along the dusky air
Homewards, I blest it! deeming its black wing . . .

Flew creeking o'er thy head, and had a charm
For thee, my gentle-hearted Charles . . .

This echoes surely the crow in *Macbeth* that makes wing to the rooky wood: but it is a rook, and so belongs to a (benign) colony and, here, is made an object of blessing and a charm, rather than a menace. In redeeming the objects (symbols) in the landscape around him, Coleridge transforms them into benignity: the fronting ('affronting'?) elms, the usurping black ivy, the wheeling bat, the black rook in the late twilight — these are turned into manifestations of life, instead of shadows of death:

For thee, my gentle-hearted Charles, to whom
No sound is.dissonant which tells of life.

Identifying with Charles and his suffering, his recent encounter with death, Coleridge escapes from his own preoccupation with his little death, his deprivation and loss of creative freedom. He gives it all to Charles and his friends, and so finds great delight in imagining their joy. Then he can look around him, and although the reality of his actual 'prison' is full of shadows, it is also full of beauty: and where the shadow of death (as it has fallen on Charles) is visible in this world, he blesses it — as the protagonist in the *Ancient Mariner* blesses the humble water snakes — and so transforms the world into a benignity, in which:

No sound is dissonant which tells of life

— in which line perhaps, with the 's's, we hear distantly the sound of the waterfall with the plants growing in it.

What have I been talking about?

Language and the texture of the poetry: its symbolism: its sources in Shakespeare, Keats and the Authorised Version of the Bible. I have said what I think the poem means, but I have tried to follow it as a record of a development of consciousness, and the exercise of the primary power of the imagination.

In this, what we follow, is the progress of a brave soul, at a moment of deep concern (about death and its effect on Charles and so on everyone), moving from self-absorption and loss, towards generosity and gratitude. We follow a subjective, or, if you like, a spiritual discipline, which satisfies and delights because it keeps so close to the *Dasein* problem, the question of the meaning of life. Having grasped this poem, we would be well equipped now to explore the period, and the intellectual movements, in which Coleridge was a major champion of the power of the imagination.*

There is no need to labour the vindication of such a discipline which is the central discipline of English — at a time when everything is threatened by a severe loss of the sense of meaning in life, and in which inner resources are so difficult and gratitude so hard to achieve.

If this latter point needs expansion, we may turn to Joan Rivers and Melanie Klein, *Love, Hate and Reparation*, and, if we need to associate it with the problem of meaning, we can study Mahler's late music — with which, I believe, we could draw parallels with Col-

*See the excellent essay on Coleridge by L.G.Salingar in The New Pelican *Guide to English Literature*, Vol. 5, p.276.

eridge's poetry, not least in the relationship between love, gratitude and finding meaning in the world.

The other problem to which poetry must be related is that of belief. Today, can we believe in anything?

This kind of question arises over a poem like Matthew Arnold's *Dover Beach*:

> The sea is calm to-night.
> The tide is full, the moon lies fair
> Gleams and is gone: the cliffs of England stand
> Glimmering and vast, out in the tranquil bay.
> Come to the window, sweet is the night-air!
>
> Only, from the long line of spray
> Where the sea meets the moon-blanch'd land,
> Listen! you hear the grating roar
> Of pebbles which the waves draw back, and fling,
> At their return, up the high strand,
> Begin, and cease, and then again begin,
> With tremulous cadence slow, and bring
> The eternal note of sadness in.
>
> Sophocles long ago
> Heard it on the Aegean, and it brought
> Into his mind the turbid ebb and flow
> Of human misery; we
> Find also in the sound a thought,
> Hearing it by this distant northern sea.
>
> The Sea of Faith
> Was once, too, at the full, and round earth's shore
> Lay like the folds of a bright girdle furl'd.
> But now I only hear
> Its melancholy, long, withdrawing roar,
> Retreating, to the breath
> Of the night-wind, down the vast edges drear
> And naked shingles of the world.

Ah, love, let us be true
To one another! for the world, which seem
To lie before us like a land of dreams,
So various, so beautiful, so new,
Hath really neither joy, nor love, nor light,
Nor certitude, nor peace, nor help for pain;
And we are here as on a darkling plain
Swept with confused alarms of struggle and flight,
Where ignorant armies clash by night.

This poem seems a very direct and sincere expression of a characteristic nineteenth century anguish. It is exceptionally not in the poetic diction of the time, but expressed chiefly in the language of ordinary speech: 'The sea is calm tonight', 'you hear the grating roar/Of pebbles which the waves draw back'. There is a little poetic inversion ('vast edges drear'), one or two poetic words ('darkling', 'tremulous'), but for the most part the voice of the poem speaks of thoughts and emotions with a simple and direct intimacy, as if in the real daily world. The words 'ignorant', 'naked' and the phrase 'long, withdrawing roar' have a strong and disturbing impact in consequence.

Belief here is an integral aspect of consciousness. In the background are the impacts of geology and Darwinian evolutionary theory, on man's relationship to the universe. Science has stripped the world of meaning, and the universe has become mere matter moving meaninglessly, without any sense of its sympathetic relationship with the human being who perceives the cosmos and responds to it.

At the beginning, the scene is one which, heretofore, might have induced a sense of awe, and of belonging.

The sea is calm, tonight,
The tide is full, the moon lies fair
Upon the straits. . .

There is an air of harmony and tranquility. In the light of Karl Stern's analysis of the psychology of our relationship with Mother Earth (in *The Flight from Woman*, 1968) we could say that there are two symbols of the Cosmic Mother here, the thalassal sea, and the moon which seems (because of her reflection in the sea) to lie on the straits as if belonging to the Earth.

There is a disturbance even in the symbolism of this scene, however. The light on the French coast

Gleams and is gone . . .

while the English cliffs stand:

Glimmering and vast

The small reassurances of human presence fade with the lights: the huge cliffs become daunting. Instead of generating a feeling of awe in the presence of God, however, what the poet experiences is a sad sense of the rhythms of the sea being merely matter in motion. The lines are a superb example of movement: so keenly does the poet recreate the scene in imagination that the words enact the movement of the waves: you hear the grating roar:

Of pebbles which the waves draw back, and fling,
At their return, up the high strand,
Begin, and cease, and then again begin . . .

What they bring in is the 'eternal note of sadness' — and a long perspective of time opens out, of the time of the geological span. (I believe Shakespeare's 'that on the unnumbered pebbles beat' is in the background.)

In the consciousness of the poet, this perspective takes him back in history to before the Christian era. He remembers something in Sophocles, inspired by the Aegean, which speaks of the turbid ebb and flow of human misery: and this now seems to stretch across the aeons, during which the waves have ceaselessly produced their 'grating roar'.

In him, the sea promotes a different thought, about religious faith. Once, religious faith was part of the universal landscape and circled the world like a sea. When one looked at a seascape like the one the poet is looking at, on Dover Beach, it would have seemed that this world was made meaningful by 'the folds of a bright girdle furl'd'. The world would have been clothed by belief.

But now I only hear
Its melancholy, long, withdrawing roar,
Retreating, to the breath
Of the night-wind, down the vast edges drear
And naked shingles of the world.

The 'grating roar' of a wave withdrawing can be a deeply disturbing sound, and here the image of the universal sea has become a universal sea of faith, which now retreats — but not like a wave, which returns, not even like a tide (which can return to 'the full'): but like a disastrous disappearance of the sea altogether, as if off the edge of the world. The night-wind seems to be a manifestation of this catastrophe, and the retreat leaves the shingles naked, that is, unadorned atomistic realities, over which no meaning can be thrown, naked in being (in Husserl's terms) stripped of meaning.

> Can we console ourselves with that? Can we live in this world, where historical occurrence is nothing but an unending concatenation of clumsy progress and bitter disappointment? *The Crisis of European Sciences*, p.7

Arnold's only defence against this 'meaningless universe, like Thomas Hardy's, is love and the values inherent in being true to one another — for the atomistic universe is also one in which values have no place, and neither do the cultural achievements of man, from Sophocles to Arnold. Without values and meaning, all human aspirations have no real existence: the world

> Hath really neither joy, nor love, nor light,
> Nor certitude, nor peace, nor help for pain;
> And we are here as on a darkling plain . . .
> Where ignorant armies clash by night . . .

'But can the world, and human existence in it, truthfully have meaning if the sciences recognise as true only what is objectively established . . . and if history has nothing more to teach us than that all the shapes of the spiritual world, all the conditions of life, ideals, norms upon which man relies, form and dissolve themselves like floating waves, that it always was and ever will be so, that again and again reason must turn into nonsense, and well-being into misery?' Husserl's words provide the perfect gloss for Arnold's poem.

In the philosophical revolution to which Husserl belonged, we can now begin to see how it may be possible to resist being daunted by the pressure upon us, of the universe as presented by modern science. By insistence on the realities of the subjective world, the complexities and special dynamics of life, and the realities of man's cultural development, we may perhaps now glimpse how, in Roger Poole's words,

> We attain a point of vantage from where we find out that we are conferring meaning on the world instead of letting the world show its meanings down to us. *Towards Deep Subjectivity*, p.92

To study how this might be possible takes us into the area of inter-disciplinary studies, such as I propose, between poetry and philosophical anthropology — in the search for something we may find ourselves able to believe.

I have tried to show, by writing about a selection of poems, the kind of elements I would try to bring out, in teaching poetry. Can we believe that, when such works of art are shared, there is no effect on the reader? Does the reading of poetry contribute nothing to our living? Some critics today simply deny that it does. For instance, Peter Ackroyd, reviewing *The Oxford Illustrated History of Literature* in *The Times*, Thursday 23 April 1987 (ironically, Shakespeare's birthday) said: 'No member of that vast army of students currently reading paperbacks of D.H. Lawrence or Geoffrey Chaucer is going to become a "better" or "more sensitive" person by doing so'. This is nonsense, and we know it to be so, even if we cannot explain why.

If we feel delight or satisfaction after reading a poem or play (say) about death, what explains our elation? Or do we feel depressed? If so, why do we? I ask the reader to close his eyes and try to imagine how it would be, if Shakespeare had never existed. —-would we have lost anything? If so, what? Of course, answers could not be given in any neurological terms, such as I.A. Richards attempted in *Science and Poetry*. But isn't it true, as Henry James wrote,'Art makes life, makes interest, makes importance?' (in a letter to H.G.Wells)

All we can say, I think, is that what we take for granted, our 'life world', our being-in-the-world is not a constant reality, or something that is ever completed, or even sustained without continual effort. It is a process, continually nourished, by symbolic activity in many ways: dreams, fantasies, and all kinds of cultural efforts.

Without this nourishment our confident sense of being would collapse.

These cultural processes sustain our relationship with the world in which we are always seeking to relate the inner reality to the outer. We are not static and passive. We are constantly sensing, judging, acting, perceiving. In our philosophical tradition, which remains atomistic and mechanistic, the mind receives sensations and impressions on a *tabula rasa*. We fail to recognise the continual positive by which any living creature sends out a team of perception into the world: of intentionality.

We sense Erwin Straus bases his profound critique of Pavlov by pointing out that there is no such thing as a passive subject, not even a dog in a laboratory. There is a dynamic there, before the scientist begins his experiments. (He also declares there is no such thing as a 'stimulus': see *The Primary World of Senses*.) And where human consciousness is concerned, if we accept that symbolism is the basis of all thought, a continual and powerful exercise of symbolism lies beneath the engagement of our consciousness with the world, in all doings. (See also Susanne Langer on dreams in *Philosophy in a New Key* passim.)

There is even, it seems, a need to dream: some researchers found that if subjects are prevented from dreaming, being woken whenever their eye movements indicate they are beginning a dream sequence, they seem to build up a need to dream, so that once they are allowed to sleep they set off on a big dream sequence. Subjects who are prevented from dreaming seem to become disorientated. This is not mere fatigue. If they are woken between dream sequences they do not suffer.

So, I believe we can say that art nourishes our dreams: nourishes all these complex inner dynamics, processes of fantasy, thought and imagining, by which we sustain a sense of identity and what Freud called 'a reality sense' and beyond that — what Leavis called 'the living principle'. But all this is a going concern: there are many things happening at once — memories of our body-life as infants, ambitions, images of yesterday's flowers. or meals, or acts of love; old phrases spoken by friends or lovers or old poets or things heard in the street: 'Spinoza and the smell of cooking', to take a phrase from T.S.Eliot: 'out of these the poet is always making new wholes.'

A good poem, or novel, or play, nourishes these continual processes, by which we build bridges between subjective and objective.

Sometimes the nourishment is good — as with a tragedy full of seriousness, full of gravity, in which the language is charged and intense, and in which the human problematic is pressed to the limit. At other times, as when we listen to a light revue or a *café chantant* song, it is trivial. It is never without its effect on our total spirit life, our *geist*: but nor can the effect of a work of art be judged simply as healthy or moral, though we must bear such questions in mind. Certainly good literature can't be regarded as having an immediate positive effect on our moral life, like eating wholemeal bread. The effect is peripheral to our whole struggle to exist: but it is real, nonetheless. And there can be no doubt that some culture can corrupt.

As I write, I am looking at a book of reproductions of the paintings of Berthe Morisot. It impels me to add that an important part of our experience of art is that of beauty and order. This is the experience of the efforts of a particular consciousness: or one can say spirit. To most of us, life passes by like a river flowing under a bridge. The artist strives to capture moments, imbue them with his or her vision, and give them a form, so that they have a meaning — and where the art is successful. that meaning will be beautiful. It may be the light on the bark of some beach trees, the water in a harbour, the light on a woman's arm as she dresses, a child in a meadow. The attempt to 'fix' the beauty of the moment, of the momentary vision, is at one with the joyful application of the brush-strokes, and the beauty is spun out of the mysterious complex of eye, the inward vision thrown out of the consciousness, the use of the brush to make paint seem a record of the world, and the awareness of the artist of how the viewer will see his or her painting. (A wonderful account of the complexity of the act of painting is given by Jean Renoir in his marvellous book *Renoir, my Father*.)

What Berthe Morisot's paintings convey is a joy in being alive. We need to recognise that she was a great genius, and it is especially satisfying for us to experience such a woman's consciousness through her paintings (even though, alas, most of them seem to be in America).

Can we come back to poetry and see it as a manifestation of consciousness that is impelled by joy, gestures towards beauty and meaning, and is a feminine kind of mystery? How old-fashioned it is, I suppose, to talk thus—-but that it is a mark of why poetry is so badly taught, why teachers in schools avoid it, why the English soul is so unpoetic (not least because of its deficiency of femininity in an age of masculinity of thought) and why we are so restless and dissatisfied.

Poetry, it would seem, is felt to be too feminine, and to be feminine is to be weak and vulnerable. We have today in Britain, substituted a kind of false male poetry for it, full of coarse language, irony, grossness and nihilism, to say nothing of what is presented in the novel or on stage and screen. If we turn to the work of women writers and artists — Emily Dickinson, Emily Brontë, Edith Wharton, Berthe Morisot, Mary Cassatt — what strength we find! What insights! What awareness of the Infinite and the tragic!

I am thinking aloud: but I shall not apologise — for a richer sense of the female modes of consciousness, numinous and poetic, is urgently necessary for us, however much such an emphasis will cut no ice with a utilitarian age and its attitudes to education and the university.

ENGLISH IN PRACTICE: THE NOVEL

Having demonstrated the essential discipline of English studies in the approach to poetry, we can next turn to the other forms of literature. Drama I will leave aside, though it is worth saying that despite the cultural decline of recent years — the decline in reading for example — students still take enthusiastically to drama. Shakespeare saves us, because we all enjoy meeting in his works, over which (without even referring to it explicitly) students happily discuss what I call existential themes, to do with the nature of being, meaning and freedom.*

But another great difficulty today is to be found over the novel — especially the long and dense nineteenth century novel, despite its importance in literature. This is partly a question of time: students feel under pressure, and so they feel daunted at the prospect of the number of long hours needed to read *Middlemarch* or *Dombey and Son*. They do not have the capacity to read dynamically and have not learnt how to skip intelligently. They have not read half the books we read as a matter of course in the sixth form. So, a good case has to be made out for the novel, in order to convince students the time and effort demanded is worth it. The analysis of prose seems to me much more difficult than that of verse, and I believe too little has been said about this problem in literary criticism and educational writing about English.

We are all practised in the practical criticism of poetry: I have to confess that I have tended to shirk the discussion of passages of prose in seminars — though I have attended to the great novels in supervisions.

In practice with students at university, our discussion of novels tends to be somewhat superficial — not least because of the problem of time. My basic book list which I send to freshers really re-

---

*This is not to say one is not dismayed by tendencies here too: of, for example, the grotesque productions of Shakespeare on today's stage. The bright sensational mixture echoes that of television, while a Shakespeare production will often confront one with blank misunderstanding. Atrocities to sensibility like *Prick Up Your Ears* raise no doubts or scruples, it seems.

quires something like ten years rather than three. In adult education classes one might spend three weekly sessions of two hours on a novel like *Sons and Lovers*. In supervisions an hour is as much as one dare spend. For our students are driven by a sense of dismay already, needing to cover literature from 1350 to the present day in four 8-week terms and two 4-week ones — 40 weeks in all. So they display considerable anxiety, if we dwell on a single novel for more than that one hour. Of course, one hopes that after an hour on *The Bostonians* or *Mansfield Park*, they will go away and read the author's other works and apply what they have learnt. But I have always found teaching the novel frustrating at university level, while I am amazed to find lecturers trying to cover (say) two major novels in one hour's session.

What one tries to do is to pick some four or five scenes which may be discussed in detail, in relation to the overall structure of the books: say, in *Sons and Lovers*, the mother being turned out into the garden; the son burning the bread; Paul and Miriam watching the sun go down; the dreadful scene of Mrs Morel's death. What one tries then to discuss is a combination of features of the art — its 'technical' qualities — and the symbolism and meaning. Then, in the end, its 'upshot', the morality, as enacted, as 'felt life' in the widest sense.

If we can show that the rich qualities of the prose art where it is best are generated because of a vital engagement with the deepest issues of being, then, I believe, we have done our job. The focus of attention, again, is the creative power of the imagination, manifest in the act of consciousness which the prose work is: the excitement of consciousness is manifest in the rhythm and the language.

What today's students find it hard to recognise is the amount of contributing participation the reading of a serious novel requires.

So, I would hope to open discussion of the novel by taking a substantial passage from a carefully chosen example, moving out from this extract to discuss the themes of the novel as a whole, to do with integrity and authenticity. There are, of course, many aspects of the novel as a literary form which a student should be aware of — the development of that exploration of the inner life of characters, from Chaucer's Criseyde on. There is the whole complex question of 'narrative' and how the story is presented, the use of a mature persona like 'Pip' in *Great Expectations* to tell the story, making a commentary on himself and his attitudes implicitly as he does so.

But here I want to concentrate on what I believe to be the central aspect of our discipline. I would hope to try to bring to the attention of students the central themes of authenticity, the question of being true to oneself, which, I believe, the good novel deals. Having done this in detail with one novel, whether it is *What Maisie Knew* or *The Reef* or *Sons and Lovers*, the student should be able to find this element himself or herself, and see the aspects of 'technique' and historical development in relation to this the essential task of this form of art.

Dickens must surely be an important figure in the consideration of the novel, though the sheer length of his works is a stumbling block for many students today, even a gripping story of great economy and force, such as *Great Expectations*. How, then, do we relate the theme of authenticity to this world of Dickens? Why, for instance, do so many of his works begin with a mother dying, a child orphaned, or otherwise neglected? The answer must surely be something to do with inheritance? Dickens has a special preoccupation with the child, lis state of existence in the family, his 'condition' (in Sartre's sense) and his expectations. The child needs, as he emphasises in *Hard Times*, a 'childhood of the mind', a particular state in which through the experience of love, kindness, and the provision of play — fantasy and imagination — he is able to develop a moral sense. This is the moral fable of *Hard Times*, that children brought up on utilitarian principles do not develop a moral sense, because that requires an imaginative training. Thus Dickens feels deeply disturbed, to contemplate a child who has no access to his or her inheritance (like Esther Summerson) or who is in some way cheated or barred from it (Little Dorrit, David Copperfield) or who is in some way falsified in gaining access to his psychic inheritance — the process of becoming that which he or she has in himself or herself to become, like Pip and Estella. So he comes to attend to the needs of being and their fulfilment.

The essential themes are struck in the first chapter of *Great Expectations*, as Pip contemplates the convict Abel Magwitch:

At the same time, he hugged his shuddering body in both his arms clasping himself, as if to hold himself together and limped towards the low church wall. As I saw him go, picking his way among the nettles, and among the brambles that bound the green mounds, he looked in my young eyes as if he were eluding the hands of the dead people, stretching up cautiously out of their graves, to get a twist upon his ankle and pull him in.

When he came to the low church wall, he got over it, like a man whose legs were numbed and stiff, and then turned round to look for me. When I saw him turning, set my face towards home, and made the best use of my legs. But presently I looked over my shoulder, and saw him going on again towards the river, still hugging himself in both arms, and picking his way with his sore feet among the great stones dropped into the marshes here and there, for stepping places when the rains were heavy, or the tide was in.

The marshes were just a long black horizontal line then, as I stopped to look after him; and the river was just another horizontal line, not nearly so broad nor yet so black; and the sky was just a row of angry red lines and dense black lines intermixed. On the edge of the river I could faintly make out the only two black things in all the prospect that seemed to be standing upright; one of these was the beacon by which the sailors steered — like an unhooped cask upon a pole — an ugly thing when you were near it; the other a gibbet, with some chains hanging to it which had once held a pirate. The man was limping on towards this latter, as if he were the pirate come to life, and come down, and going back to hook himself up again. It gave me a terrible turn when I thought so; and as I saw the cattle lifting their heads to gaze after him, I wondered whether they thought so too. I looked all round for the horrible young man, and could see no signs of him. But, now I was frightened again, and ran home without stopping. (End of Chapter One)

The relationship between the desperate escaped convict and the child is, of course, powerfully dramatic — and done imaginatively in such a way that we see things from the child's level (at the very beginning Pip sees everything upside down because the convict holds him upside down). The whole of Pip's life is altered, because of this chance meeting on the marshes — and what he meets is man reduced to a 'poor bare fork'd animal', in desperate straits:

> he hugged his shuddering body in both his arms — clasping himself as if to hold himself together . . .

It seems to Pip that the dead people in the graves were 'stretching up cautiously out of their graves, to get a twist upon his ankle and to pull him in.' Magwitch lives on the verge of death all through the novel, and so presses upon us the problem of 'the point of life' — in relation to which question develops the massive falsification of Pip's life, by Magwitch's patronage, in reward for the succour he provides for the escapee under divers menaces and threats of death. (The novel is full of murder.)

The scene at the end of this chapter has a powerful symbolism, in relation to the themes of the novel. Pip 'makes the best use' of his legs — he is free: the man limps painfully, because he is cold, and sore from being in irons — an outcast from the human world, and though 'free' as a fugitive, 'hemmed in with threats to that freedom', the right to which he has sacrificed by his criminal acts.

So, in the scene, there are two 'black things': one is the beacon by which the sailors steered, a cask upon a pole which is an 'ugly thing': the other is the gibbet which once held a corpse. It is as if the passage through life is painful anyway — even the sign which makes navigation possible is ugly. The other landmark is uglier — the gallows which has held the body of an executed criminal which has rotted away, and to which now the escapee seems to be moving towards, to 'hook himself up again'.

Seen as through the child's imagination, the scene seems an allegory of a painful life that limps between an ugly 'true' path, and doom. Magwitch's 'young man' is not (yet) Compeyson (though he is on the marshes, too): that fantasy presence gives another touch of murderous menace to the scene — and later, of course, Compeyson turns out to be the man who has blighted Miss Havisham's life. Mortality saturates the scenery of this novel from the beginning. The starkness of the scene thus has an apocalyptic quality:

> The marshes were just a long black line then . . . the river was just another horizontal line, not nearly so broad nor yet so black; and the sky was just a row of long angry red lines and dense black lines intermixed.

The angry red lines perhaps evoke a distant image of the weals of whipping and wounds: the black is the black of death: land, river and sky are reduced to bleak elemental forms, into which the hunted man looms. The black horizontal lines also evoke the theme of freedom, for as the man limps towards them, he seems to move towards infinite space, and yet to be barred or confined by the dark horizontal lines. We get something of the same effect in Emily Dickinson's poem:

> I'll tell you how the Sun rose —
> A Ribbon at a time —
> The Steeples swam in Amethyst —
> Till when they reached the other side
> A Dominie in Gray
> Put gently up the evening Bars
> And led the flock away . . .

That is, the sunrise or sunset becomes a setting, full of significance, for a human scene, in which life becomes a drama.

Moving out from local analysis of rich passages of this kind, to discuss the drama of a whole book like *Great Expectations*, it is easy to see that it cannot be understood without attention being paid to the 'unconscious factors' — the dream-like elements, the symbols of fantasy. The persistent image of the phantom hanging woman, the rivalry between Compeyson and Magwitch, the burning of Miss Havisham, Estella's cold-heartedness obviously have a symbolic meaning (as D.S. Brewer sees in his *Symbolic Stories*). This meaning relates to the inner reality, to aspects of the psyche, like dreams.

So, as we examine Pip's story, we are inevitably involved in deep questions of being. In discussing problems of expectations and choice in life, we are involved in questions of existential freedom, and these are inseparable from problems of psychology and models of man. Existential freedom, if it is to be true freedom, cannot be exerted in a superficial way; it needs to take account of the complex nature of man, each individual's psychic inheritance, each man's 'condition' — and, ultimately, his biological existence, on earth, in time.

What is the relation of love to a meaning in the whole life, to man (and woman) as 'beings-in-world'? How does what happens between man and man, and between man and woman, relate to our life- tasks, to the society in which these may be taken up, and to life in the universe? F.R. Leavis has commendably drawn our attention to such problems, as problems to which literature addresses itself and this is why literature matters. But such questions cannot be discussed in terms of literature alone.

We may take, for example, the whole investigation in psychology of the self-other relationship. One important insight here is that our capacities to relate to others are bound up with the development of a special capacity which is that of concern. Concern requires the experience of painful recognition of the possible consequences of one's own hate — a kind of pain which can be a pain of consciousness. Love, true love, is only possible through the painful experience of the reality of the 'other's being'. Here is the vast philosophical problem of 'finding' the other.

It is this which is the theme of Dostoevsky's *Crime and Punishment*: to escape from his predicament of not knowing whether he is a man or 'vermin' Raskolnikov has to kill the old woman. Dostoevsky had to have this painful fantasy, to try to escape from his own schizoid condition, and find love. But the consequent process of experiencing love brings a deep anguish, because the adult, his protagonist with whom he identifies, is going through processes normally completed in infancy, but because he is an adult he is aware of the risks as the infant is not. In the light of this it is possible to discuss a novel like *Great Expectations* in part as a dramatisation of intrapsychic dynamics, which is, if we are to believe W.R.D. Fairbairn, what our dreams are. Every character can be seen as dynamic of the 'I': the art is a quest to bring these disparate energies in the psyche to meaningful, reconciliation, and the central themes are the capacity to find others and to develop concern: that is, the theme is love, in relation to the problem of finding the reality of the self and the world.'*

Pip's problem is to find himself capable of genuine love, as for Joe Gargery, without denying such affection through snobbery—- the feeling that he has risen, as an incipient 'gentleman', above Joe's sphere. This impulse to deny the heart through snobbish aspirations to 'rise' is sewn in Pip by Estella's contempt for him as a rough boy. In Estella herself the capacity to love has been inhibited by Miss Havisham, whose fulfilment as a woman has been thwarted. But Estella is the daughter of two criminals, one a murderess and the other possibly a murderer. If we are to try to explain Pip's associations of Estella and the brewery and Miss Haversham with murder, we have to take unconscious factors into account, as we shall with Old Orlick's attempts to murder Pip's sister and Pip himself, and the way Estella, so distressingly, humiliates herself by marrying the gross Bentley Drummle. In the undercurrents of the book are deep and dark feelings in Dickens, about woman, sex and murder — and our understanding of these preoccupations can never be fully unravelled. In the end, Pip is confronted by true love between Joe and Biddy, in his own feelings for Magwitch (associated in Dickens's mind obviously with the injunctions found in the New Testament to love the sinner) and, ultimately, at least in one version, in his final union with Estella. All the way through the book (as Mrs Leavis pointed out) Pip grows in self-knowledge.

Undergraduates today as I have said have to be trained to read— however angry they may be if we say so publicly. It is not their fault: reading is not at a premium at any stage of education or field of culture. Moreover, the kind of reading we require is a particularly alert kind — capable of responding to complex symbolism, for example. I have always found this passage a useful example, to prompt the kind of attention I require:

---

*These sentences also apply, I am aware, to *Wuthering Heights*, which needs to be read as a creative dream. I shall not have room to discuss this novel here but examine it at length as a drama of the inner world of Emily Bronte in *Wuthering Heights — A Drama of Being*. Sheffield Academic Press. 1991. See *Charles Dickens and Woman* by the present author, New York University Press, 1993

Next day the clothes I had ordered all came home, and he put then on. Whatever he put on, became him less (it dismally seemed to me) than what he had worn before. To my thinking there was something in him that made it hopeless to attempt to disguise him. The more I dressed him, and the better I dressed him, the more he looked like the slouching fugitive on the marshes. This effect on my anxious fancy was partly referable, no doubt, to his old face and manner growing more familiar to me: but I believed too that he dragged one of his legs as if there were still a weight of iron on it, and that from head to foot there was Convict in the very grain of the man. The influences of his solitary hut-life were upon him besides, and gave him a savage air that no dress could tame; added to these were the influences of his subsequent branded life among men, and, crowning all, his consciousness that he was dodging and hiding now. In all his ways of sitting and standing, and eating and drinking — of brooding about, in a high-shouldered reluctant style — of taking out his great horn-handled jack-knife and wiping it on his legs and cutting his food — of lifting light glasses and cups to his lips, as if they were clumsy pannikins — of chopping a wedge off his bread, and soaking up with it the last fragments of gravy round and round his plate, as if to make the most of an allowance, and then drying his fingers on it, and then swallowing it — in these ways and a thousand other small nameless instances arising every minute in the day, there was Prisoner, Felon, Bondsman, plain as plain could be.

It had been his own idea to wear that touch of powder, and I conceded the powder after overcoming the shorts. But I can compare the effect of it, when on, to nothing but the probable effect of rouge upon the dead; so awful was the manner in which everything in him that it was most desirable to repress, started through that thin layer of pretence, and seemed to come blazing out at the crown of his head. It was abandoned as soon as tried, and he wore his grizzled hair cut short.

Words cannot tell what a sense I had, at the same time, of the dreadful mystery that he was to me. When he fell asleep of

> an evening, with his knotted hands clenching the sides of the easy-chair, and his bald head tattooed with deep wrinkles falling forward on his breast, I would sit and look at him, wondering what he had done, and loading him with all the crimes in the Calendar, until the impulse was powerful on me to start up and fly from him. Every hour so increased my abhorrence of him, that I even think I might have yielded to this impulse in the first agonies of being so haunted, notwithstanding all he had done for me and the risk he ran, but for the knowledge that Herbert must soon come back. Once, I actually did start out of bed in the night, and begin to dress myself in my worst clothes, hurriedly intending to leave him there with everything else I possessed, and enlist for India, as a private soldier.
>
> I doubt if a ghost could have been more terrible to me, up in those lonely rooms in the long evenings and long nights, with the wind and the rain always rushing by. A ghost could not have been taken and hanged on my account, and the consideration that he could be, and the dread that he would be, were no small addition to my horrors. When he was not asleep, or playing a complicated kind of Patience with a ragged pack of cards of his own — a game that I never saw before or since, and in which he recorded his winnings by sticking his jack-knife into the table — when he was not engaged in either of these pursuits, he would ask me to read to him — 'Foreign language, dear boy!' While I complied, he, not comprehending a single word, would stand before the fire surveying me with the air of an Exhibitor, and I would see him, between the fingers of the hand with which I shaded my face, appealing in dumb show to the furniture to take notice of my proficiency. The imaginary student pursued by the misshapen creature he had impiously made, was not more wretched than I, pursued by the creature who had made me, and recoiling from him with a stronger repulsion, the more he admired me and the fonder he was of me.

The context is, of course, the way in which Abel Magwitch has tried to mould Pip in *Great Expectations* to his idea of a gentleman, so threatening his authenticity and corrupting him into a falsification of himself. Something in him makes him ashamed of being a common and coarse boy (which is how the cruel girl Estelle sees him — she who is in any case Magwitch's daughter by an alleged murderess).

The novel is pervaded by all that is meant by Newgate, and when his benefactor appears Pip recognises the convict he helped to find food and a file, and did not betray, on the marshes as a child.

As he watches the sleeping Magwitch Pip becomes aware that it is 'hopeless to disguise him': his fugitive life as a transport has left its marks upon him: 'there was Convict in the very grain of the man'.

It is easy to see how this relates to the theme of authenticity: what is one? And at the unconscious level we may extend this to the underlying themes of the book. We follow Pip in his advancing self-knowledge from child to man, and we suffer with him great shocks to his awareness — the discovery that it is a convict who has made him a rich idler: that it is Miss Havisham who has misled him and ensnared his heart to the cold and emotionally impotent Estella: that Joe still loves him and is prepared to nurse him through a dangerous fever, even though he despises him: that Biddy has come to love Joe and his condescending affection for her is futile, since she is going to marry the blacksmith. But the underlying bafflement is about human nature itself — what am I? Do I have within me the brutality of an Orlick? The oafishness of a Bentley Drummle? And what of woman (and my own feminine element)? Can woman be heartless? So frustrated she can live a life of desperate privation and revenge? Can she be ever-forgiving, out of devotion to one's potential true self (as Biddy is)? And can one even forgive the sinner who has corrupted one's own sense of oneself (as Pip forgives and comes to love Magwitch)?

This kind of underlying preoccupation generates the poetic 'disguise' of 'gentleman' himself. In this passage the theme is 'done': 'taking out his great horn-handled jack-knife and wiping it on his legs and cutting his food — of lifting light glasses and cups to his lips, as if they were clumsy pannikins — of chopping a wedge off his bread, and soaking up with it the last fragments of gravy'. Body-language of this kind is important throughout the novel, from the first moments when the slouching convict holds Pip upside down in the marshes, until the last moments when Magwitch and Pip, as the former is dying, communicate by squeezes of the hand. Habit and experience become embodied in us: and so, too, are they so, in the 'psychic tissue': to learn in such a way as to find oneself is consequently painful, as Pip finds, not least over his hopeless love for Estella.

The 'powder' is wonderful: to Magwitch this is a trick of the gentleman: the effect is of rouge on the dead (perhaps Dickens was recalling: 'And, Betty, give this cheek a little red:

> 'One sure would not be frightful when one's dead.'
>
> Pope, *Moral Essays*)

His true nature seems to 'start through' the 'thin layer of pretence', and so Dickens picks up the Shakespearean themes of appearance and reality, from:

> 'there is no art to find the mind's construction in the face'

to:

> . . . Man, proud Man,
> Dressed in a little brief authority
> Most ignorant of what he's most assured . . .

Magwitch is a 'dreadful mystery', not least because his idea of a gentleman is so complex and strong (his motives being to put one over 'society' and to redeem his own value) that he is prepared to die for it.

And of course Pip never knows what he has done: because of this. he can only deal with the situation at times by contemplating flight. So Magwitch is worse than a ghost — not least because he can be 'taken and hanged on my account'. Pip hides from the man's reality by putting his hand before his face (more body-language; children, of course, do this) but then peeps between his fingers, to watch him 'appealing in dumb show to the furniture' (since he cannot appeal to the public) 'to take notice of my proficiency'. Pip himself feels like the 'misshapen creature' made by Frankenstein, and at depth the perplexity is what strange motive impels Magwitch to take over a young man's life in this way — not least because he may have been a murderer — for murder haunts the book.

The vivid realisation of Magwitch's presence is done in language that has a Shakespearean vitality (cf. 'Patience with a ragged pack of cards') and every phrase can be examined for its sinewy life: but this sinewy life comes from the heat of Dickens's imagination, in developing his drama of true being, and the threat to it.

The quest for authenticity in *Great Expectations* makes it a book of more than 'social' or 'political' relevance: *Great Expectations* is a work of art very much concerned with freedom, as an inward condition of spirit. Of course, 'society' in *Great Expectations* is a society of injustice, and this is physically manifest in the recurrent symbolism of being manacled —- while some of the characters like Magwitch and Estella's mother bear the scars and mannerisms of the convict all through their lives.

The hulks, out beyond the marshes, symbolise the way in which society puts beyond the bounds the creatures it has brought down by its own darkness and moral miasma. These characters have forfeited their freedom, or have had it destroyed (which is why Magwitch wants to enshrine freedom in Pip).

Throughout the book Pip fears the loss of freedom and authenticity as a death — it is that which this society threatens one with, the death of one's potentia. Estella says 'I must be taken as I have been made' and this relates to the central theme of the 'natural heart'. The heart might be said to be a beacon, while the alternative is the gallows: throughout Pip has a recurrent image of a suspended death such as is symbolised in those opening passages of poetic prose which we have examined.

Pip is threatened throughout the book, with the threat of a contamination from this world of the criminal — which is the threat (as I would put it) of 'false solutions' — the false solutions of hate, violence, and murder; but also of money and 'manners makyth man' in the wrong and superficial sense. Of course, Pip is not likely to fall into crime but he suffers from the defects of those who ruin other people's lives as a consequence of their own false solutions.

At the end of Chapter XXXI Pip feels this contamination, as Wemmick shows him Newgate.

> I consumed the whole time in thinking how strange it was that I should be encompassed by all this taint of prison and crime; that, in my childhood and on our lonely marshes on a winter evening I should have first encountered it; that it should have re-

> appeared on two occasions, standing out like a stain that was faded and not gone; that, it should in this new way pervade my fortune and advancement. While my mind was thus engaged, I thought of the beautiful young Estella, proud and refined, coming towards me and I thought with absolute abhorrence of the contrast between the jail and her. I wished that . . . I might not have had Newgate in my breath and on my clothes. I beat the prison dust off my feet as I sauntered to and from and I shook it out of my dress, and I exhaled its air from my lungs.
>
> So contaminated did I feel . . . that . . . I was not yet free from the soiling consciousness . . . when I saw her face . . . what *was* the nameless shadow which again in that one instance had passed?

Of course Pip has the shadow of Newgate on him, and Estella is daughter of a criminal woman and Pip's criminal patron. But at another level revealed by the psychoanalytical analysis of symbolism, I believe we can say that there is a sense in which the 'shadow' is the shadow in Pip of his own male libidinousness, his sexual aggressiveness, which he also recognises to be mirrored as the animus in Estella (and which she fulfils in her sado-masochistic marriage to Bentley Drummle). In his quest for meaning Dickens includes the search for sexual wholeness, libidinal and ideal united, which he pursues through all his work culminating perhaps in *Our Mutual Friend*.

We need to extend our insights here beyond Freud, however. Psychoanalysis has taken in a more positive approach from the 'new' existentialism. We may say that Pip's problem (like Dickens's) was to come to terms with woman, including the woman (or anima) in himself. This means, too, to come to terms with the ideal and libidinal in woman: to find woman both as an angel and inspiring force, and as a sensual embodied creature with sexual needs of her own. Estella, whose light early on 'comes along the passage like a star' is beautiful and seemingly ideal, but cold and heartless (being trained in this by the frustrated Miss Havisham. who has in consequence of her sexual rejection turned to hate.) The clue to Dickens's association throughout his writings of woman with murder seems to have to do with a dread of sexuality (hence his obsession with the murder of Nancy). Like many Victorians he displays a dread of the libidinal, as if sexuality could destroy one — behind which must surely lie something like the infant fear of sex as eating embodied in the infant fantasy of the Combined Parents (Melanie Klein).

There are two aspects of the libidinal which are explored in this book. One is the natural (sexual) heart represented by Biddy: Biddy's name means 'the libidinal'. Of course, Freud devised the term long after Dickens wrote — but the word 'biddy' for a libidinal girl is found in *Twelfth Night* ('Ay, Biddy, come with me', 'biddy' here meaning a chicken, with a sense of 'poule'). Pip is blind at first to Biddy's natural female affection: when he decides to go and propose to Biddy, it is too late, for he has thrown his hopes away on the ideal but cold Estella. It is inauthentic now for him to turn to Biddy, for he has not courted her, and merely assumed — arrogantly — that she is 'available'. Biddy's love, like Joe's, is true love: his love for Estella belongs to his falsification of himself until (as it were) she has been exorcised and refined by her self-humiliating suffering as the wife of Bentley Drummle.

The other aspect of the libidinal is the problem of homosexuality. Or, to put it in a more meaningful way, Pip's acceptance of the female element in the male, the emotional polarities beween men. The relationship between Pip and Joe Gargery is homosexual in this sense: 'What larks!' exclaims Joe, whose delight in Pip seems to belong almost to the stage of play between adolescents of the same sex which everyone goes through, in normal development. There are also strong, homosexual elements in Pip's relationship with Herbert and with Magwitch, 'homosexual' in that they are like the deep feelings between brothers or between father and son. The last tenderness of Pip to Magwitch as he is dying is that of homosexual love, in this sense. In the pattern of intrapsychic dynamics, we may speak of Dickens learning to love his maleness: which is (as in Mahler) loving the father in oneself.

Between Joe and Pip, and Magwitch and Pip — even between Jaggers, Wemmick and Herbert and Pip — this man-to-man element is positive and enrichening. But with Orlick and Bentley

Drummle the male potentiality is seen to be sadistic and brutal, and impelled by envy. Behind all these preoccupations we may, detect primitive fears of the aspects of man and woman as manifest in father and mother and in the self. In this novel he seeks to come to terms with them all, in his quest to find genuine love and concern, and the truth of self-being.

Those sexual elements may be linked with the 'freedom ' theme of the book thus; it is possible for the natural heart to be influenced by both male and female, by both mother and father, and among these dynamics one must find inauthenticity within oneself.

Great Expectations is a satisfying novel, gripping and touching: a masterpiece in the canon. The problem always in English in a university course is that of time: one always has to withdraw from becoming deeply involved in a novel, because there isn't time to 'do' everything in such depth. but perhaps my approach, as outlined, can suggest ways in which, selecting works from the canon, one can use them to work one's way into moral issues, and involve oneself in the historical setting in which the work was written.

Another example comes to mind, over a somewhat neglected novel, Mrs Gaskell's *Ruth*. This could well be used to involve English students in a discussion of modes of sexual behaviour of a time very different from ours, and so stretch their perspectives on both art and life.

I recently received a request from a research worker about whether I considered that English teaching should be a vehicle for teaching about 'human rights'. Of course, I replied, if English is taught as a Humanities subject, discussions will inevitably arise, about human rights, and it should propagate sympathy in such a way that torture and the denial of freedom should become unthinkable. But at the same time I could see behind the request an impulse to use English as a source of examples, for propaganda about human rights issues. This must lead to an avoidance of the true function of the English teacher.

That role is to ensure the possession of imaginative works, and this means putting young people in touch with creative symbolism. In this process, we do not know fully what is happening: an important part of the whole process is the unconscious factor and the unknown processes of the consciousness. The child seizes gratefully on the opportunity, to use symbolism to ask, 'What is to be human?' and 'What is the point of life?' — but how these questions are pursued is never quite clear.

Teaching is an art. But there is an important aspect of this process. If works are merely used as examples to teach something else, 'rights' or whatever, we may be avoiding the issue altogether: the politicisation may be an avoidance of those painful developments of self-awareness which can really contribute to a concern about human rights, value and freedom. For if English is taught properly, it should be impossible to avoid involvement — the recognition that 'there but for the grace of God go I': that we have in ourselves, everyone, what makes a Goneril, or a Coriolanus, or Raskolnikov or a Rasumov or a Gauleiter.

What we seek to promote teaching English as a Humanities subject is an open and painful recognition of the realities of human nature. To teach human rights, with literary works as mere illustrations, may be to avoid the problem, in a newly untruthful way, as much as to ignore the question altogether. So, we need to take into account the unconscious factors in all education.

Teaching English as a humanities subject doesn't just stop at reading literature: a teacher is bound to indicate implicit criticisms of his civilisation — as (say) in the claims made for 'being' by Blake and Dickens. Any attempt to relate the values inherent in great literature to life in Leavis's sense as he outlines in *Education and the University* is bound to raise enormous difficulties today with students. The trouble is that the very world one is often resisting and criticising by implication in our work with students is their world, or, rather, one they feel to be theirs.

So, there are profound problems of relationship in learning, at the university. This is a very delicate and complex subject, because the most powerful dynamics are involved, yet these are tacit and must remain tacit: they are largely unconscious and can only remain so. The young person who is a student needs for one thing to get clear of dependence on the adult: yet at the same time he (or she) needs the adult to be 'there', and needs to feel that the adult is dependable. and knows what his (or her) values are. The university student is beyond adolescence and yet not beyond adolescence: he (or she) wants to be treated like an adult, in an adult-to-adult way: yet there is not really a completely free 'equality' in this relationship, as the student feels that the adult must take the responsibility, not least if and when the student is not willing to be responsible or accept anything of the kind.

Moreover, as Winnicott argues, society needs the irresponsible idealism of the adolescent — while we must at the same time keep our ends up. The student still needs to play the game of 'I'm the king of the castle — get down you dirty rascal' while the adult must simply display a determination to survive. Against our continuing existence the student sharpens his or her personal values.

While the student needs the adult, and the adult must be 'there', the student is happiest when he can simply take this 'presence' for granted, in the background — perhaps never drawing on it. Then, he departs — however much he has needed the adult throughout his university course — and happily forgets and casts the adult off. The adult on this part must simply be willing to bear both the intense (and often unspoken) need, and the ultimate rejection. What enables both to bear it is the body of assumptions for which the university stands: that is, the body of philosophical anthropology it sustains, whether it knows it or not — its implicit philosophy of man and being.

Some students find it difficult to transfer from the kind of relationships they experience at school to the university. In the sixth form students see their staff every day. In English at school they may work with the English teacher for an hour or more every day. Thus a close relationship develops, in which care is experienced as a quotidian thing, and the student will give his or her work to a teacher every working day. The adult-child relationship persists even into the sixth form.

One aim of university teaching by contrast is to get students working on their own: to do their own learning, to educate themselves. So, they have to be pushed away, while the 'care' must be established as a feature of their lives which is very much in the background. They see their supervisor perhaps for one or two hours a week, and the relationship with him or her is much more distant, and directed more towards abstract, intellectual, and technical aspects of the work. Of course, emotional issues tend to be larger and more dramatic among young adults, and so there is also a need to be available, as adult to adult, on such occasions.

But the relationships are very different. I think students like to 'see' the senior staff with whom they are in contact, but at a distance, as in hall taking meals, so they can see when they get their hair cut, or who they're talking to. But for my part, I am happiest when I see students ignoring 'us', earnestly arguing or joking among themselves, not giving us a thought: and, as I know, sometimes they argue all night into the small hours or go off 'underground' as it were for a term, taking part in a play, or pursuing a love affair. Even so, there is a sense in which they can do such things, because we are there, and they can trust us to allow them to be irresponsible, idealistic, confused or hard-working — however the mood takes them.

I believe that this tacit form of trusting relationship, which at best is a matter of human beings leaving one another alone, while 'meeting' in the task of studying in the humanities, with all the assumptions that lie behind it, is an important political element. It is the guarantee of their self-realisation and freedom. and is an aspect of the intangible atmosphere of trust upon which democracy depends (this trust depending, as Winnicott argues, on a certain kind of family structure).

We have a great advantage, where this turmoil of youth is concerned, in our subject. There is no doubt that, in a Humanities subject, people are changed by their learning: if English is successful it should surely enable students to become more human, more aware of human needs, even though the effects of teaching on sensibility are by no means as direct as Leavis thought them. But, of course, the learning can't be separated from the relationships we establish, and the way we treat our students.

Perhaps the most important word in my discussion of this movement is trust. In the young adult, the need for someone to 'receive' his work is not as pressing as it is for the child, who actually needs to come to you, for response and praise. The young adult wants to go off to begin work on making sense of his or her world, by himself or herself.

But they do seem to require an imago of you, a sense of your trustworthy presence, to make this possible. With that ghostly presence, they need to feel that certain things are shared — and what is shared is the assumption that the serious play activity of literary studies is worth it, worth it in the deepest ontological sense. Only establish this sense of shared assumption, of the grave primacy of our attention to symbolism — and even if they only see you for an hour a week, students will be released to make their own creative explorations, of self and world. And an important aspect of our response to them is gratitude, a gladness for their living voyages, in their unique self-fulfilment.

The disillusionment which F.R. Leavis suffered later in his life possibly resulted from his own failure to recognise the complexity of the relationship between 'mind' (or 'intelligence'), the 'psychic tissue', the 'condition' (in Sartre's terms), the upbringing, the character, the genetic inheritance, the creative uniqueness, of each man (and woman!). I think his very devoted idealism itself led him to attempt to dominate his students too much and then to be bitterly disappointed with the decree of loyalty he created. In his book, in discussing the value of a literary education, he assumes that the value of making choices in 'English' will be straightforwardly transferred to making choices in life:

> The more advanced the work, the more unmistakeably is the judgement that is concerned inseparable from the profoundest sense of relative value which determines or should determine the important choices of actual life. *Education and the University*, p.35

Not even a Jesuit, surely, would claim as much? It is surely only possible to work in education, hoping that a tiny amount of the culture to which one draws students' attentions may, minimally, affect their capacities for choice in life? Leavis evidently felt that a reading of *Middlemarch* and *Macbeth* should make it possible, directly, for an individual, 'with a trained mind', to behave properly: and when human beings revealed that they were as maddening and unpredictable, as susceptible to degeneracy as (say) Lydgate or a David Copperfield or a Macbeth, he turned against them and condemned them.

We must allow human beings to be themselves, to make what they can of themselves: this is the first principle, and it requires gratitude (in Melanie Klein's sense) — the capacity to let others go into their own freedom, and be glad for them. Leavis's attitude seems often to have been, by contrast, motivated by envy, leading to the impulse to control others, albeit for their own good, an impulse leading inevitably to frustration and despair.

Philosophical anthropology, especially psychoanalysis (and most especially *Daseinsanalysis*) makes clear that in our relationship to others, loving and letting go, is a primary principle — in the search for a sense of meaning in life, and in the quest for freedom.

When I returned to Downing College as Director of English Studies in 1981 I found the students I had taken over projected over me the image of a stern Leavisite, demanding discipleship, and likely to offer a dogmatic, censorious approach. We experienced severe and serious difficulties in establishing trust. In the end it was some of them who were trying to bring me to accept some of Leavis's views, which I preferred to reject, after our very open debates!

But in the course of this painful experience, I came to see, as I thought, that there was a profound difference between my method and that of Leavis. When all is said and done, Leavis's approach appeared to be based on fear. In his reviewing, in his asides, and even in his teaching, he seemed to persuade others to his point of view by inducing the fear of being thought 'unintelligent'. By contrast, I believe, we have to learn to base our work on a shared pursuit of truth, rooted in love and gratitude.

However, the whole complex of trust which I have discussed, can, I found, be disturbed by encountering the very problem with which I began this chapter. If one criticises the society (as being an 'unpoetic' one) and registers the deficiencies in the students' own sensibilities in consequence — that is, if one discusses publically the problems of one's work, students become upset and take it as an insult. There is thus a radical division between generations.

To defend themselves against a harsh world, students tend to take on the self-protective defensiveness of a Holden Caudfield (in *Catcher in the Rye*). Even those most concerned to befriend you, the lesson is, will all too easily betray you: and so, on the least excuse, or at the least prompting by anyone trying to stir up trouble, students will cast you off. And today, because so many cultural influences are disturbing Oedipal feelings and exploiting them, there can be murder in the air. This involves responsibilities and the recognition of inner needs, but it is this that our society's culture has seriously falsified. Here the Dutch psychiatrist Joost de Meerlo has made some important contributions to our understanding of our predicament.*

He is especially useful in discussing the problems of young adults such as we teach at the university. In his discussion of political issues Meerlo believes that what threatens democracy is the failure to mature. We must recognise that coming to maturity is itself a taxing and painful process:

> Becoming conscious of the entity we call ego or self or I is a painful mental process. It is not a matter of chance that the feeling of endless longing, of *Weltschmerz*, is traditionally connected with

*De Meerlo, like Frankl, survived Auschwitz.

> adolescence. The process of becoming an autonomous and self-growing individual involves separation from the family. To achieve internal democracy, the adolescent must separate himself from his protective environment . . . *Mental Seduction and Menticide*, p.297

At this stage, whether or not an individual can achieve internal democracy obviously depends upon whatever his mother and family, and his teachers, have enabled him, by their love, to create within himself. But it is just at this stage, as we see today, strong cultural forces converge on the youth, offering him a hedonistic culture of distraction, while society often denies him positive opportunities to realise his potentialities, and to find authenticity.

Agencies of all kinds can take advantage of the adolescent at this stage Meerlo says because he is not merely intoxicated with his sense of growth and emancipation; he is also filled with a sense of fear and loneliness. He is entering a new world in which he must henceforth assume mature responsibility for his actions. A personal grudge against growing up may lead him to forsake the struggle for personal maturity (pp.297-8).

Meerlo believes our ways of bringing up children in the West may emphasise this problem. Whereas primitive groups impose some measure of social responsibility upon the child early in life and increase it gradually, our middle-class culture segregates him completely in the world of childhood, nursery and schoolroom and then plunges him precipitately into adulthood to sink or swim.

At this turning point, many young people shrink from such a test. Many do not want a freedom that carries with it so many burdens, so much loneliness. They are willing to hand back their freedom in return for continued parental protection, or to surrender it to political or economic ideologies which are in fact displaced parental images (p.298).

It is in such a context that we work and we must be aware of this. In doing so we must accept the painfulness of certain unconscious elements. Bearing difficulties with our students is a price that we may for fostering democracy itself.

D.W. Winnicott discusses in an important essay in *Playing and Reality* how adolescents have a need for 'confrontation'. What he means by this is a real, warm-hearted, confrontation: he does not mean 'getting on the side of the young'. Much of what happens both in our education and our culture today is a falsification of relationships which pushes on young people a false early, precocious, responsibility. Inevitably, the young person must 'lose spontaneity and play and carefree creative impulse', but these shouldn't be driven out of them by a too-early false adulthood. 'One of the most exciting things about adolescent boys and girls', Winnicott says, 'can be said to be their idealism'. If we force too early responsibility on them, this idealism may be lost. 'Responsibility,' he says, 'must be taken by parent figures'.

If parent figures abdicate, then the adolescent must make a jump into a false maturity and lose their greatest asset: freedom to have ideas and act on impulse. In our time a culture which seems to offer liberation is rather a form of what Marcuse called 'repressive desublimation'—-a means of exploiting young people more easily by seeming to offer then. a more permissive world.*

Winnicott says 'the adolescent striving that makes itself felt all over the world . . . need not be given reality by an act of confrontation'. Confrontation must be personal. 'Adults are needed, if adolescents are to have life and liveliness. Confrontation belongs to containment that is non-retaliatory, without vindictiveness, but having its own strength.' It is salutary he says to remember that genuine radicalism among the young (says Winnicott) may in part be a product of the better attitudes we are glad to have achieved towards baby care and child care.

> 'Let the young alter society, teach grown ups how to see the world afresh: but where there is the challenge of the growing boy or girl, they let the adult meet the challenge. And it will not necessarily be nice . . . ' 'In the unconscious fantasy these are matters of life and death.' (p.150)

Difficulties arise when (as in the sixties) a false radicalism was pro-

*See Charles Parker, *'Pop', the Manipulated Ritual* in *The Black Rainbow*, ed. Peter Abbs, Heinemann 1975.

moted among the young, while many adults opted out. Here Meerlo's words may be taken to bear on Winnicott's.

> . . . the youth's surrender of individuality is no guarantee against fear or loneliness. The real outside world is in no way altered by his inner choice, therefore the youth who relinquishes his freedom to new parent figures develops a curious, dual feeling of love and hate towards all authority . . .
>
> The duality is an endless one, for one side of his nature continually seeks to overstep the limits which his other, submissive side has imposed. The man who fails to achieve freedom knows only two enemies: unquestioning submission and impulsive rebellion.
>
> Conversely, the individual who is strong enough to embrace mature adulthood enters into a new kind of freedom . . . an ambiguous concept since it involves the responsibility of making new decisions and confronting new uncertainties . . . (p.298)

Meerlo's view is important, as it makes plain the unconscious and psychic connections between that personal culture which is linked with the sense of identity, and the capacity for an individual to 'contribute in' to a democracy. Where we find cultural deadness, commercial exploitation of the adolescent and child by 'displaced parental images' (like the leaders of 'pop'), we have a threat to democracy itself.

Moreover, the solution itself appears in the light of Meerlo's analysis as a cultural one. The inner harmony between social adaptation and self-assertion has to be reformed in every new environment. Such individual has to fight over and over again the same subtle battle that started during infancy and babyhood. The ego, the self, forms itself through confrontation with reality. Compliance battles with originality, dependence with independence, outer discipline with inner morale. No culture can escape this inner human battle.

Yet youth is often persuaded that these necessary struggles may be escaped — and this persuasion is combined with the march towards triviality is under commercial-industrial pressures. The following observation applies, of course, not only to youth, but to us all:

> Radio and television catch the mind directly, leaving children no time for calm. dialectic conversation with their books. The view from the screen doesn't allow for the freedom-arousing mutuality of communication and discussion. Conversation is the lost art. These inventions steal time and self-awareness. What technology gives with one hand —easiness and physical security — it takes away with the other. It has taken away affectionate relationships between men. Technical intrusion usurps human relationship as if people no longer had to give one another attention and love any more . . . The impersonal machine replaces human gesture and mutuality . . .

Those who question the march of technology must feel despair today. But, as Meerlo asks,`What is the ultimate result of technical progress?' Is the ultimate result living by proxy: instead of living and labouring and creating (one's own world)? We must keep in mind that every step in personal growth needs isolation, needs inner conversation and deliberation and a reviewing within the self. But ours, in English and other humanities, is the realm of 'calm, dialectic conversation with books' — and this is our trump card.

If we pay attention to the subjective realities, our world seems to menace creativity and freedom at large. Inevitably, as Meerlo says, 'the world of tomorrow will witness a tremendous battle between technology and psychology. It will be a fight of technology versus nature, of systematic conditioning versus creative spontaneity.'

What the implications are for us, I am not sure. Students do mostly seem to feel that 'their' culture, which is powerfully influenced by technological requirements, is primary, while ours is really antique, and need only be tolerated for the purposes of passing the examination. At times, however, one does make a breakthrough, and perceives a real development of a critical sense, turning against the spurious culture of our time. At other times students seem to be slipping, seduced into the meretricious culture of the commercial world.

All one can do in this case is to work and hope: meeting in the possession of a work where one can, hoping that its message will go home. This can be at best an enriching experience for young adult and teacher, since it is in this sphere of 'meeting' that the literary culture 'lives'. Even so, the student can withdraw and become hostile, and in any case, at the end of his course, disappears, often displaying an unwillingness ever to return. The degree to which a university teacher is cast off even seems at times a mark of his or her success, as perhaps it is with a psychotherapist. Our penalty is an endless castration complex!

In a sense it is all very artificial: people talk of 'loving their students', but it is a strange love that shows itself capable at times of episodes of distrust, and that ultimate castration.

Oddly enough, the major continuing reality in all our lives is the biggest abstraction — upheld by many tacit assumptions, and embodying behind it generations of critics and teachers: the syllabus, the assumed body of work in our subject to which we pay attention and share. In this, even though we may not be aware of it, we still work and sustain our universities within the influence of the original *telos* of Ancient Greek civilisatien — in which our kind of attention to outer and inner truth, and our kind of democracy, had its beginnings. A subtle and delicate complex, it could be lost (as Karl Jaspers knew) but our natural feeling for the collaboration between maturity and youth as part of democracy will, I am sure, preserve it.

AN ENGLISH SYLLABUS

In my approach to English studies I have emphasised what I believe to be the essential discipline: the phenomenological one. What about the encyclopedic aspect of English? Some will feel that there does not seem perhaps enough in this contribution to the idea of English in a university course, about 'life and thought', about the sense of history, and the relationship between literary works and the 'background'. This is a complex problem: as Marjorie Cox says in her essay on The Background to English Literature 1603-1660 in the *Pelican Guide* (Vol.3), 'the relationship between literature and the society in which it is created eludes any easy definition or even description.' This is not, however, a reason for neglecting the problem.

While reading her essay I noticed a number of things happening to me, as I was preparing once more to teach Jacobean drama and the Metaphysicals. I had been studying *Four Quartets* with a student, and also Leavis's long account of those poems in *The Living Principle*. As I read about the time of King James, King Charles, and the Civil War, I found some of Eliot's lines from *Little Gidding* were echoing in my mind: 'History is now and England', and

> We cannot restore old policies
> Or follow an antique drum . . .

I recalled the tormented sense, which runs throughout *Four Quartets*, as to whether human choices and acts, such as are evoked in the poems at *Burnt Norton*, and *East Coker*, have any significance at all. For Eliot, of course, this question relates to the apprehension of another reality altogether, beyond flesh, time and place. But yet, too, from Eliot we gain a powerful sense of the presence of history, and the living presence for him, of the efforts of the poets and writers of the past, who tried to find meaning in life, through language.

With this sense of history in Eliot went his enormous effort in literary criticism, and to 'purify the dialect of the tribe', in part by promoting a new apprehension of the work of the poets he found important to his own creative efforts. In this, I thought, we can see that the reason for the historical sense and for other forms of encyclopedic investigation in English is in terms of what it contributes to our existential problem of the here and now.

The other thing that I found happening, as I read Marjorie Cox's excellent short survey, was a recognition of the importance of the period she was outlining, to the philosophical problems which I have examined above. There were decisive changes in the history of thought in the seventeenth century, as the old cosmology was shifted, and as new modes of thinking took over: the 'new philosophy' was beginning to be fashionable, and only now are we beginning to become aware of its significance: Mariorie Cox sends us to F.A. Burtt's *The Metaphysical Foundations of Modern Science*, Basil Willey's *Seventeenth Century Background*, H. Butterfield's *The Origins of Modern Science*, Sir W.C. Dampier's *A History of Science and its Relations with Philosophy and Religion* and A.R. Hall, *The Scientific Revolution, 1500-1800*. Concern about these fundamental questions of attitude to the world were, of course, central to Eliot's interest, as they have been to Leavis, and to L.C. Knights.* Leavis recommended in his work, often, that students should pay special attention to the changes in attitudes to man and the world that emerged in the seventeenth century and the scientific revolution.

My kind of emphasis, on English as a Humanities subject, belonging to philosophical anthropology, places its emphasis on the moment of consciousness, in the 'I', at this moment when we are moving forward in time, where 'men's curiosity searches past and future' and may contemplate 'the point of intersection of the timeless/With time'. Is there a future? And what kind of future might it be? It is not extravagant to say that the new modes of thinking which came into being through the scientific revolution of the seventeenth century have brought us to a situation in which we contemplate daily the possibility that there may not be a future. Man began to see, in that century, the possibilities of gaining power over the world. There have been many gains, and none of us would wish to return to a state before scientific advance: none of us want to live our lives without anaesthetics or painkillers, disinfectants

*See *Literature and the Study of Society*, Inaugural Lecture, University of Sheffield, May 1947, an excellent statement of the connections.

and drugs that cure. But there is no escaping the fact that in certain areas, by the sheer effectiveness of technology and scientific advance, we have filled our lives with dread — dread of the monstrosities which might be manufactured by genetic and molecular manipulation (which even scientists are now worried about), dread of the consequences of nuclear fission, and dread of the ecological consequences of environmental and chemical manipulation.

No Humanities subject can, surely, ignore this terrible situation? For we are surely able to see that it has meant that man's power has far outstripped his capacity to deal with the kind of problem of living well in the world, with which Shakespeare grappled? Again and again, in our work in English, we encounter the perplexities of the individual consciousness of the 'I', caught in the toils of the modern dilemma:

> Poppies whose roots are in man's veins
> Drop, and are ever dropping;
> But mine in my ear is safe,
> Just a little white with the dust . . .

Isaac Rosenberg's *Break of Day in the Trenches* records the perplexing irony of a moment when a man, condemned to die in trench warfare, momentarily claims his humanness, his state of being alive and able to choose, by sticking a poppy and sticking it behind his ear. But what he records is the characteristic present-day dilemma, of feeling a victim of man's folly, unable to act in such a way as to alter circumstances, and arrest their catastrophic progress towards disaster: only to reconcile oneself to them.

The predominant truth of our time is that we now have the power to put an end to ourselves. The passionate belief in the potentialities of the future, which we display to a greater or lesser extent in education, must surely take account of the possibility of there being no future, unless we do something about it. Above all, it is important for us to feel that we are actors: that we are not the victims of impersonal forces, either outside or within us, which we cannot alter. This has philosophical implications which spring directly out of our considerations of 'literature, life and thought', not least around the major changes, in the seventeenth and nineteenth centuries, towards a 'functional' view of man.

This book has been mainly directed at the problem of the basic problem of teaching literature to undergraduates, and, as I have said, much of what we do is what used to be done in the sixth form. By Part I of the English Tripos we have done today what used to be achieved fifty years ago in a good sixth form at a grammar school. In Part II there are some opportunities to develop a wider enquiry of a 'Humanities' kind, into considerations of the nature of human existence, as in the Tragedy paper. But what I feel to be lacking, at Cambridge at least, is a further development of the processes of learning and study, in this wider perspective. There are no post-graduate courses, and there is little interest in inter-disciplinary work. In English itself, an increased 'professionalism' even rejects the wider interest in culture in relation to civilisation which was a feature of the *Scrutiny* movement in the thirties, as manifest in *Culture and Environment* and *Scrutiny* itself. The possibility of such developments is worth examining.

Some years ago I conducted a series of informal seminars, held in the Psychology department by the tolerant permission of Professor Oliver Zangwill, for undergraduates, research graduates, and staff, as between poetry, philosophy and psychology. At these sessions we discussed records of human experience, and passages of thought about them, in an open way, not knowing where it might lead. We discussed poems, case-histories (such as some from Winnicott's work), and chapters from books on philosophy and psychology.

To our surprise, the discussions brought together a number of needs. Perhaps the most important was to find another mode of enquiry into human truth other than the strictly positivistic, objective, empirical one — and to establish the validity of other approaches. This, members have told me since, meant an enormous amount to them. Then we needed to establish connections between the records of experience in poetry, and accounts of a phenomenological kind from elsewhere: such as, for instance, the light cast on Coleridge's *Frost at Midnight* by Winnicott's theories of 'creative reflection', male couvade, and the relationship between the I-Thou and our creative perception of reality.

Here, of course, ideas of intentionality, and the relationship between subjective and objective come in as do ideas of what consciousness is and how we explore it: phenomenology. One week we would discuss Martin Buber's essay *Distance and Relation*, the next Sylvia Plath's *The Night Dances*, then Victor Frankl from *Against Reductionism*, and then Winnicott's account of the meaning of an infant's gestures in his clinic. One week we listened to Gustav Mahler's *Kindertotenlieder*, to explore the reason why he should wish to write songs about dead children: and here, of course, questions emerged of the *Dasein* and being-unto-death, which led in turn to Heidegger.

The scope of these explorations of an interdisciplinary kind are discussed elsewhere, and have been edited into a course book: there is also an explanatory volume (*Education and Philosophical Anthropology*). The strangest aspect of this development which is essentially in the nature of Leavis's hint at a special background library in the Humanities — is the intense resistance they encounter. However, there is a project in one university education department, for an interdisciplinary course with graduates, on lines suggested by my work: an experimental course based on some course-books I have prepared, has been tried out at the School of Education at the University of Bath. There, I am told, the subject has to be vigorously defended, against hostility displayed by those devoted to the limited pragmatism in a University aligned to 'practical ends': computer science and other 'technological' directions.

However, at least the project was at least 'allowed'. One of the most extraordinary aspects of the situation in education today, one finds, is the militant hostility in some areas, of science and technology, to attempts to raise questions of the investigation of aims, values, goals or even the nature of being human. Fortunately, there are enough people who understand the value of the humanities sufficiently to defend them. In our crisis today, we need subjects like English more than ever: that is what I hope to show here.*

*At the moment of editing this book I hear a conservative politician being interviewed on the radio about the 'new blood' provision of funds for universities. He spoke of how the money was going mainly to subjects which are 'really useful' rather than the Arts and Humanities, a revealing phrase.

Though it is no doubt a Utopian view, my own belief is that in present circumstances, to really train a student in an English course really fit to be called 'Honours', one would need five years. There is the decline of general 'Humanities' education in school, the decline of reading as a habit, and the triumph of a barbaric culture and atmosphere at large. In this five-year course, the first year would be foundation work, of the kind we used to do in the forties in the sixth form: discussions and essays on general Humanities topics; learning to write an essay; getting down to the basic reading (including Dickens, George Eliot, etc.); learning the basic terms of prosody; obtaining some sense of the structure of language; learning to co-operate in seminar work. The fifth year (following the ordinary three-year Honours course) would be an interdisciplinary course, in which ideas from philosophical anthropology were discussed alongside works of literature, drama, ballet, music, painting and architecture. Philosophical anthropology would include post-Kantian philosophy; post-critical philosophy; psychoanalysis (with object-relations psychology, existentialist psychoanalysis, *Daseins-analysis* and *Gestalt* psychology); philosophical biology; phenemonology; and existentialism. Students would be invited to opt to take this course, which might be part of an 'Education year' for the P.G.C.E.

With the economy in a state of chaos, perhaps subjects which deal with inner resources and the quality of life are the useful ones?

At the moment, however, when there is such an unwillingness on the part of the state to safeguard the future of British civilisation by providing adequate funds for higher education and research, and such pressure for higher education to be more 'functional', there seems to be a general reluctance to experiment. Publishers with an educational list tend also to think in terms of assured markets, and will not take risks. Because of these tendencies, there is a widespread mood of conservatism, and it even seems at times as if the very expression of interest in unorthodox approaches is felt to be in some way improper or ill-advised. Yet it is surely yet another mark of the lack of confidence in English, that there are so few signs of new developments. If the Humanities are to be defended, they must show themselves aware of the need to promote further advances in the task in hand. Edmund Husserl, urging nothing less than a massive reintegration of the subjective realities in our perspectives, points to an enormous task which is hardly yet begun, and I believe the acceptance of English as a Humanities subject is a necessary and important step in this task.

THE WEEKLY WORK IN ENGLISH

The kind of approach we hope to promote is not that of the old-fashioned academic grammar school or a course which is the preparation for an academic life, but of a University in which English belongs to the Humanities. The kind of person we hope to turn out is not a narrow academic specialist, but someone who has a living sense of the bearing of literature as an art, on life and civilisation: on human meaning.

We believe that the impulse in education to which our work belongs originated in the *telos* of Greek civilization, when (in our era) men set out to discover the truth about themselves and the world. English as a subject in the Humanities sets out to answer such questions as:

What is it to be human? and What is the point of life?

A student who is excited by the way in which his acquaintance with literature enhances his capacity to pursue these questions will have no difficulty about doing well in the examinations. And he will incidentally be a good person for research, if research is to have any use or significance.

Of course, students have to do well in the examinations, and prepare themselves to get employment in the world. These considerations will not be neglected.

But it is far more important for us to be what Edmund Husserl called 'functionaries of mankind', devoted to understanding the manifold efforts great minds have made, to find a sense of meaning in life: and to contribute to this, if we can, in our discussion of literary works (for in such discussion they come palpably alive) and our own creative work.

If the world remains as cruel and unpromising as it is at the moment, at least an English student will have inner resources to draw upon, in order to cope with it. For the essential component of all our work is the human imagination and its products. It is a phenomenological discipline.

A university makes a powerful challenge to students in two respects:

> First, their time is largely their own, and their possession of the literature and its 'background' is their business. An enormous amount of reading must be done.
>
> Secondly, students must become articulate in their own voice, about their response to literature. This is practised in supervisions and seminars.

While most students have worked hard to get to the university, this has often been on a very narrow range of literature: the set books. Ours is not a reading age (in an article at the time of writing, it says that Gladstone in his working life must have read 80,000-100,000 books! Most MPs today are 'too busy' to read serious books: a survey not long ago showed that MPs had not read the great literature of the English tradition, like Dickens, while their reading of the classics of their political spectrum was slight).

Students have to develop new habits of voluminous reading, and attentive reading. They must do a great deal of systematic reading (making notes as they go). It is not unusual today even to find candidates for a university place in English who have (say) never read a novel by Dickens or George Eliot, and in 1981 I found several third year men who had not read *The Ode to Autumn*, *The Waste Land* or *Dombey and Son*.* Today students have to achieve at the university reading which used to be done in earlier years.

It is perhaps worth saying that while a Director of Studies will try to see that a student covers everything he should cover, students should not expect to be taught everything, as perhaps they were at school. The best supervision is one during which the students do most of the talking, having prepared themselves by digging into a subject, rather than waiting for the supervisor to tell them about it.

Students should also try to expose themselves to as many minds as possible, among the lecturers

*I hear that this year one candidate for a place in English had never heard of Jane Austen while another characterised his main reading as ''orror'. (1990)

It is not possible for 'teaching' to cover all the authors and periods required for the English Tripos, in detail. The student has to cover the ground himself or herself. At the university, students are expected to work according to their own pace and interest. Supervision hours and classes are meant to be for stimulation in depth, but the main dynamics should come from the student. The student should come to his supervision ready to present his own discoveries and comments on the work he has read: he should be prepared to argue with fellow-students, and to be challenged by his supervisor — and to have his views extended. The supervisor will ask, have you read this poem by the same author, or someone who is very different, or have you seen J on P, or do you know what Leavis said or Eliot said? A student who sits and waits with pen poised for his supervisor to teach him, to fill the hour with instruction talk, is not functioning in a proper university way: he is trying to force things back to the school pattern, and the A level 'right answer' situation. In English there are no right answers, and the more perplexed we are by the fundamental questions of meaning, the better. In supervisions we should share the perplexities of our responses, and our curiosity about the meanings and implications of works.

At the same time, it has to be said that students do seem to need help with even the most elementary techniques of how to read, and how to prepare an essay. They need to discuss how to read a book, how to cut, how to make notes and what to do with these. Some, of course, are well away, but students should not mind discussing these simple matters.

They also need to be equipped with the basic terminology of critical discourse — and to develop their understanding of words- like rhythm, tone, diction, symbolism, intention, as well as specifically technical terms like enjambment, synecdoche, iambic pentameter, anacoluthon and onomatopoeia.

The seminar is the most important medium of work. At a weekly seminar a poem is presented and read, and may be an 'unseen'. We wait until people begin to speak — often a painful proceeding. The pain is part of the educational process. The problem is, of course, what it is possible to say. And so, we move between discussions of what the poem says and its 'technique', the way it says it. From this arise questions of quality and value ('sentimentality', 'sincerity') and wider philosophical issues of the nature and purpose of art, questions of belief and of being.

I find that, at first, students have to learn, step by step, how to collaborate in such a seminar. All I can say is that it is only possible here to learn by doing, and that there is no substitute for our kind of painful application. Adult class students and teachers in training courses can do this kind of work well, and I am reminded by going off occasionally to such groups (in between student seminars) that it is a question (as with riding a bicycle) of developing tacit powers, the powers of an art, which cannot be learnt by explicit instructions. (Parallels are recognition in biology and the art of diagnosis in medicine.)

When I.A. Richards wrote his book *Practical Criticism* he devised a method for a particular purpose. It seems a little puzzling that it has become such an expertise, and even a mystique. There are many people offering classes in 'practical criticism'. In our seminars what we practise is the attempt to understand the meaning of a poem, using whatever concepts of a technical kind we know, to that end — a discipline which we believe yields in the end the best results, when students are faced with poems and passages for comment.

FIRST TERM: MEDIAEVAL PERIOD

We have (say) eight weeks in which to 'do' the mediaeval period. The possible subjects are:

Chaucer's *Canterbury Tales*	The Miracles and Mystery Plays
Troilus and Criseyde	The Moralities
Langland's *Piers Plowman*	Dunbar and Henryson
Sir Gawaine and the Grene Knight	Malory
Pearl	Wyatt

The studente also has to read some material on 'background', such as the essays in the *Pelican Guide* by Derek Brewer and John Speirs, and perhaps C.R. Owst on the sermon tradition, Muscatine on Chaucer, Speirs on *Sir Gawaine* and two or three other books on religion, war, plague or economic and social life in this period. He will then hope (say) to write answers on passages for comment on work by Chaucer, *Sir Gawaine*, The mediaeval theatre and/or religion, knowing that these will almost certainly crop up. All this amounts to a fair first term's work. However, besides satisfying the requirements of the examinations, students ought still to be able to ask themselves relevant questions, in English as a Humanities subject, which relate the subject to the modern world.

Q The mediaeval world was dominated by religion — in the sense that all human actions were in some sense looked at as manifestations of Adam sinning or Christ redeeming. (Brewer says, 'All existence was significant because each individual soul was acting out his or her part in a cosmic drama.') In our agnostic or humanistic age, what have we lost or gained by reaching our very different attitudes to the significance of human acts?
Q In the light of recent medical understanding of the roots of 'wickedness', how do you respond to the last scenes of a mediaeval mystery cycle (the last judgement). Is the loss of the idea of Hell a social catastrophe? or the mark of a great advance in consciousness?
Q Compare the opening lines of T.S.Eliot's *The Waste Land* and Chaucer's *Prologue* and discuss the implicit differences in common attitudes to man's relationship with the natural world. Why is this relationship important?
Q If you read Chaucer (and, say, D.S.Brewer's *Chaucer and His World*) you will perhaps be amazed to find how much people travelled, and how European a man like Chaucer was. He was exceptional, but it is also clear that many people travelled a great deal — as on pilgrimages. Of course there are many huge differences (the whole population of Britain was only one to three million) but the transmission of important ideas and cultural influences seems more significant than it does in our time, despite the modern speed of travel communication. Discuss this, and explore the effects of the invention of printing and other ideas from McLuhan. What was lost by the passing of a vernacular culture?
Q Discuss the attitude to time, in mediaeval poetry and music, and compare it with our own. Take into account the time of natural science: the escape from time in Mahler's music: time in the philosophy of Martin Heidegger (*Sein und Zeit*, *Being and*

Time) and of Maurice Merlean-Ponty: time in T.S.Eliot's *Four Quartets*, and in the Chinese poetry translated by Pound and Arthur Waley.

SECOND TERM: RENAISSANCE PERIOD : 1550–1620

The possible subjects here are as follows:

Edmund Spenser, *The Fairy Queen*
The Shepherd's Calendar
Poetry from Wyatt and Surrey to Sidney and the university wits
The influence of Petrarch
Translation of the Bible from Tyndale (1525) to the Authorised Version (1611)
The Book of Common Prayer 1550
Popular writing and journalism (Dekker, Nashe); translations (Seneca);
The rise of the theatre (*Gorboduc* to Kyd)
Christopher Marlowe, *Tamburlaine*, *Edward II*, *Doctor Faustus*
Dramatists:
Greene, Peele, Heywood, Drayton,
Shakespeare, His *Venus and Adonis* and *Rape of Lucrece* should perhaps be read at this point.
The *Sonnets*.
Ben Jonson, *The Alchemist*, *Volpone*
Chapman's translation of *The Iliad* (1598)
Drayton, *Endimion and Phoebe* (1595)
Raleigh, poems and *The History of the World*
Jacobean tragedy:
Middleton's *The Changeling*, *Women Beware Women*
Tourneur, *Revenger's Tragedy*
Webster, *The White Devil*, *The Duchess of Malfi*
Massinger, Beaumont and Fletcher
Burton, *Anatomy of Melancholy*
Bacon, *The Advancement of Learning*
Montaigne, translation by Florio
Hooker, *Ecclesiastical Policy*
Castiliogne, *The Book of the Courtier*
Composers: Thomas Morley, Wilbye, Gibbons, Campian, Dowland, Farnaby, Weelkes, Ferrobosco

This is but the barest sketch: but it indicates that in one term an undergraduate is expected to acquaint himself intimately with one of the richest periods of literature in the whole of European history! Impossible: so, again, judicious selection is necessary.

In the eight weeks available one might hope to deal with the following:

The achievement of Spenser: (selections from *The Fairy Queen*)
Some Elizabethan verse Marlowe's *Dr Faustus*
Ben Jonson — *The Alchemist*, *Volpone*; some poems
Tourneur — *Revenger's Tragedy*
Some passages from translations of the Bible
Middleton's *The Changeling*

Discussion of the decline of tragedy. It should be noted that although this term is given to the 'Renaissance' (1550-1620) the Part I paper includes the whole period 1550-1700 — so we still have 80 years to go.

(In the light of the implied pace of the above work, it seems to me extraordinary and pretentious, that Tripos questions should be set like: 'Write on the relation between "Mind" and the natural world in the works of one or more writers of the period'.)

The kind of 'background' questions which a student needs to bear in mind here might include the following:

How the Renaissance in England was bound up with the consolidation of the Tudor regime.

The vitality of popular language traditions and interest in language: and the reasons for the growth of drama as a predominant art form.

The nature of the new humanistic culture of the Renaissance, and the way in which it dislodged the mediaeval world view: new intellectual sources in antiquity, in deference to Scripture, versus the authority of Aristotle, Aquinas and scholasticism.

The new pragmatic approaches, linked with the rise of capitalism.

The influence of Machiavelli. 'Human motives were no longer judged in the old way.'

Castiglione's *The Courtier* and Neo-Platonism

The rise of the new science: 'the new Philosophy calls all in doubt' Donne wrote in 1611

The decline of the moment of tragedy with Beaumont and Fletcher: 'the age of a national drama was over'

The effect of printing during this period.

I suppose the prudent student might calculate to be able to satisfy the examiners if he has really covered in depth: Spenser's *Fairy Queene* and the *Shepheardes Calendar*; Marlowe's plays; Jonson's drama; some Elizabethan verse; some revenge tragedy (Tourneur, Middleton, Webster) and Shakespeare's *Sonnets* and poems.

But a student who is trying to relate his subject to the modern world will also ponder, out of his reading in this period, the following questions:

Q Machiavelli's 'realism' influenced Bacon and Raleigh and represented a new pragmatism which cut away the ground from religious theories as the basis for political thought. Trace this 'realism' through to contemporary Realpolitik: see Michael Polanyi's essays on nihilism in *Knowing and Being*.

Q The Puritans refused to recognise any authority in religion outside the Bible. Today not even university students have read the Bible, while science is now virtually the one remaining recognised authority. Trace the origins of this change to the period (Copernicus, Harvey, Kepler, Hakluyt, Gilbert on magnetism, Gallileo, Raleigh, Bacon) and the 'adoration of the human intellect'. Have any important aspects of truth been lost sight of, in the historical progress of 'the advancement of learning'?

Q Examine T.S.Eliot's concept of 'the dissociation of sensibility' in the light of this age: the Elizabethan approach to the problems of life (as in Shakespeare's tragedies) is a 'whole' one and their idea of an educated man was one in which many accomplishments were included, from ability in music and poetry to an interest in the new science. There was also a kind of seriousness, of gravity, of moral interest, which made tragedy possible — and which declined after Jacobean tragedy. Was there a disastrous decline in sensibility after the period in question? And why? What are the contemporary manifestations of this?

R.H. Tawney's *Religion and the Rise of Capitalism* seems to me a key work here (and his *The Acquisitive Society*): see also L.C. Knight's D*rama and Society in the Age of Jonson*. See also the essays by L.A. Cormican on 'The mediaeval idiom in Shakespeare' in *Scrutiny*, XVII. T.S. Eliot, *Selected Essays*.

SHAKESPEARE

Shakespeare does seem to be the one literary subject on which students today are still well educated at school, and which they enjoy. Usually, however. students have read only a few of Shakespeare's plays and have studied only one or two in depth.

The main concern here is to get students aware of the nature of the development of Shakespeare's verse: comparing, for example, the more stilted, elaborate and diffuse qualities of the earlier writing, with the intense concentration of meaning in the great tragedies. *Richard II* is a useful introduction to the origins and development of the tragic moment: *Henry IV*, parts one and two, enables students to appreciate the vigour and depth of Shakespeare's prose, and also the remarkable combination of vitality, realism and deep moral concern.

Students need to explore the comedies and consider in them the treatment of love and relationships (leading to the remarkable mature play *Measure for Measure*). They need to look at Shakespeare's treatment of politics, and the way in which he explores problems of power, will and appetite, from the history plays to *Macbeth*, *Othello*, and *Lear*. *Antony and Cleopatra* is a useful tragedy to study, as it cannot be fitted into any of the categories of tragedy while its human problems remain insoluble, and its point seems to remain baffling — despite its profound insights into human nature.

The purpose of work at this stage is to enable students to discard all their narrow and facile 'A' level approaches to Shakespeare and to enable them to be really disturbed and enriched by the plays.

The ramifications around this subject are too numerous to be mentioned. S.L. Goldberg's *An Essay on King Lear* will be a useful foil. Also relevant are Dr.Johnson's critical comments on Shakespeare and F.R. Leavis's essay *Tragedy and the Medium*. This raises the question of What is Tragedy? — a question which becomes central.

One hopes that students will read two or three good critical books on Shakespeare, including those by Traversi, and L.C. Knight's 'Hamlet' and other Shakespearean Essays: J.F. Danby's *Shakespeare's Doctrine of Nature* and A. Righter, *Shakespeare and the*

Idea of the Play. Questions which Shakespeare's work raises for the modern world are the following:

> Q If we look realistically at man's nature and his capacities for good and evil, can we hope for solutions to the problems of social organisation and ethical living?
>
> Q In the chaos which can follow from an outburst of moral inversion, or hate, in human affairs, may it not appear that life has no meaning? In what can such meaning be said to exist, if it does? Does the loss of faith in God and a spiritual realm mean that such meanings can no longer be found?
>
> Q In *Lear*, *Timon* and other plays Shakespeare expresses deep problems in attitudes to women. What does this tell us, about problems of woman in the unconscious life? And how do these relate to the problem of being?

Period 1620-1700: Again, we have a period of enormous richness which has to be dealt with partly in the third term of the first year and in the first term of the second year, even as the second year braces itself to take on the eighteenth century, perhaps the most remote in mode from our own.

Fortunately, the Metaphysical poets are most congenial to our own sensibility, and many students have done work on them before coming up. But the period also contains the massive enigma of Milton: Dryden's difficult work, huge quantities of pamphlets and occasional writings, the dry and solid prose of Hobbes and Locke, and John Bunyan. In this period, too, are the significant origins of modern approaches to psychology, particulate and atomistic approaches in science and the Hobbesian paradigm of reductionism.

The works pre-eminent in this period are:

John Donne. *Songs and Sonnets* and religious poems
John Donne, Sermons
Ben Jonson's poetry and *Timber* (prose)
George Herbert, *The Temple*
Henry Vaughan, Thomas Traherne
Richard Crashaw
The Cavalier Poets (Herrick, Carew, Suckling, etc.)
Milton, *Comus*, *Paradise Lost*, *Samson Agonistes*
Andrew Marvell
Hobbes, *Leviathan*
John Bunyan, *Pilgrims Progress*, *Grace Abounding*
Abraham Cowley, John Locke,
Lancelot Andrews, Sir Thomas Browne
Dryden, *Marriage à la Mode*
John Dryden, *Absalom and Achitophel*, *All for Love*

Restoration Comedy:
Sir George Etherege,
She Would if She Could
William Wycherley, *The Country Wife*
William Congreve, *Way of the World*
Sir John Vanburgh, *The Relapse*
George Farquhar, *The Beaux Stratagem*
Shadwell, *The True Widow* (1678)
Collier, *A Short View of the Immorality and Profaneness of the English Stage*

Again, an enormous act of selection is called for. Most students will surely want to study John Donne and Andrew Marvell. Those with an interest in religious poetry Herbert, Vaughan and Traherne. Herbert will be the subject of seminars, inevitably, because of his supreme honesty and simplicity, and it is important to see how he relates to Bunyan, and belongs like Bunyan to a tradition that persists from the Middle Ages.

Milton's *Paradise Lost* and his special place in the century and in English literature must be grasped. Dryden's position must also be understood. The other areas of literature are surely a matter of taste, especially Restoration Comedy. But the philosophical and religious issues in this century are of very considerable importance, as are the profound changes in taste. These are usefully discussed in Professor Basil Willey's *The Seventeenth Century Background* which surely every student will wish to read.

This is the century of the English Civil War — the pain of which is evident behind Marvell's retreat into a green shade. (*The Horatian Ode* is a key poem.) Milton's huge ambitions to justify the ways of God to man may be contrasted with Herbert's humility: Milton's grandiloquence with Herbert's plainness.

The King had been put to death, and there were subsequently endless debates on what now might be the basis of the right to rule, and of the moral law.

Important figures in prose are Lord Herbert of Cherbury, John Selden, Samuel Pepys, John Evelyn, and Lord Halifax. Halifax's account of Charles II (*The Character of a Trimmer*) indicates a significant difference between the Restoration Court and the Court of Charles I which had a 'central and magnetic position in society' and had regained 'something more than the dignity of Elizabeth's Court.' Charles II's 'mob of civilised gents' was quite different.

There are other important themes: the fanaticism of the Puritans for example (Jeremy Prynne) and the radical political ideas which emerged in the Civil War (Winstanley's Diggers, Lilburne and the Levellers, Colonel Rainborough, Puritan Millanarianism, the 'Parliament of Saints' — with its sequels in America) the development of scientific and philosophical ideas.

Modern themes which emerge from this century are clearly visible throughout the literary criticism of T.S. Eliot and F.R. Leavis. See also E.A. Burtt, *The Metaphysical Origins of Modern Physical Science*: H. Butterfield, *The Origins of Modern Science*, Sir W.C. Dampier, *A History of Science and its Relations with Philosophy and Religion*, on education see W.T. Costello on *The Curriculum at Seventeenth Century Cambridge*.

Christopher Hill's work from a Marxist point of view on the English Revolution is interesting: *Puritanism and Revolution*. See also the anthology, *The Good Old Cause*, ed. C. Hill and E. Dell.

THE EIGHTEENTH CENTURY : 1700–1830

Students should study the aims of the Augustans, and their attitudes to Nature and Reason: a study of them illuminates so much of English architecture, landscape and townscape. (Visit Holkham Hall). Pope is a satisfying poet to study, between Marvell and the metaphysics, and Wordsworth. Swift is a fascinating figure. Samuel Johnson is a great man in English literature. Crabbe is an important poet. A few things by Gray and Collins deserve attention. Blake is a highly significant figure belonging to this century — and, of course, Jane Austen belongs here. We need to understand something of the origins of the novel in Richardson, Smollett, Fielding, and Defoe. Goldsmith's *She Stoops to Conquer* and Sheridan's *The School for Scandal* and *The Critic* represent a fruitful moment in drama as does Gay's *Beggar's Opera*.

So, for this paper, let us set out our aims, for the eight week term:

Dryden, *The Hind and the Panther*, *All for Love*
Pope, *The Rape of the Lock*, *Windsor Forest*, *On the Death of an Unfortunate Lady*, *Moral Essays*
Augustanism and the classics (Horace),
'What oft was thought but ne'er so well expressed'
Swift, *Gulliver's Travels*

Richardson, *Pamela*
Fielding, *Tom Jones*
Crabbe *The Lover's Journey, Peter Grimes, The Borough, Procrastination*
Gray, *Elegy in a Country Churchyard*
Collins, *Ode to Evening*
Johnson, *London* and *Vanity, On the Death of Dr.Levet*
Preface to Shakespeare and notes on Shakespeare's plays
Lives of the Poets: Cowley, Milton, Pope
Blake, *Songs of Innocence and Experience*
Jane Austen, *Mansfield Park, Emma, Pride and Predujice.*
Goldsmith. *She Stoops to Conquer*

While these provide more plenty for supervision discussion and essays, students should also try to read some of the following:

Pope. *Essay on Man: Essay on Criticism*
Dryden, *Absalom and Achitophel*
Joseph Addison, some essays from 'The Spectator'
Akenside, *The Pleasures of the Imagination*
James Boswell, *Life of Johnson*
Samuel Butler, *Hudibras*
Congreve, *The Way of the World*
Cowper, *Moral Satires*
Daniel Defoe, *Moll Flanders, Roxana, Robinson Crusoe,*
Henry Fielding, *Tom Jones, Joseph Andrews*
John Gay, *The Beggar's Opera*
Oliver Goldsmith, *The Deserted Village, She Stoops to Conquer*
William Law, *Serious Call*
Samuel Richardson, *Clarissa* and *Pamela*
Rochester, *Satyr Against Mankind*
Sheridan, *The Critic, The Rivals*
Swift, *Tale of a Tub, A Modest Proposal, Journal to Stella* (some)

For the purposes of this period, Wordsworth, Keats, and Coleridge come within its compass: also Scott and the Gothic novel. The Romantic movement comes in this period: most students have done a good deal of work on this, fortunately, at school.

The interesting thing about the Eighteenth Century, as far as 'background' is concerned, is the confidence with which the Augustan values were held. 'Reason', it was believed, should control even poetical fancy and religious faith. (Boileau, however, complained that Descartes had 'Cut the throat of poetry'). The culture of the period belonged of course, to a limited group: it was not (like Elizabethan drama) a national culture. 'Taste' was established in circles where social distinction, political importance, and classical reading predominated. There was a definite 'reading public' to be addressed: and there was also a growing popular public, too. (Johnson declared, 'the knowledge of the common people of England is greater than that of any other vulgar'.)

There was a reaction against the fanaticism, Civil War and rebellion of the last century, and a concentration on economic growth, order and trade. (Though Crabbe and Goldsmith recorded the poverty of the countryside.)

The deepest belief of the Augustan era was that there was a moral and intellectual absolute: God — so it was man's duty to discover and obey these moral laws. 'Natural laws' were evidence of God's beneficence (a view shaken, all the same, by the Lisbon earthquake of 1755 which killed tens of thousands of the devout at their prayers). There was a fundamental spiritual goodness accessible to man through his conscience: 'natural philosophy' (science) was subservient to purposes of a higher kind.

As is commonly recognised, beneath this preoccupation with order ('Whatever is, is right') there was a suppression of large regions of experience. This may be discussed round the attitudes of Dryden and Johnson to Shakespeare. The deeper aspects of the psyche, and the bleaker problems of the world, did not go away of course (cf. the statistics in *The Gentleman's Magazine*. of infant mortality, disease, executions. etc.). Johnson was afraid of madness: Swift's agitated hatred runs beneath the surface of all his work: Jane Austen had a problem of living in close promixity to people you hate ('regulated hatred'), Blake had problems of madness and incoherence, while Christopher Smart's *Jubilate Agno* is the imaginative documentation of his own madness.

The Romantics, the Gothic novel, and Gothic in architecture were all reactions against the limitations of Eighteenth Century reason. Should man impose his own disciplines on Nature? or should he be in humility before Nature, and recognise the mysteries and irrationalities of his mind and the world? An aesthetic distrust tended at last to dissociate the aesthetic from the rational.

In the seventeenth century (as in Hobbes' *Leviathan*) emerged a new materialism and a potential atheism. In our own time, some believe that we must begin from a recognition of the meaninglessness of existence. (See Bertrand Russell — 'man is the product of causes which had no prevision of the end they were achieving . . . his beliefs, are but the outcome of accidental collocations of atoms — '*A Free Man's Worship*). In its concentration on sound sense, and on a society of humane proportions, did the eighteenth century cut itself off from 'tragic experience' and so from some of the essential existential problems of the meaning of life? And are we any nearer trying to solve them? General reading: A.R. Humphreys, *The Augustan World*; Basil Willey; J.W.Bate, *From Classic to Romantic*.

The Romantic Movement needs to be seen as a rediscovery of important aspects of the human spirit: of the mysterious resources of being (cf. *Kubla Khan*), of touch with childhood and the origins of consciousness (*Tintern Abbey*, *Ode on the Intimations of Immortality*. *The Prelude*, *Frost at Midnight*). and what may be called the existential problems.

1830–THE PRESENT DAY

Today, when students seem to acquire the reading habit late, the nineteenth century seems to present the biggest problem, while the twentieth century branches out into a bewildering diversity. The solution is perhaps for students to start on an intense programme of reading in the works of this period from the very first moment, during the year before they even begin work at university.

Dickens seems to be one of the most difficult figures: students seem to find it hard to bear his sentimentality and his reliance on coincidence: he is also very long-winded. But he is an important artist, concerned with being (in the Blake — D.H. Lawrence tradition). So, the following should be read:

Dickens: *Hard Times, Great Expectations, David Copperfield, Bleak House, Dombey and Son, Little Dorrit, Our Mutual Friend,*
George Eliot: *Scenes of Clerical Life, Adam Bede, Middlemarch, Daniel Deronda, The Mill on the Floss,*
Thomas Hardy: *Under the Greenwood Tree, Tess of the d'Urbervilles, Jude the Obscure, The Trumpet Major, The Woodlanders, Return of the Native,*
Emily Brontë: *Wuthering Heights*
Charlotte Brontë: *Jane Eyre, The Professor, Villette*
Anthony Trollope: *Barchester Towers, The Warden*
Elizabeth Gaskell: *North and South, Mary Barton, Wives and Daughters*
Benjamin Disraeli: *Sybil*
Also of interest are Mark Rutherford, George MacDonald (*Phantastes*),
Thackeray, Samuel Butler (*Erewhon*), and William Morris.
Victorian poetry which should be read includes:
Matthew Arnold: *Dover Beach, The Scholar Gypsy*
Robert Browning: *My Last Duchess, Two on the Campagna, Meeting at Night*
Emily Brontë: *Poems*
Thomas Hardy: *Veteris Vestigea Flammae*, Poems 1912-13
Gerard Manley Hopkins: *Collected Poems*
Rudyard Kipling: *Barrack Room Ballads*
Christina Rossetti: *Poems*
Algernon Swinburne: *The Triumph of Time*
Tennyson, Alfred, Lord: *In Memoriam, Mariana, Maud*
Oscar Wilde: *The Ballad of Reading Jail*

In supervision work perhaps we shall tackle: Dickens' *Great Expectations*; George Eliot, *Middlemarch*; Hardy, *Tess*; Emily Brontë, *Wuthering Heights*; poems by Arnold, Browning, Hopkins and Hardy.

The great 'background' problem of the nineteenth century is Utilitarianism — which is fundamentally a problem of attitudes to human nature and being. A key work here is F.R. Leavis's *Mill on Bentham and Coleridge*, and his book on Dickens.

What we must not underestimate, however, is the great advances in the nineteenth century of democracy, local government, education and social care. We may also reflect soberly on the extent and stamina of the reading public (figures will be noted of the circulations of the leading nineteenth century reviews).

Matthew Arnold's *Culture and Anarchy* and his *Essays in Criticism* are important. See also Carlyle (*Signs of the Times* 1829) and Ruskin.

Religious dispute was prodigious. And one major debate spills over into our time — the impact of ideas from science, especially Darwinism, on attitudes and beliefs. The major theories from geology and astronomy, the Second Law of Thermo-dynamics, and Evolutionary Theory totally demolished the established Christian world-view, and began to replace it with a mechanistic, atomistic universe devoid of all meaning. This philosophical problem surely lies behind the separation of poetry and the imagination from the 'real' world (Bentham called poetry 'push pin"). This is why so much Victorian poetry retreated to the world of the scholar gypsy and Arthurian legend: to this some of Browning, Arnold's *Dover Beach*, Hopkins and Hardy are honourable exceptions with problems of being and the inner life (as do some of the fantasists like George MacDonald).

Other important books on the Nineteenth Century:

G.M. Young: *Portrait of an Age*
John Stuart Mill: *Autobiography*
Edmund Gosse: *Father and Son*
Q.D. Leavis: *Fiction and the Reading Public*
Sir L. Stephen: *The English Utilitarians*

THE TWENTIETH CENTURY

Many new themes introduce themselves with the twentieth century. Some believe that civilisation itself collapsed in 1914. Certainly in Mahler's music (e.g. the Ninth Symphony, 1911) we seem to near the collapse of empires and of faith. The 'reading public' begins to collapse, while the age of 'communications media' begins. It is the age of the common man, but of no common values: of intense political moral fervour, but also of apathy, disillusionment, moral turpitude and amoralism — even in the Arts. Nihilism and Realpolitik triumph: Marxism breeds tyrannies.
Key works for discussion must surely include:

T.S.Eliot: *The Waste Land*, *Four Quartets*
E.M.Forster: *A Passage to India*, *Howards End*,
Where Angels Fear to Tread
D.H. Lawrence: *Sons and Lovers*, *The Rainbow*, *Women in Love*
Joseph Conrad: *Heart of Darkness*, *Under Western Eyes*,
The Secret Agent
James Joyce: *Ulysses*, *Portrait of the Artist as a Young Man*
Arnold Bennett: *The Old Wives' Tale*
Henry James: *What Maisie Knew*, *Portrait of a Lady*
Edith Wharton: *The Reef*, *The Custom of the Country*,
The House of Mirth,
Other works by poets: W.B.Yeats: especially *Byzantium*,
Sailing to Byzantium, *Among Schoolchildren*, *A Prayer for my Daughter*
Ezra Pound: *Hugh Selwyn Mauberley*, *Poems*
Edward Thomas: *Collected Poems*
Isaac Rosenberg: *Poems*
And the following writers should be read:
Virginia Woolf: *To the Lighthouse*, W.H.Auden, Samuel Beckett,
Walter de la Mare, L.H.Myers (*The Near and the Far*);
Wilfred Owen, George Orwell, J.M. Synge

But this is now beginning to look like a year's work, before we have even considered the modern age since 1945.

The following are important general works to read on this period:

Q.D. Leavis: *Fiction and the Reading Public* (again)
George Bourne: *The Wheelwright's Shop*
Robert Graves: *Goodbye to all That*
Sigmund Freud: *Civilization and Its Discontents*
David Riseman: *The Lonely Crowd*
Richard Hoggart: *The Uses of Literacy*
F.R. Leavis and Denys Thompson: *Culture and Environment*
Raymond Williams: *Culture and Society*
D.H. Lawrence: *Phoenix*
F.R. Leavis: *The Common Pursuit*
G.S.Fraser: *The Modern Writer and his World*
W.W. Robson: *Modern English Literature*
William Walsh: *A Human Idion: Literature and Humanity*
David Holbrook: *Lost Bearings in English Poetry*
J. Fletcher: *Novel and Reader*
ed. P. Abbs: *The Black Rainbow*
Per Gedin: *Literature in the Market Place*
T.S. Eliot: *Notes Towards a Definition of Culture*
F.R. Leavis: *Revaluation* and *The Living Principle*

General problems of this century are too complex and enormous to list: but attention will need to be given to problems of belief and nihilism: the investigation of the nature of consciousness in psychoanalysis and its effects on attitudes to human nature: the fragmentation of culture and problems of symbolism and meaning: the suggestion from philosophers (e.g. Susanne Langer) that man is the *animal symbolicum* whose primary need is culture and meaning; the reconsideration of the nature of knowledge (Polanyi, Husserl, Marjorie Grene) and the attempt to reconsider the Newtonian universe (see *The Albach Seminar*, ed. Koestler and Smithies).

It may be of interest to give here a note on the weekly seminar.

As a teaching method, it derives from adult education. In such work the established course tended to be a breathless lecture-rush through the canon: some lecturers came to believe that adult students came in to classes because they wanted to discover the relationship between literature and 'life', its relevance to their own experience. It was important to give them the opportunity to report on their experience of works of literature, to say what it meant to them, and the tutor would then take the discussion from there, to return to the text, to examine its language, to elucidate difficulties, and to try to place the work in its wider context. But the essence of the work was 'the common pursuit of true judgment', and collaboration. Students were asked to read the texts and then begin sessions by talking about them.

With undergraduates the approach is slightly different. To ask them to work in this way is more arduous, because they have less experience to draw on and are more diffident about their experience. (I vividly recall the report of an adult woman student who had gone home from a class on *Antony and Cleopatra* to be asked to help a neighbour lay out a corpse. This kind of experience isn't common among undergraduates!). On the other hand, students should have keener and better trained minds, and are more 'intellectual' than 'experiential' in their approach to literature. They also have specialisms and often know more about a subject than the supervisor.

They also feel pressed by exam requirements and become anxious about whether they are covering the work: to give up an afternoon to talk about one poem seems to some a wicked luxury or a waste of precious time. Some find the detailed attention to one work a great strain.

However, there are many tacit or unseen elements in the seminar which are valuable in training response to literature.

First is the uncertainty itself. Of live performances of music, Stravinsky spoke of the important of the element of 'risk'. The very possibility that no-one may have anything useful to say, that the seminar may not 'work', is an important component of the experience. The very fact that we can 'meet' in the experience of a poem is itself an indication of the real existence of a shared cultural experience, of 'a man speaking to man'. In practice, seminars which are genuinely of the kind at which the students do the talking do usually 'work', and this is incidentally a valuable experience for students who ultimately have to face unseen passages on many examination papers. No-one who has attended seminars regularly should have any problem in being articulate in a Practical Criticism examination.

One of the most valuable aspects of the seminar is the experience of the poem or passage 'coming alive' during the afternoon, often in depth. It is this close experience, and the subsequent debate that has, perhaps months later, become the germ of a good dissertation: one student's dissertation on Coleridge *Frost at Midnight* and on his theories of perception is a case in point. This student found his thesis developing out of an argument over this poem at the seminar a couple of years before he wrote his thesis. The deep experience of some poems also enables them to be used as sign-posts throughout other work in supervisions, and as examples in critical theory. The experience of reading and discussion also helps with theoretical considerations, of where a poem 'is', what it can do for us, what it is valid to say about it and what its social implications may be.

All this in itself helps to make the study of literature 'real', a genuine experience. It is important, in a utilitarian world in which universities face severe threats especially in the Arts, for us to feel that our discipline has a justifiable value. Here, the benefit of the seminar is that all years participate, and when it happens I find a great satisfaction in this. Much of the friendly cohesion of the 'English' students in a College is established by the experience of collaboration in the seminar, and the all-year group unites us all not least in the feeling that literature is never exhausted — that however many years we have studied it, there are still perplexities, and the art remains unexhausted, ineffable, new. It can challenge us afresh, even when we are somewhat stale with a surfeit of reading for examination purposes.

It can be very exciting when a third year student is challenged by a first year one, or when the supervisor's opinion is questioned by a student. The best moments are when students disagree, and the most successful are when the supervisor says hardly anything. (Yet from the supervisor's point of view this way of working is, in fact, the most exhausting, since one has to listen with acute attention, yet resist the impulse to fill in the time with talk, or to avoid the pain of silence or of waiting for students to speak.) Even those who attend the seminar and make no contribution experience this close attention too. The best part of the seminar is often the period of attentive silence in the first ten or fifteen minutes.

Such seminars also challenge the widespread window-dressing which established 'English' for exams tends to generate. We all know that both exam papers and student essays tend to suggest that the student knows much more, is wiser and better informed than he really is. In a seminar anything one says may be challenged: and yet students also often say the most marvellous and insightful things.

But they are real reports on the experience of the poem, and so (as I like to think) the seminar is a training in authenticity of comment, in sincere literary comment. Though this is painful, it seems to me likely to contribute to effectiveness — so that students ask themselves, 'What is worth saying? What can be usefully articulated?' and so should be capable of greater economy, which has a practical value in the world, not only for exams.

I hope these notes will help students to regard the seminars as an important part of their weekly work. The problem is that the elements of the experience which are beneficial are 'tacit' and not easily apparent: but nonetheless valuable, I believe. For discussions of this kind of approach see *Reading and Criticism*, Raymond Williams; Simon Stuart, *Say* (Nelson); and there is a verbatim account of a seminar on a child's poem in *The Exploring Word* (CUP 1967) by the present author.

THE SEMINARS

The following poems have been discussed in open seminars (two hours) with all years present.

S.T. Coleridge: *Frost at Midnight*
Ben Jonson: *Ode to Himself*
Edward Thomas: *Old Man*
George Herbert: *The Collar*
W.B. Yeats: *Among School Children*
Thomas Hardy: *After a Journey*
Sylvia Plath: *The Night Dances*
Keats: *Ode to Autumn*

The purpose of these seminars was to allow the students to do the talking. The best part being the long initial silence in which students are attending to the words on the page. It is difficult to bear, but waiting for them was the essential discipline on the tutor's part; after that his role was to guide the ensuing discussion — and occasionalllv to check irrelevancies, or suppress destructive facetiousness which might destroy the atmosphere of serious attention. One problem, of course, is that if a supervisor waits in silence, or is self-effacing throughout a session, some students conclude he has nothing to say!

Those who have gained most from this method are those who needed help to become much more articulate and coherent; and those who had to be asked to justify some of their generalisations. Some of the first year found a strength in themselves in trying to uphold their points of view in the company of older years (several students tend to talk off the top of their heads too easily).

One second year proved the most difficult. At a seminar in the summer which I took with them alone they would give nothing, and remained doggedly silent, a phenomenon I have never experienced before (fortunately one third year man was with us and broke the ice). During the term. they have been a great problem. Some of the girls who are more shy have not taken to the seminar. One very left-wing, intelligent man has used the seminar for attacks on what he supposes to be my position, declaring that there can be no literary judgements, and that there can be no moral connection between literature and life. This is, of course a proper area of discussion: but to this student's response there has been a strong personal element of hostile rejection of what he supposes to be my position. (It is certainly strange to conduct seven 'open' seminars listening to students, to be told afterwards one is trying to impose a viewpoint on them!) When he has forgotten to be contentious in a personal way, however, this student has made many useful contributions. Another third year man has also made many intelligent contributions, but has also nearly wrecked some of the seminars by destructive facetiousness, with an undercurrent of distrust and antipathy.

One third year man who was active in the theatre seems not to have enjoyed the seminars, though he had in supervisions enjoyed close discussion of the texts of plays like *King Lear*: even there, however, he said he felt it was like 'working with a bulldozer', a response I found it hard to understand. Another who seemed to have enjoyed working in the seminars, had made contributions which were sometimes bizarre (of Thomas Hardy's *After a Journey* he opened by saying 'This is a mad kind of poem . . . ') and at the last seminar he wrecked it compIetely by describing for half an hour how I was using my choice of poems to 'get' at him, and I was in league with others in the group against him. This seems really quite paranoid.

I chose substantial works, but it was clear that the poems were often too difficult for the students. I found it hard to believe that two students had never read Keat's *Ode to Autumn* before I chose this poem because (I supposed) it would be well known, and is positive and easily 'accessible' to them. But they simply could not read it well. One student did not know what a gleaner was, and it had to be explained that the gleaner is carrying a big sheaf of gathered grain on stalk across a plank bridge. I take this example because it was the last, after a term's work, and because the poem is such a simple, beautiful and well-known one. Students apply the 'practical criticism' 'technique' in an absurd way: because of 'the soft-dying day', some said, the poem displayed a 'death wish': others because of 'oozings' said it was 'full of rot and corruption'. One student declared it was so cloying and sickening that he hated it, and found it full of 'death'.

When I tried to point out the way in which the poetry does what it says, by its textural richness and its movement, they declared I was being 'partisan', in favour of poetic language (Milton's) which did not have these qualities but was equally valid. I was surprised how many students disliked Yeats.

Some alleged that in using Keats I was again trying to impose upon them, a 'Leavis' approach. My reference to Leavis's remark that the moss'd cottage trees gave the 'feel in the mouth', of biting a ripe apple was greeted with ridicule, while my remarks on the double 'm's in the last line of the first stanza,

> For summer hath overbrimmed their clammy cells . . .

as making one feel one honey in one's mouth was also ridiculed. 'Clammy', they said, made them think of a corpse. One girl ridiculed the suggestion that the words 'treble soft' gave, onamato-poetically, the very sound of the robin's song; and, indeed, denied that there was any 'onamatopoeia' in the poem at all.

What I am trying to indicate is that (a) the students own responsiveness to words is very poor — their errors of reading are about ten times as grotesque as those made by students in I.A. Richards's *Practical Criticism*. Yet they enlisted this disabilitv (b) in an assault on my kind of choice and my kind of attention to the language. Moreover (c) they continually make wild and rather subversive generalisations.

Compared with similar seminars I have given in the past, these were lacking in the friendly spirit of collaboration. In the background I sensed a rival teaching which went so far as to oppose even my very concept of what poetic language is, so that the establishing of common response was undermined in a quite artificial way.

The best seminars were on *Frost at Midnight*, *Old Man* and *The Night Dances*, though the last was a heated one. The worst were on 'Hardy's *After a Journey* which many found to have too many archaisms ('Hereto', 'life lours', 'whither') for which they could not make allowances: these seemed to them to indicate a fundamental insincerity. They could make little sense of *Among School Children* — they couldn't put the elements of the poetry together (though one man — the man active in the theatre was good, I remember, on the last stanza.) This reveals, I believe, that their 'philosophical' pretensions are empty: their theoretical postures are so much wind, and when they come to a real problem of working out meaning, their minds are full of blockages and they fall down before the essential problem. Usually, with *Night Dances*, it takes forty minutes for a group to find that it is about a baby: this group took one hour twenty minutes; and then they were furious with me for not telling them, beforehand — believing that I played some kind of trick on them. Even though explained that what we had been through was what any reader has to go through, on reading the poem for the first time. One rather disturbed girl 'found the baby': she is a quiet but very astute reader, though somewhat elusive.

I was delighted that students collaborated so well across the three years.

My purpose in supervisions this term, with each year, was to

'meet' students' minds, in certain chosen texts. I hoped to get their noses into 'the words on the page' and there to establish,between my reading and theirs,a sense of a common language, in which to talk about literature. I also hoped to get up some 'signposts' by which students might begin to find their way about the topography of English Literature: and to develop a dynamic in the students, with which they could then turn to any subject necessary for the examination, and get to grips with it. I was careful to choose texts which would also be useful for examinations and dissertations. central texts which any English student ought to know. Armed with this work, I thought, we could then move on to 'periods': but I also choose work which raised questions of 'literature, life and thought', of the relationship between the creative imagination, consciousness, society and civilisation. Each work would thus raise critical problems, which would be explicitly discussed when we turned to literary criticism for certain required papers.
The works covered by me have been as follows: First Year

Isaac Rosenberg: *Break of Day in the Trenches.*
Seventeenth Century Metaphysical poetry:
Donne's: *Aire and Angels*; *The Flea*; some *Holy Sonnets*;
Some poems from Herbert's *The Temple*;
Vaughan: *The Retreat*;
Marvel: *Little T.C. In a Prospect of Flowers*, *To His Coy Mistress.*

(For these, students were asked to read T.S. Eliot on *The Metaphysical Poets* and Samuel Johnson's *Life of Cowley*. I also told them about a review by William Empson of John Carey's book on Donne in the *New York Review of Books*, and urged them to read *The Seven Types of Ambiguity*).

The last few seminars have been on D.H. Lawrence's *Sons and Lovers*, an important tragic novel of our time. I have been trying to make links between the creative artist's engagement with human experience, at the level of 'being', and the defence of being against all those forces, in society, and in the way in which men think of themselves: this in turn is a question of language and the way in which it is inseparable from thought and feeling. One question here is that unity of thought and feeling which is to be found in

Donne and Marvell which interested T.S. Eliot, and which was revived in the literary critical movements of our century: this is a major feature of 'Cambridge' English. (I have continuaily referred to Eliot's *Essays*, and of course Leavis). I have, I hope, left lines hanging in the air, by which (next term) to connect our reading of Donne and the Metaphysics with Shakespeare — and later further twentieth century works. Lawrence's depth and symbolism should be a good introduction to the greater English novels.

However, I am in general disturbed by the deficiencies in the reading of students. I conducted a survey of student's reading and I found most gaps in the nineteenth century novel. One cannot understand (say) Joyce, Lawrence and E.M. Forster in this century without knowing Dickens, George Eliot, Conrad and Henry James, at least.

I was shaken to find that (for example) not one of my 22 students had read *Dombey and Son* (while 2 third- year men had never read *The Waste Land*) I am anxious at once to remedy this and have urged the first year to read a selection from Dickens, and the other authors mentioned, over Christmas, to fill in this terrible gap. (Imagine a student faced with a passage from *David Copperfield* on a practical criticism paper, and not recognising it!)

The work with the second year has consisted of the following:

After some preliminary discussion of poems, to establish rapport and a language between us, I asked them to read *Hard Times* and then *Great Expectations*.

I supposed this would be a simple procedure, leading us on to discussions of language, of 'creativity', and the upholding of 'being' or individual authenticity, against those forces in social organisation and the thoughts of men(e.g. utilitarianism) which manifested against it.

This could lead to a discussion of Dickens's 'Shakespearean' qualities as an author concerned with the question of 'what men live by': his relation to Blake and Wordsworth as champions of human potentiality (and especially that spirit which is found in the child): the way he leads on to the other great novelists of the nineteenth century, and to Lawrence in our own time. He is a major signpost.

I asked the students to read *Mill on Bentham and Coleridge*, as presented by Leavis, and John Stuart Mill's *Autobiography*. I xeroxed some of this material to be passed round the students.

To my horror and dismay, the students disliked Dickens, because they could not bear his sentimentality and his Victorian faults, like impossible melodrama and coincidence. One left-wing student denounced Dickens as a mere entertainer and told me that since his generation had been immersed in 'sardonic' novels like *Catcher in the Rye*, they couldn't take 'positive' novels any more — and in any case the novel as literature was 'redundant'.

Few of the students had ever read Dickens before. One girl said she had seen the old black and white film of *Great Expectations* but found the book 'disappointing'. Another said she had tried *Bleak House*, but hadn't been able to get beyond the first two chapters.

Only two students wrote the essay I asked for on Dickens: one on *Great Expectations* and another on *Hard Times*. I was delighted to hear from the latter that I had converted her to Dickens.

All students were asked at the beginning of term to write a note on why they were studying a university course. These were disturbingly poor, and only two were interesting.

From Dickens, although I was deeply unsatisfied with the work we did on him, we went on to Wordsworth. I turned to Wordsworth to get back into the eighteenth century which the students were wanting to cover. Two students simply refused to read Wordsworth — one put a note through my door which told me 'she had nothing to say about Wordsworth'. After a discussion of 'Surprised by Joy', and 'Margaret', both of which I found almost too moving to read aloud, another girl declared 'Why do we have to read Wordsworth? — all this stuff about flowers — he's like Patience Strong!' This was in response to the lines about the signs of neglect in Margaret's garden which seem to me among the most harrowing in English literature (*Margaret* is a poem sometimes discussed in the Tragedy Paper for Part II).

It should be emphasised that one reason for my choice of Wordsworth was that students must, for the Practical Criticism paper in Part I, know the *Preface to the Lyrical Ballads*. They cannot obviously discuss this unless they know Wordsworth's poetry, and the way in which he sought a new kind of poetic language (closer again to

Shakespeare) in revolt against the constraints of poetic diction. I tried to get this over to the students by using an essay written by Edgell Rickword, the poet and Editor of *The Calendar of Modern Letters*. We discussed Wordsworth in relation to the French Revolution, Godwin, the Age of Reason, Blake and Romanticism. Later, of course, I was going on to Blake, and (incidentally) back to Jane Austen: moreoever, I hoped students would have found how, to John Stuart Mill, Wordsworth's poetry offered the 'very culture of the feelings'.

Later I would take this theme up in my discussions of Matthew Arnold, whose *Essays in Criticism* must also be studied for the Practical Criticism paper in Part I. Arnold found Wordsworth's poetry a healing power — and a grounds for his championship of poetry as a cure for the nation's ills — which leads us in turn to many critical considerations, of the work of Eliot, Leavis and others.

All this very complex sense of the relevance of Wordsworth to the literary topography was wrecked, by the students, refusal to 'take' Wordsworth. One of the consequences of the campaign being conducted against my approach was to make some of the more sensitive students terribly anxious. Some would continually accost me whenever I crossed the College Court: 'Can I talk to you about my work' — but yet they had nothing to say. Some began to speak of an 'unfortunate situation' and only in the last week or so of term did I realise that it was not the students' own dissatisfaction that was in question, but a campaign against me in which they had been enlisted.

One student even said he did not trust me enough to give me back a questionnaire on his reading. He has no cause for this view: I had given him an extra 'hour' to listen to a remarkable essay of fifteen pages on *Under Western Eyes*. I also lent him my *Education, Nihilism and Survival* to help him deal with the moral and philosophical problems we discussed.

The third year have presented me with prodigious difficulties — yet have been in the end less trying and hostile than the second. They are more mature and are able to collaborate as adults — speaking out when they feel like it, mostly without hostility.

I tried to choose works which reflected their maturity, but which would raise important questions of creativity and 'life, while still relating to specific papers and projects. These included:

> *The Waste Land* (which few had read)
> *King Lear*, *Macbeth*, *Hamlet*, *Timon of Athens*
> The Poetry of W.B. Yeats

We have spent most of the time on *Lear* and it has been a great delight to dwell for three or four supervisions on the meaning of the poetry of one of the greatest of all literary works.

The problem with this vear has been to practise basic reading and response without making it seem an insulting five-finger exercise. *King Lear* did this for us! One student at least said to me 'I have been enjoying it enormously' (in week seven).

I was particularly anxious to help the Third Year to get some sense of the central issues in the Tragedy paper (as it used to be when its purpose was understood) — the pressing of the problem of the meaning of life, to its ultimate, by confronting Death. This, I believe, we have achieved between us, by explanations of *King Lear* and other plays.

At their request I gave some students time on W.B. Yeats, but here I found were hampered by their poor abilities to read complex poetry. I do not of course say this to them, and on their part I realise that they would like me to talk more about Yeats' interest in occultism, Maud Gonne and Madame Blavatasky. One has a great interest in Baudelaire, Kafka, Mallarmé, Verlaine, Rimbaud, Flaubert and others, for which I hope to provide some fertiliser: but I make a mental note that, confronted with magnificent lines such as

> The salmon falls, the mackerel-crowded seas

and:

> Oh, chestnut tree, great rooted blossomer
> Are you the leaf, the blossom or the bole?

Despite his alleged interest in Yeats, he was not very forthcoming on the meaning of the words. On 'A Prayer for My Daughter' he was better, though we had some wild nonsense from him over the lines about Venus throwing herself away on 'a bandy-legged Smith' (i.e. Vulcan, who was thrown out of heaven and broke his leg) which (he said) showed Yeats to be a 'fascist'.'

The worst aspect of the whole situation is the way students try to apply 'A' level expedient calculations to bucking the system. It is possible to avoid a whole period in Part I, by offering a dissertation. The student thus hopes to avoid the eighteenth century, and others the whole modern period. Thus a dissertation on Jane Austen will obviate the need to study Johnson, Fielding, Swift, Pope, Crabbe, Blake and a dissertation on (say) Conrad will cut out Dickens, Henry James, George Eliot, the Brontës, Hopkins, D.H. Lawrence, Joyce and T.S. Eliot. Students protest 'Oh, I don't want to do Dickens, because I am not doing that paper.'

It is then possible in Part II to avoid (say) the nineteenth century novel — so a student could leave Cambridge with an English Honours degree without ever having read the major writers of that century: I have checked with the Faculty and my opinion is confirmed that the Faculty wishes students to be educated in the literature, life and thought of all periods.

Students find that in other colleges the work is neatly parcelled out, so that the mediaeval period is tackled in the first term, the 1550-1700 period next, and so on — leaving all modern work until the Third Year. Though concessions may be made to this approach it seems absurd to stick rigidly to it, as there is a constant need to make connections (e.g. Donne — Eliot; Blake — Dickens — Lawrence; Shakespeare — Keats). But I confess I do not find it easy to cover the literature from 1300 to the present day in two years with undergraduates when today they have to start more or less from scratch — and this problem is not likely to get better.

It may perhaps be illuminating to give the results of a survey of students' reading made in all three year of an English Honours Course of seventeen students.

r = have read or studied this book or poet
n = have never read it at all

T.S. Eliot, *The Waste Land*	rrrrrrrrrrrrrr	nnn
Charles Dickens, *Hard Times*	rrrrrrrrrrr	nnnnnn
Bleak House	rrrrrrrr	nnnnnnnnn
Dombey and Son	r	nnnnnnnnnnnnnnnnn
Great Expectations	rrrrrrrrrrr	nnnnnn
David Copperfield	rrrrrrrrr	nnnnnnn
Little Dorrit	rr	nnnnnnnnnnnnnnn
George Eliot, *Mill on the Floss*	rrrrrrrrr	nnnnnnn
Adam Bede	rrr	nnnnnnnnnnnnnn
Middlemarch	rrrrrrrr	nnnnnnnn
Henry James, *What Maisie Knew*	rrrrr	nnnnnnnnnnnn
Joseph Conrad, *Heart of Darkness*	rrrrrrrrr	nnnnnnnn
The Secret Agent	rrrrrrrr	nnnnnnnnn
Thomas Hardy, *The Woodlanders*	rrrrr	nnnnnnnnnnnn
Tess of the d'Urbervilles	rrrrrrrrrrrrrr	nnnn
Tolstoy, *War and Peace*	rrrrrrr	nnnnnnnnnn
D.H. Lawrence, *The Rainbow*	rrrrrrrrrrrrr	nnnn
Edward Thomas's Poetry	rrrrrrrrr	nnnnnnnn
Wordsworth's Poetry	rrrrrrrrrrrrrr	nnn
E.M. Forster, *Howards End*	rrrrrrrr	nnnnnnnnn

EPILOGUE

In some of my comments on teaching I feel I may have given an unfair impression of my own students, which is unfortunate, since I have learnt so much from them.

I don't budge from my main argument, which was concerned with the welfare of students in the Humanities in general. Ours is an unpoetic world: that is, in my terms, a world which less and less seems to concern itself with the needs of being, the need for individuals to feel that their life has significance. There does seem to be a decline in the schools, of the kind of general debate there used to be in the sixth form, on human issues and values. As Dr P.J. Bayley of Gonville and Caius College said in a letter to *The Times* there is 'a nationwide drift towards narrow and unadventurous specialization in the post A-level stage', and from his own experience he detects a process whereby schools select a very narrow range of texts for study from the lists of literary options, and coach their pupils to respond to them in 'drearily predictable critical terms'. 'Nor do the sterotyped general essays offer much evidence of reading'. In interviews recently I came across an intelligent young man whose only topic among the whole of twentieth century literature was George Orwell. He said insightful things about George Orwell, but he knew nothing else from the last 100 years of our literature.

In such a situation, it does seem that we begin with many disadvantages, and my point was that what is needed is a course which emphases wide, sound reading — and not a flight from this into abstruse literary theories, using the texts as excuses for intellectualisation. I also believe we need a philosophy of English which vindicates this — in the wake of F.R. Leavis's insistence that the poem is not the 'black marks on the page'. but the revivifying of the poem, in discourse, 'in the criss-cross of utterance between us'. Unless the poem or whatever is 'there', in our minds ('my words echo thus in your mind . . . ') there is nothing to talk about.

I think we need to develop the theory somewhat beyond that, we need to face up to some of the psychological issues more realistically in terms of what a reading of a literary work can do for us, for anyone: and some of the philosophical issues, of the moral effect of creative art. One of the strangest aspects of the attitudes of some students today is their resistance to the assumption that literary art has to do with what Leavis calls 'life', with actual questions of moral choice in existence, with questions of morality and values. So, as I see it, it is an uphill job, establishing between us a 'possession ' of a novel like *Mansfield Park*, which is quite clearly based on very firmly held moral convictions, to do with how the failure of 'active principle' in living can harm and damage individual lives seriously and disastrously.

What must be said, however, is that among Cambridge English students, at least the ones I have worked with, I find a passionate sincerity, and a deep and genuine interest in literature. I would be sorry to give any other impression. And when they get here, they take off in no mean fashion. I paid tribute to what I know of the work of others in the faculty, and there is no doubt that English Literature is alive and well — indeed, one would not be driven to go on with one's criticisms and attempts to debate critical assumptions and so forth, unless this were so.

There are difficulties of 'meeting' in the way I have emphasised, not least when a teacher has strong opinions: my students feel that my selection of literature is strongly prejudiced by my own preferences. But, I tell them, they would find this with anyone who was really engaged. Where my interests have met theirs,we have entered into a possession of work with — to me at any rate — great satisfaction. I think particularly of one afternoon on *Kubla Khan*, about which I had been nervous, because, although I had read *The Road To Xanadu*, I didn't feel I could give a finally satisfactory account of that poem. But, working from their own natural capacities for responding to poetic meaning, they recreated the poetic logic and meaning of the work. One learns a great deal from such an experience. As will be clear, a central practice in my own teaching was to present a poem, usually unseen, in this way, in a seminar at which the students do the talking. What came out of this was often very heartening, not because of displays of specialist knowledge, or 'brilliance': but a recognition that, given the opportunity, young people can exercise their skills of understanding the meaning of the words. It is certainly a valuable antidote to the pessimism into which Leavis fell into his late years. One's students, even when one disagrees with them, give one hope for the future.

It is also encouraging to note that the official documents which come round endorse the 'involved' approach: examiners report a desire to see students'engaged, or troubled, or. . . . interested' and led towards 'independent critical thinking', by contrast with being trained in 'depressing generalisations. . .'.

We managed best, I thought, to 'meet' in Shakespeare. Even if students today seem less well trained in poetry, and reject our emphasis on the nineteenth century novel,they respond with enthusiasm and warmth to Shakespeare, and to drama in general.Moreover, as with a perplexing play like *Anthony and Cleopatra*, they don't mind being left unable to reconcile the final 'upshot' of the play: they don't want its message, or even its overall metaphorical patters, to be summed up, and they find the criticism of 'our' generation (Mason, Wilson, Knight, Knights, Leavis, Traversi) too apt to bring things to conclusion in this way. They prefer Sam Goldberg, in his essay on *King Lear*. This speaks a great deal for their inner security, and their critical scrutiny of any 'position', and their earnest desire to make up their own minds.

Because some students have done so much work on their own enthusiasms, and because they are, some of them, much more intelligent than oneself, one learns a great deal that is new, often somewhat painfully. One student, for example, powerfully challenged my Leavisite indifference to Robert Browning, and drew my attention to some of his best poetry and this has led to a reconsideration of the whole question of Browning and his influence. In the same way I have been drawn into the heart of Dr Johnson's criticism of Shakespeare as never before, as well as into Eliot's *Four Quartets*, and Leavis's criticism of these poems. Keen students reveal one's own illiteracy — one's laziness, in failing to respond to poets who were not in the'canon' of one's own mentors: and the gaps in one's own reading. It was a matter of disdain, to one of my students, that I had not really read Pound's *Cantos*, for example. In my part, I have had some of them rushing out to buy George Crabbe, or Pope, or working their way into the contortions of

Leavis's discussions of George Santaya on 'Tragedy and the Medium'. At first, my own students were deeply suspicious of the Leavis connection: now, they find his reading of *Marina* magical. while being dismayed at his bad arguments in *The Living Principle* over Eliot. He has come alive for them, albeit subjected to their own discrimination and valuable iconoclasm.

Readers will be, I hope, taking in what kind of experiences I had, feeling generally that I was being given frequent kicks in the pants, not least in needing to make my own written criticism and teaching to their needs.

One obstacle to progress was the deep anxiety about the world, which we all share. The backwash of unemployment even sweeps into the supervision room, as students hear of last year's graduates not getting jobs, and it then seems somewhat irrelevant to attend to a mere sonnet about the moon. This anxiety often makes them intensely wary of us, the older generation.

Where we triumph, I believe, is when we share the delight of a literary text between us, which illuminates the human condition, and build a genuinely educational collaboration on that point of meeting.

BIBLIOGRAPHY

Abbs, P. (ed.) (1975), *The Black Rainbow*, London, Heinemann.

Allport, Gordon (1955), *Becoming: Basic Considerations for a Psychology of Personality*, Newhavens, Conn., Yale University Press.

Balint, Michael (1952), *Primary Love and Psychoanalytical Technique*, London, Tavistock.

Berdayev, Nicolai (1950), *Dream and Reality: An Essay in Autobiography*, London, Bles.

Binswanger, Ludwig (1922), *Introduction to the Problems of General Psychology*, Berlin, Springer.

Binswanger, Ludwig (1951), *Sigmund Freud, Reminiscences of a Friendship*, New York, Grune and Stratton.

Binswanger, Ludwig (1963), *Being-in-the-World*, New York, Basic Books.

Boss, Medard (1963), *Psychoanalysis and Daseinsanalysis*, New York, Basic Books.

Bowlby, John (1953), *Child Care and the Growth of Love*, Harmondsworth, Penguin.

Brentano, Franz (1960), Chapters translated in *Realism and the Background of Phenomenology*, Chisholm R.M. (ed.) Glencoe, Ill., Free Press.

Bretall, Robert (1951), *A Kierkegaard Anthology*, Princeton, Princeton University Press.

Brewer, D.S. (1970), *Symbolic Stories*, Woodbridge, Suffolk, Brewer and Boydell.

Brink, Andrew (1977), *Loss and Symbolic Repair*, Hamilton, Cromlech Press.

Brink, Andrew (1982), *Creativity as Repair*, Hamilton, Cromlech Press.

Buber, Martin (1937), *I and Thou*, Edinburgh, Clark.

Buber, Martin (1947), *Between Man and Man*, London, Kegan Paul.

Buber, Martin (1964), *'Distance and Relation', in The Knowledge of Man*, Friedman, M. (ed.) London, Allen and Unwin.

Buber, Martin (1969), in Schlipp, P.A. and Friedman, M., *The Philosophy of Martin Buber*, La Salle and London, Open Court and Cambridge University Press.

Bugental, J.F.T. (1967), *The Search for Authenticity*, New York, Holt, Reinhart and Winston.

Burtt, E.A. (1932), *The Metaphysical Foundations of Modern Physical Science*, London, Allen and Unwin.

Burtt, E.A. (19670), *In Search of Philosophic Understanding*, London, George Allen and Unwin.

Buytendijk, F.J.J.. (1958), *Das Menschliche*, Stuttgart, Koehler.

Buytendijk, F.J.J. (1962a), *Pain: Its Modes and Functions*, Chicago, University of Chicago Press.

Buytendijk, F.J.J. (1935), *The Mind of the Dog*, London, Allen and Unwin.

Buytendijk, F.J.J. (1965), *Woman*, Glen Rock, NJ, Newman Press.

Buytendijk. F.J.J. (1962b), Essay on the phenomenological approach to problems of feeling and emotion, in Ruytenbak, H. (ed.), *Psychoanalysis and Existential Philosophy*, New York, Dutton.

Buytendijk, F.i.j. (1967), in O'Connor, D. and Lawrence. N. (eds.), *Readings in Existential Phenomenology*, Englewood Cliffs, NJ, Prentice Hall.

Buytendijk, F.J.J. (1952), *Phenomenologie de la Rencontre*, Paris, DescIée de Brouwer.

Camus, Albert (1942), *The Outsider*.

Carline Richard (1968), *Draw They Must*, London, Edward Arnold.

Cassirer, Ernst (1963), *An Essay on Man*. New Haven, Yale University Press.

Chaloner, Len (1963), *Feeling and Perception in Young Children*, London, Tavistock.

Collingwood, R.G. (1938), *Principles of Art*, Oxford, Clarendon Press.

Collingwood, R.C. (1945), *The Idea of Nature*, Oxford, Clarendon Press.

Curtis, B. and Mays, W. (eds.) (1978), *Phenomenology and Education, Self-consciousness and its Development*. London, Methuen.

Drury, M. O.C. (1973), *The Danger of Words*, London, Routledge and Kegan Paul.

Erikson, Erik (1950), *Childhood and Society*, New York, W.W.Norton.

Esterson, Aaron (1970), *The Leaves of Spring*, London, Tavistock.

Fairbairn, W.R.D. (1952) *Psychoanalytical Studies of the Personality*, London, Tavistock.

Farber, Leslie H. (1966), *The Ways of the Will*, London, Constable.

Foudraine, Jan (1974), *Not Made of Wood*, London, Quartet.

Frankl, Victor (1963), *From Death Camp to Existentialism*, Boston, Beacon Press.

Frankl, Victor (1965), *The Doctor and the Soul*, New York, Knopf.

Frankl, Victor (1967), *Psychotherapy and Existentialism*, New York, Washington Square Press.

Freud, Sigmund (1914), *On the History of the Psychoanalytical Movement*, in (1924), Collected Papers, Vol.I, p.287, London, Hogarth.

Friedman, Maurice (ed.) (1964), *The Knowledge of Man*, London, Allen and Unwin.

Fromm, Erich (1942), *Escape from Freedom* (The Fear of Freedom), London, Kegan Paul.

Fromm-Reichmann, F. and Moreno, F.J. (eds.) (1956), *Progress in Psychotherapy*, New York, Grune and Stratton.

Grene, Marjorie (1948), *Dreadful Freedom*: An Introduction to Existentialism, Chicago, University of Chicago Press.

Grene, Marjorie (1957), *Martin Heidegger*, London, Bowes and Bowes.

Grene, Marjorie (1976), *Philosophy In and Out of Europe*, Berkeley, University of California Press.

Grene, Marjorie (1974), *The Understanding of Nature*, Boston, D. Reidel.

Grene, Marjorie (1969), *The Anatomy of Knowledge*, London, Routledge.

Grene, Marjorie (1966), *The Knower and the Known*, London, Faber and Faber.

Grene, Marjorie (1959), *Introduction to Existentialism*, University of Chicago, Chicago.

Guntrip, Harry (1961), *Personality Structure and Human Interaction*, London, Hogarth Press.

Guntrip, Harry (1968), *Schizoid Phenomena, Object Relations and the Self*, London, Hogarth Press.

Heidegger, Martin (1949), *Existence and Being*, Chicago, Regnery-Gatway.

Heidegger, Martin (1962), *Being and Time*, trs. J. MacQuarrie and E. Robinson, London, Sc.M.

Hodgkin, R.A. (197), *Reconnaissance on an Educational Frontier*, Oxford, Oxford University Press.

Holbrook, David (1971), *Human Hope and the Death Instinct*, Oxford, Pergamon.

Holbrook, David (1972), *Sex and Dehumanisation*, Pitman.

Holbrook, David (1975), *Gustav Mahler and the Courage To Be*, Athlone, London, Vision.

Holbrook, David (1976), *Sylvia Plath: Poetry and Existence*, London, Athlone.

Holbrook, David (1987), *Evolution and the Humanities*. Aldershot, Gower.

Holbrook, David (1988), *Further Studies in Philosophical Anthropology*, Aldershot, Gower.

Holbrook, David (1987), *Education and Philosophical Anthropology*, Cranbury, NJ, Associated University Presses.

Holbrook, David (1980), *English for Meaning*, Reading, N.F.E.R.

Holbrook, David (1977), *Education, Nihilism and Survival*, London, Darton, Longman and Todd.

Husserl, Edmund (1970), *The Crisis of the European Sciences and Transcendental Phenomenology*, Evanston, Ill., Northwestern Univ. Press.

Jaspers, Karl (1933), *Man in the Modern Age*, New York, Henry Holt.
Jaspers, Karl (1950), *The Perennial Scope of Philosophy*, New York, Philosophical Library.
Jaspers, Karl (1932), *Philosophie*, Berlin, Springer.
Jaspers, Karl (1960), *The Idea of the University*, London, Owen.
Jung, C.G. (1928), *Contributions to Analytical Psychology*, London, Routledge and Kegan Paul.
Kaufmann, Walter (1956), *Existentalism from Dostoevsky to Sartre*, Cleveland, World.
Kaufmann, Walter A. (1950), *Philosopher, Psychologist Anti-Christ*, Princeton, Princeton University Press.
Kierkegaard, Søren (1941), *Concluding Unscientific Postscript*, Princeton, Princeton University Press.
Kierkegaard, Søren (1941), *Philosophical Fragments*, Princeton, Princeton University Press.
Klein, Melanie (1932), *The Psychoanalysis of Children*, London, Hogarth Press.
Klein, Melanie (1941), *Contributions to Psychoanalysis*, London, Hogarth Press.
Mackillop, Ian (1995), *F.R. Leavis: A Look at Criticism*, London, Allan Lane
Mackillop, Ian (1995), *F.R. Leavis: Essays and Documents*, Sheffield, Academic Press
Maslow, Abraham (1959), *New Knowledge* in *Human Values*
Maslow, Abraham (1968) *Towards a Psychology of Being*, New York, Van Nostrand.
May, Rollo (1950), *The Meaning of Anxiety*, New York, Ronald.
May, Rollo (1953), *Man's Search for Himself*, New York, W.W.Norton, London, Souvenir.
May, Rollo (1969), *Love and Will*, New York, W.W.Norton.
May, Rollo (1972), *Power and Innocence*, New York, W.W.Norton.
May, Rollo (ed.) and with Angel, Ernest and Ellenberger Henri F. (1958), *Existence — A New Dimension in Psychiatry*, New York, Basic Books.
Meerlo, Joost de, *Mental Seduction and Menticide*, Merleau-Ponty, Maurice (1962), The Phenomenology of Perception, London, Routledge and Kegan Paul.
Merleau-Ponty, Maurice (1969), 'The Child's Relation with Others', in Edie, James M. (ed.), *The Primacy of Perception*, Evanston, Ill., Northwestern University Press.
Milner, Marion (1969), *The Hands of the Living God*, London, Hogarth.
Milner, Marion (1950), *On Not Being Able to Paint*, London, Heinemann.
Moustakas, Clark (1966), *Existential Child Therapy*, New York, Basic Books.

Naevestad, Marie von (1979), *The Colours of Rage and Love*, Oslo, Norway, Universitetsforlaget.

Nietzsche Friedrich, The Gay Science in *The Complete Works of Friedrich Nietzche*, ed. Oscar Levy, 18 vols, London, T.N.Foulis, 1901-13.

O'Connor, D. and Lawrence N. (1967), *Readings in Existential Phenomenology*, Englewood Cliffs, NJ, Prentice Hall.

Pivevic, Edo (1970), *Husserl and Phenomenology*, London, Hutchinson.

Polanyi, Michael (1970), *The Tacit Dimension*, London, Routledge and Kegan Paul.

Polanyi, Michael (1946), *Science, Faith and Society*, Chicago, University of Chicago.

Polanyi, Michael (1969), *Knowing and Being*, London, Routledge and Kegan Paul.

Polanyi, Michael (1958), *Personal Knowledge*, London, Routledge and Kegan Paul.

Polanyi, Michael (1975) and Prosch, Harry, *Meaning*, Chicago, University of Chicago Press.

Poole, Roger (1972), *Towards Deep Subjectivity*, London, Allen Lane.

Read, Herbert (1945), *Education Through Art*, London, Faber and Faber.

Ricouer, Paul (1966), *Freedom and Nature*, Evanston, Ill., Northwestern University Press.

Ricouer. Paul (1970a), *Freud and Philosophy*, New Haven, Conn., Yale University Press.

Ricouer. Paul (1970b), *Husserl: An Analysis of his Phenomenology*, Evanston,, ill., Northwestern University Press.

Robinson. Ian (1973), *The Survival of English*, Cambridge, Cambridge University Press.

Robinson. Ian and Knight. Roger (1988), *My Native English*, Retford. Brynmill.

Roubiczek,, Paul (1969b), *Existentialism: For and Against*, Cambridge, Cambridge University Press.

Roubiczek, Paul (1969b), *Ethical Values in the Age of Science*, Cambridge, Cambridge University Press.

Ruggiero, Guido de (1946), *Existentialism: Disintegration of Man's Soul*, New York,, Social Sciences.

Ruytenbeck, H. (1962) (ed.), *Psychoanalysis and Existential Philosophy*, New York, Dutton.

Ryle, Gilbert (1949), *The Concept of Mind*, London, Hutchinson.

Sampson, George (1921), *English for the English*, Cambridge, Cambridge University Press.

Sartre, Jean Paul (1948), *Existentialism is a Humanism*, New York, Philosophical Library.

Schlipp, P.A. and Friedman, M. (eds.) (1969), *The Philosophy of Martin Buber*, La Salle and London, Open Court and Cambridge University Press.

Singh, G (1995), *F.R. Leavis: A Literary Biography*, London, Duckworth.

Spiegelberg, Herbert (1965), *The Phenomenological Movement*, The Hague, Nijhoff.

Spiegelberg, Herbert (1972), *Phenomenology in Psychology and Psychiatry*, Evanston, Ill., Northwestern University Press.

Stern, Karl (1968), *The Flight From Woman*, London, Allen and Unwin.

Straus, Erwin (1963), *The Primary World of Senses*, Glencoe, Ill., Free Press.

Straus, Erwin (ed.) (1964), *Phenomenology*, Pure and Applied, Pittsburgh, Dusquesne University Press.

Straus, Erwin (1966), *Phenomenological Psychology*, New York, Basic Books.

Straus, Erwin (1969), *Psychiatry and Philosophy*, New York, Springer.

Strickland, Geoffrey (1981), *Structuralism or Criticism?*, Cambridge University Press.

Suttie, Ian D. (1935), *The Origins of Love and Hate*, London, Routledge and Kegan Paul.

Tillich, Paul (1952), *The Courage To Be*, New Haven, Yale University Press.

Tomlin, E.W.F. (1947), *The Approach to Metaphysics*, London, Routledge and Kegan Paul.

Tomlin, E.W.F. (1955), *Living and Knowing*, London, Faber and Faber.

Tomlin, E.W.F. (1985), *Psyche, Culture and the New Science*, London, Routledge and Kegan Paul.

Tomlin, E.W.F. (1986), *Philosophers of East and West*: The Quest for the Meaning of Existence in Eastern and Western Thought. London, Oak Tree Books. Foreword by Kathleen Raine.

von Uëxkull, I.J. (1926), *Theoretical Biology*, London, Kegan Paul.

Wahl, Jean (1944), *A Short History of Existentialism*, New York, Philosophical Library.

Whitehead, A.N. (1927), *Symbolism*, Cambridge, Cambridge University Press.

Whitehead, A.N. (1933), *Adventure of Ideas*, Cambridge, Cambridge University Press.

Whitehead, A.N. (1938), *Modes of Thought*, Cambridge, Cambridge University Press.

Whitehead, A.N. (1929), *Process and Reality*, Cambridge, Cambridge University Press.

Wild, John (1955), *The Challenge of Existentialism*, Bloomington, Indiana University Press.

Wild, John (1963), *Existence and the World of Freedom*, Englewood Cliffs, NJ, Prentice Hall.

Wilshire, Bruce (1968), *William James and Phenomenology*, Bloomington, Indiana University Press.

Wilson, Colin (1966), *Introduction to the New Existentialism*, Boston, Houghton Mifflin.

Winnicott, D.W. (1957), *The Child and the Family*, London, Tavistock.

Winnicott, D.W. (1957b), *The Child and Outside World*, London, Tavistock.

Winnicott, D.W. (1958), *Collected Papers: Through Pediatrics to Psychoanalysis*, London, Tavistock.

Winnicott, D.W. (1965), *The Family and Individual Development*, London, Tavistock.

Winnicott, D.W. (1966), *The Maturational Processes and the Facilitating Environment*, London, Hogarth Press.

Winnicott. D.W. (1970), *The Piggle*, London, Hogarth Press.

Winnicott, D.W. (1971), *Playing and Reality*, London, Tavistock.

Winnicott. D.W. (1971), *Therapeutic Consultations in Child Psychiatry*, London, Hogarth Press.

Wisdom, John (1952), *Philosophy and Psychoanalysis*, Oxford, Basil Blackwell.

Yalom, Irvin D., (1980) *Existentialist Psychotherapy*, New York, Basic Rooks.

ARTICLES AND CHAPTERS

Burtt, E.A. (1963), 'Descriptive Metaphysics', *Mind*, vol. LXXII.
Holbrook, David (1984), 'F.R. Leavis and the Sources of Hope', in *The Leavises*, ed. Denys Thompson, Cambridge, Cambridge University Press.

Knights, L.C. (1947), *Literature and the Study of Society*, Inaugural lecture, University of Sheffield.

Leavis, F.R., (1974), "Believing In" the University', *The Human World*, vols.15-16, p.98, Brynmill.

Polanyi, Michael (1967a), 'Life Transcending Physics and Chemistry', *Chemical and Engineering News*, 56 (August 21).

Polanyi, Michael (1970), 'Science and Man', *Proceedings of the Royal Society of Medicine*,. vol. LVIII (September), pp.969-76.

Poole, Roger (1974), 'From Phenomenology to Subjective Method', *Universities Quarterly*, vol.29, no.4, Autumn 1975, p.912.

Poole, Roger (1974), on Merleau-Ponty, *Universities Quarterly*, vol.28, no.4, p.488.

Ryle, Gilbert (1986), on Husserl and Phenomenology, *Philosophy*, vol..XXI.

Salinger, L.G. (1982), 'Coleridge: Poet and Philosopher' in *The New Pelican Guide to English Literature*, ed. Boris Ford,.p.276.

Saunders, Wilbur (1986), on literary theory, *Universities Quarterly*, vol.40, no.5 (summer).

INDEX

Abbs, Peter: 175fn. 203
Absalom and Architophel: 194, 197
Ackroyd, Peter: 148
Acquinas, Thomas: 191
Acquisitive Society, The: 192
Adam Bede: 216
Adam: 66
Addison, Joseph: 197
Advancement of Learning: 190
After a Journey: 30, 20, 209, 30
Against Reductionism: 183
Aire and Angels: 210
Akenside, Mark: 197
Alchemist, The: 190
Alice in Wonderland: 112
All for Love: 198
Alpach Seminar: 203
Among School Children: 202, 209
Anatomy of Melancholy: 190
Ancient Mariner: 129, 140, 143
Andews, Lancelot: 194
Andrews, Michael: 130
Anna Karenina: 32,
Antony and Cleopatra: 73-81, 124, 193, 204, 219
Approaches to a Philosophical Biology: 7
Aristotle: 191
Arnold, Matthew: 14, 17, 56, 61, 17, 87, 144ff, 200, 201
Athens: 53, 58
Auden.W.H.: 202
Augustan World: 199
Austen, Jane: 83, 153, 186ff. 194, 196, 197, 198
Authorised Version of the Bible: 86, 134-5, 190, 192
Autobiography, John Stuart Mill: 212

Babbitt, Irving: 54
Bach J.S.: 5
Bacon, Francis: 190, 192
Bahktin: 52
Barchester Towers: 200
Barnard, Eric: 49
Barthes: 37, 44
Basic Books: 13, 15
Bate, Walter Jackson: 44
Bath, University of: 34
Baudelaire: 214
Bayley, John: 36, 84
Bayley: P.J. 217
Beaumont, Francis: 190, 191
Beaux Stratagem, The: 195
Beckett, Samuel: 202
Beggar's Opera: 196, 197
Being and Time: 190
Believing in the University: 156fn
Bennett, Arnold: 5, 9, 13, 32, 83, 89, 103, 169
Bentham, Jeremy: 9, 62, 201
Berkeley Bishop: 136fn. 137
Beveridge: 90
Binswanger, Ludwig: 23
Birtwhistle, Harrison: 130
Black Rainbow, The: 203, 175 fn.
Blake, William: 57, 63, 64, 65, 66, 67, 68, 69, 70, 190, 197, 199, 211, 213, 218,
Blavatsky, Madame: 214
Bleak House: 200, 216
Boileau: 198
Boleyn, Ann: 48
Book of Common Prayer: 86, 119
Book of the Courtier, The: 190
Borough, The (Crabbe): 197
Bostonians, The: 153
Boswell, James: 197
Bourne, George: 203
Bradbury, Malcolm: 35
Break of Day in the Trenches: 181, 210
Brewer, Derek: 53, 188, 189
Brewer, Reuben: 43
Brontë, E.: 151, 200
Brontës, The: 215
Browne, Sir Thomas: 194
Browning, Robert: 200, 201, 219, 108ff.
Buber, Martin: 3, 5, 12, 106

Buddha: 17, 56
Bunyan, John: 194, 195
Burnt Norton: 179
Burtt, L.A.: 9, 180, 196
Butler, Samuel: 197, 200
Butterfield, H.: 180, 196
Buytendijk, F.J.: 59
Byzantium: 202

Calendar of Modern Letters, The: 213
Cambridge Review: 53fn
Cambridge: 10, 182
Campion, Thomas: 190
Canterbury Tales, The: 188
Cantos, (Ezra Pound): 219
Carew, Thomas: 94
Carey, John: 197, 210
Carlyle, Thomas: 201
Carroll, Lewis: 112, 197
Cassatt, Mary: 151
Cassirer, Ernst: 2, 3-4, 9, 14, 24, 32
Castilione: 190, 191
Catcher in the Rye, The: 173
Caudfield, Holden: 173
Chaloner, Len: 112, 113, 138fn, 148 183, 184
Changeling, The: 190
Chapman, George: 190
Character of a Trimmer: 193
Charles Dickens and the Image of Woman: 159fn
Charles I, King: 195
Charles II, King: 195
Chaucer and His World: 189
Chaucer, Geoffrey: 24, 153
Christ, Jesus: 12, 41, 48, 89, 189, 197, 205, 206,
Civilisation and its Discontents: 203
Clarissa: 192, 197
Coleridge, S.T.: 111, 120ff., 132ff. 143fn, 182
Collier, Jeremy: 190, 195, 197, 198
Collingwood, R.G.: 68
Collins, William: 196, 197
Colours of Rage and Love, The: 57
Common Pursuit, The: 203
Comus: 194
Concept of Anxiety, The: 202, 211, 216,
Confucius: 54
Congreve, William: 195
Conrad, Joseph: 80
Copernicus: 192
Coriolanus: 168
Cormican, L.A.: 135fn
Costello, W.T.: 196
Country Wife, The: 195
Courage to Be: 32
Cowley, Abraham: 194
Cowper, William: 197
Cox, Marjorie: 179, 180
Crabbe, George: 139, 201 215
Crawshaw, Richard: 194
Crime and Punishment: 158
Crisis in European Sciences, The: 147
Critic, The: 196, 197
Culture and Anarchy: 201
Culture and Environment: 182
Culture and Society: 203
Curriculum at Seventeenth Century Cambridge, The: 196
Custom of the Country: 202

Dampier, William: 180, 196
Danby, J.F.: 193
Daniel Deronda: 200
Darwin, Charles: 5, 45
David Copperfield: 154, 172, 200, 211, 216
Dawson, Christopher: 60
De la Mare, Walter: 202
De Man, Paul: 42, 44
Defoe, Daniel: 194, 197
Dejection, an Ode: 129, 141, 142
Dekker, Thomas: 190
Delacroix: 130
Dell, E.: 196
Descartes, Rene: 60, 63, 72
Dialogue between the Body and the Soul: 50
Dickens, Charles: 1, 5, 9, 12, 14, 24, 32, 62, 66, 83, 86 152, 154, 169, 184, 186, 199
Dickinson, Emily: 13, 100ff., 106fn., 157, 200

Die Stellung de Menschen im Kosmos: 3
Disraeli, Benjamin: 200
Dvorak: 82
Doctor Faustus: 190
Doll's House, The: 25
Dombey and Son: 186, 200, 211, 216
Donne, John: 110, 115, 130, 191, 194, 195, 210, 211, 215
Dostoevsky, Feodor: 10, 86 158
Doughty Society, The: 47
Dover Beach: 14, 56, 200, 201
Dowland, John: 190
Downing College: 14, 43, 47, 53, 172
Drama and Society in the Age of Jonson: 192
Drayton, Michael: 190
Dryden, John: 194, 197, 198
Duchess of Malfi: 190
Dunbar, William: 188

East Coker: 179
Ecce Homo: 32
Ecclesiastes: 135
Eccliastical Polity: 190
Edge: 99
Education and Philosophical Anthropology: 183
Education and the University: 10, 30fn., 53, 59, 68 169, 172
Education, Nihilism and Survival: 213
Edward II: 190
Elegy in a Country Churchyard: 197
Eliot, George: 19, 135fn 184, 200, 211, 215, 216
Eliot, T.S.: 2, 23, 63, 67, 70, 150, 179, 180, 189, 196, 201, 203, 210, 211, 213, 215, 216, 219
Emma: 197
Empson, William: 76, 91, 104, 210
Endimion and Phoebe: 190
English for Maturity: 5
English Utilitarians, The: 201
Erasmus: 54
Erewon: 200
Essay on Criticism: 197, 201, 213
Essay on King Lear: 193
Essay on Man: 26, 197
Etteridge, Sir George: 194
Eve of St Agnes: 92ff. 97ff
Evelyn, John: 195
Existence and Being: 19
Existence: a New Dimension in Psychiatry: 15, 24, 61
Existential Philosophy: 62
Existential Psychotherapy: 15
Exploring Word, The: 206
Experimental College, The: 54

Fairbairn, W.R.D.: 155
Fairy Queen, The: 190, 191
Farnaby, Giles: 190fn.
Farquar, Sir George: 194
Father and Son: 201
Feeling and Perception in Young Children: 131, 138fn.,
Ferrobosco: 190
Fiction and the Reading Public: 207
Fiedler, Leslie: 44
Fielding, Henry: 196, 197, 215
Flaubert: 214
Flea, The: 210
Fletcher, J.: 22
Flight from Woman, The: 145
Florio, John: 190
Forster, E.M .: 202, 211, 216
Fortunes of Richard Mahoney: 131
Foudraine, Jan: 33
Four Quartets: 23, 67, 70, 79, 190, 201
Frankl, Victor: 32, 86, 173fn., 183
Franklin's Tale, The: 111, 112
Fraser, G.F.: 203
Free Man's Worship: 198f.
Freud, Sigmund: 10, 20, 24, 27, 33, 61, 90, 111
Freville, de: 194
From Classic to Romantic: 198
Frost at Midnight: 6-7, 111, 120fn., 129fn., 136, 204, 205, 209
Further Stud. in Phil. Anthropology: 42

Galileo: 8, 62, 192

Gaskell, Elizabeth: 200
Gay Science, The: 32
Gay, John: 196, 197
Gentleman's Magazine, The: 198
Gibbons, Orlando: 190
Gilbert: 192
Gladstone, W.G.: 156
Godwin, William: 213
Gogh van, Vincent: 130
Goldberg, Sam: 193 219
Goldsmith, Oliver: 176, 197, 198
Goneril: 168
Gonne, Maud: 214
Gonville and Caius, College: 217
Good Old Cause, The: 196
Gorboduc: 190
Gosse. Edmund: 201
Gothick Novel: 197, 198
Grace Abounding: 194,
Grainger, Percy: 131
Graves. Robert: 203
Gray, Thomas: 196
Great Expectations: 150ff. 200 211, 212, 216
Greece, Ancient: 42 178
Greene, Henry: 190
Grene, Marjorie: 7, 8, 9, 59, 65, 67, 69, 185, 203
Gulliver's Travels: 196
Guntrip, Harry: 33,

Hakluyt, Richard: 37, 108, 147, 185, 192, 203
Halifax, Lord: 30, 83, 147, 195, 200, 201, 206, 216
Hall, A R.: 85, 89, 107, 180, 183, 190
Hamlet: 66, 111, 154, 200, 210, 212, 216
Hard Times: 12, 131 200, 201 215
Harding, D.W.: 61
Hardy, Thomas: 97
Harvard Magazine: 42
Harvey, William: 192
Heart of Darkness, The: 202
Hegel: 24, 21
Heidegger, Martin: 11, 214
Henry IV: 192
Henryson, Robert: 180fn., 188, 196
Herbert of Cherbury, Lord: 195
Herbert, George: 195
Herrick, Robert: 194
Heyward, Thomas: 190
Hill, Christopher: 196
Hind and the Panther, The: 196
History of Science and its Relations with Philosophy and Religion: 180
History of the World: 190
Hobbes, Thomas: 199, 206, 210
Hockney, David: 130
Hoggart, Richard: 203
Holbrook, David: 203, 206
Holkham Hall: 190
Holy Sonnets: 201
Hooker, Richard: 190
Hopkins, Gerard Manley: 13
Horation Ode on Cromwell's Return from Ireland: 195
House of Mirth: 402
How to Teach Reading: a Primer for Ezra Pound: 51
Howards End: 202
Hudibras: 197, 216
Hugh Selwyn Mauberley: 202
Human Hope and the Death Instinct: 61
Human Idiom: Literature and Humanity: 203
Human World, The: 5, 6, 63 and fn
Humphreys A.R. :198
Husserl, Edmund: 8, 9, 19, 22fn., 27, 28, 33

Ibsen, Henrick: 25
Idea of a University, The: 15, 30
Iliad, The: 190
Images of Woman in Literature: 50
In Memoriam: 200
In the Hands of the Living God: 57

Jacobean Drama: 119
James, Henry: 23, 81, 100fn., 148, 153, 154, 202, 211, 215, 216
James, P.D.: 86

Jane Eyre: 200, 62
Jaspers, Karl: 18-23, 31fn., 34
Johnson, Samuel: 193, 190
Jonson, Ben: 190, 191, 194, 219
Joseph Andrews: 197, 198, 210, 215, 219
Journal of the History of Ideas: 62
Journal to Stella: 197
Joyce, James: 178, 208
Jubilate Agno: 198
Jude the Obscure: 83, 200
Jung, G.: 10, 211

Kafka, Franz: 80, 86, 168, 207, 214, 217
Keats, John: 48 57, 92ff., 166, 172
Kekulé: 89 135, 143, 156, 208
Kierkegaard, Soren: 12, 24, 25, 26, 27, 28, 29, 30, 31
Kindertotenlieder :140, 141, 183, 198, 215, 218
King Charles: 179
King James: 179
King Lear: 7, 14, 168, 194,
Kipling, Rudyard: 200
Klein, Melanie: 10, 192, 193, 219
Knights, L.C.:180 and fn
Knowledge of Man, The: 5, 6
Kubla Khan: 92, 198
Kyd, Thomas: 190

Lady Chatterley's Lover: 67, 53-71, 76, 84, 107, 108, 120, 135, 149
Lamb, Charles: 140ff.
Langer, Susanne: 3, 4, 56, 62, 64, 67, 83, 84, 113, 148, 153, 154
Law, William: 197
Lawrence, D.H.: 5-6, 9, 12, 13, 28, 32, 35, 56, 62, 65, 67, 83, 86, 113, 148, 153, 154, 198, 210, 211, 215, 216
Leavis, F.R.: 6, 20, 23, 24, 25, 27, 28, 30fn, 35, 44, 47, 95, 158, 169, 172, 173, 179, 180, 187, 211, 212, 213, 217, 229, 220
Leavis Q.D.: 159
Leavises, The: 54, 58fn
Levellers, The: 196
Leviathan: 194
Li Po: 56
Liebnitz: 108, 216
Life of Cowley: 210, 201, 203
Life of Johnson: 197, 187, 193, 196, 200, 203, 208, 203
Life versus Death in the Later Criticism of F.R Leavis: 60fn
Lilburne: 196,
Lime-tree Bower my Prison, The: 132ff
Lisbon Earthquake: 198
Little Athens, A: 200
Littie Dorrit: 148, 154, 203
Liturgy, The: 131-2
Living Principle, The: 203
Livingstone Lowe, John: 92
Locke, John: 64, 67 202, 203, 210, 211, 215 216
London: 197
Lonely Crowd, The: 203
Lost Bearings in English Poetry: 2, 6, 29, 220
Lover's Journey, The: 197
Love, Hate and Reparation: 143

Macbeth: 32
MacDonald, George: 200, 201
Machievelli: 191, 192
Mahler, Gustav: 100, 106, 128, 143, 166, 183, 189, 202
Mallarmé: 214
Malory, Sir Thomas: 188
Manifesto: 113-4,
Mansfield Park: 48, 153, 197, 218
Marcel, Gabriel: 28
Marcuse: 175
Margaret: 212
Mariana at the Moated Grange: 200
Marina: 63, 70, 220
Marlowe, Christopher: 191
Marshall: 189
Marvell, Andrew: 56, 98, 115, 124, 132, 196, 198, 210, 211,
Mary Barton: 200
Marx, Karl: 1, 26, 50 107, 196, 202
Maslow, Abraham: 32

Mason, H.A.: 219
Massinger, Philip: 190
Maud: 200
May, Rollo: 15, 23, 24, 135fn., 152, 172, 200
McGilchrist, lan: 45ff. 74
McLuhan, Marshall: 189
Meaning of Anxiety, The: 27, 61
Meaning: 6, 8, 120, 200, 212
Measure for Measure: 192
Meerlo, Joost de: 173 & fn, 174
Meeting at Night: 200
Melville, Herman: 13
Mental Secduction and Menticide: 174
Merleau-Ponty, Maurice: 107, 190
Metaphysicals, The: 179
Metaphysical Foundations of Modern Science: 9, 180, 196
Metaphysical Poets, The: 210
Micklejohn, Alexander: 54
Middleton, Thornas: 190, 191
Middlemarch: 14, 216
Middletown: 60
Mill, John Stewart: 201, 212, 213,
Mill on the Floss: 200
Mill on Bentham and Coleridge: 32, 190, 191
Milner. Marion: 56, 124
Milton, John: 11, 150, 157 184, 195, 197, 209
Moby Dick: 13, 69, 142, 172, 192, 214
Modern English Literature: 203
Modern Literary Theory: its Place in Teaching: 36
Modern Writer and His World, The: 203
Modest Proposal A: 197
Moll Flanders: 197
Monet, Claude: 130, 141
Montaigne: 190,
Moral Essays: 196
Moral Satires: 197
Morisot, Berthe: 130
Morley, Thomas: 190
Morris, William: 200
Mozart, Wolfgang Am.: 98, 106, 139
Muscatine: 188
Myers, L.H.: 202

Naevestad von, M.: 10
Nashe, Thomas: 104
Nazis: 18, 31
Near and the Far, The: 61, 202
New Heaven and Earth: 115
New Knowledqe in Human Values: 32
New Universities Quarterly: 41fn.,
New York Review of Books: 210, 203
Newman, John Henry: 19-20
Newton, Isaac: 64, 67, 71
Nietzsche: 19-20, 24, 25, 26, 27, 30, 31, 32,
Night Dances, The: 183 206, 209
North and South: 200
North, Sir Thomas: 72-85
Not Made of Wood: 33

Ode on the Intimations of Mortality: 199
Ode to Autumn: 135
Ode to Evening: 197
Ode to Himself: 206
Old Man: 186, 200, 208, 209
Old Wives Tale, The: 83, 84, 202
On Not Being Able to Paint: 124
On the Death of an Unfortunate Lady: 196
On the Death of Doctor Levett: 197
Origins of Love and Hate: 60
Origins of Modern Science: 196
Orwell, George: 202
Othello: 192
Otis, Brooks: 55
Our Mutual Friend: 154, 165
Owen, Wilfred: 202, 217
Owst, G.R.: 188
Oxford Illustrated History of Literature: 148
Oxford: 55

Portrait of a Lady: 100fn
Pamela: 197
Pantin, Professor C.F.: 131
Paradise Lost: 194, 195

Passage to India, A: 202
Pascal, Blakie: 23, 25
Pavlov: 148
Pearl: 188
Peele, George: 190
Pelican Guide to English Literature: 143ff 179
Pepys, Samuel: 195
Personal Knowledge: 28, 39-41, 131
Peter Grimes: 197
Phantastes: 200
Philosophy in a New Key: 4, 148
Philosophy and Psychoanalysis: 38fn
Phoenix: 203
Piers Plowman: 183
Pilgrims Progress, The: 194
Plath Sylvia: 99, 183, 206
Playing and Reality: 175
Pleasures of the Imagination: 197
Plumed Serpent, The: 67
Plutarch: 72-3
Polanyi, Michael: 3, 6, 7, 8, 22, 28, 38, 39, 41, 42, 46, 47, 59, 65, 68, 69, 70, 84, 89, 90, 91, 131
Poole, Roger: 27, 28, 52, 60, 61, 148
'Pop' the Manipulated Ritual: 175fn
Pope, Alexander: 13
Portrait of a Lady: 100fn., 202,
Portrait of an Age: 201
Portrait of Little T.C. in a Prospect of Flowers: 210
Portrait of the Artist as a Young Man: 202
Pound, Ezra: 53, 130, 190, 202, 219
Practical Criticism: 188, 209
Prayer for my Daughter: 202
Preface to the Lyrical Ballads: 212
Prelude, The: 39, 198
Prick up your Ears: 152fn
Pride and Prejudice: 197
Primary Maternal Preoccupation: 118fn
Primary World of Senses: 52, 148
Principles of Literary Criticism: 62
Procrastination: 197
Professor, The: 200
Prologue to the Canterbury Tales: 189
Prynne, Jeremy: 195
Psalms, The: 135
Puritanism and Revolution: 196

Rainborough, Colonel: 196
Rainbow, The: 67
Raleigh, Sir Waiter: 190, 191, 192
Rape of Lucretia, The: 190
Rasimov: 168
Reading and Criticism: 85, 92, 202, 216, 218
Receivinq Woman: 97
Reef, The:12, 54, 202
Renoir, Jean: 150
Renoir, my Father: 150
Retreat, The: 210
Return of the Native: 200
Revaluation: 203, 202, 210
Revenger's Tragedy, The: 190
Richard II: 193
Richards, I..A.: 7, 89
Richardson, Samuel: 197
Richter, Anne: 194
Rickman, H.P.: 34
Rickword, Edgell: 213
Rimbaud: 214
Riseman, David: 203
Rivers, Joan: 143
Road to Xanadu, The: 92, 130
Robinson Crusoe: 197
Robinson, lan: 56 and fn
Robson, W.W.: 203
Rosenberg, lsaac: 181
Rossetti, Christine: 200
Rothko: 130
Roxana: 97
Ruskin, John: 201
Russell, Bertrand: 198
Ruth: 167
Rutherford, Mark: 200

Safe in their Alabaster Chambers: 100ff
Sailing to Byzantium: 202
Saint Augustine: 23

Salingar, Leo: 143fn
Salinger, J.D.: 212
Samson Agonistes: 194
Santayana: 220
Sartre, Jean-Paul: 31 138
Satyr Against Mankind: 197
Say: 206
Scenes of Clerical Life: 200
Scheler, Max: 3, 26
Scholar Gypsy, The: 200
Scholes, Robert: 5, 51
School for Scandal, The: 196
Schumann, Robert: 100
Science and Poetry: 89, 148
Scientific Revolution, 1200-1800, The: 180
Scott, Walter: 197
Scrutiny: 30, 45fn, 136fn, 141, 182, 192
Secret Agent, The: 202, 216
Selden, John: 195, 198
Selected Essays: 192
Seneca: 190
A Serious Call (Law's): 197
Seven Types of Ambiguity, The: 76, 91, 210
Seventeenth Century Background: 180, 195
Shadwell, Thomas: 195
Shakespeare, William: 13, 14, 23, 32, 69, 73-81, 83, 86, 97, 111, 124, 130, 132, 135fn., 139, 142, 146, 148, 152fn., 163, 166, 190, 193fn., 194, 197, 198,
Shakespeare and the Idea of a Play: 194
Shakespeare's Doctrine of Nature: 194
Shaller Brown: 131
Shame as a Historiological Problem: 118-9
She Stoops to Conquer: 196, 197
She Would if She Could: 195
Shepherd's Calendar: 190, 191
Shepherd's Hay: 131
Sheridan, Richard Brinsley: 196
Schoenberg: 130
Short View of the Immorality and Profanity of the Englısh Stage, A: 195
Sidney, Sir Philip: 190
Signs of the Times: 201
Sir Gawaine and the Green Knight: 188
Smart, Christopher: 198
Smithies: 203
Smollett, Tobias: 196
Socrates: 54, 70
Song of a Man who is not Loved :115
Song of the Earth: 128
Songs and Sonnets: 110, 194
Songs of Innocence and Experience: 197
Sickness unto Death, The: 25, 27
Sons and Lovers: 153, 158, 202, 210
Sontag, Susan: 44
Sophocles: 145, 147
Southey, Robert: 136
Spenser, Eduundv 190, 191
Spiers, John: 158
Spinoza: 24
Stephen, Sir Leslie: 201
Stern Karl: 148
Stockhausen: 130
Straus, Erwin: 50 118, 149
Stravinsky, lgor: 204
Strickland: 44, 52
Structuralism or Criticism: 52
Stuart, Simon: 206
Suckling, Sir John: 194
Sunflower, The: 63
Surpris'd by Joy: 212
Surrey, Henry Howard, Earl of: 190
Suttie, lan D.: 10, 60, 61 & fn.
Swift, Jonathan: 196, 215
Swinburne: 200
Sybil: 200
Synge, J.M.: 102

Tacit Dimension, The: 54, 58fn., 203
Tale of a Tub: 197
Tamburlane: 190, 192
Tawney, R.H.: 25
Temple, The: 194, 210
Tennyson, Lord Alfred: 148 117
Tess of the d'Urbervilles: 36, 47, 50, 72
Thackeray, William M.: 216
Thomas, Edward: 202
Thompson, Denys: 54, 58fn.,
Thought after Flexner: 55
Thought, Words and Creativity: 8, 200, 216

Tillich: 24-25, 32, 200
Timber: 194
Times Literary Supplement, The: 42, 44
Times, The: 49
Timon of Athens: 80
Tintern Abbey: 198, 220
To His Coy Mistress: 98
To Little T.C. in a Prospect of Flowers: 124
Todorov, Tzvetan: 50, 210
Tourneur: 190, 191
Tolstoy, Leo: 32
Tom Jones: 197
Towards Deep Subjectivity: 148
Tragedy and the Medium: 193
Traherne, Thomas: 193, 194, 195
Traversi, Derek: 219
Triumph of Time, The: 200
Troilus and Cresseyde: 113, 188
Trollope, Anthony: 200
True Widow, The:195, 206, 216
Trumpet Major, The: 200
Twelfth Night: 166
Two in the Campagna: 108

Uexküll, J. von: 3
Ulanov, Anne:97
Under Western Eyes: 81, 168
Use of English, The: 34, 217
Uses of Literacy, The: 203

Vanity of Human Wishes: 197
Vaughan, Henry: 194, 195
Venus and Adonis: 190
Verlaine: 214
Vestigea Veteris Flammae: 202
Victory: 86
Villette: 200
Volpone: 190

Whitehead, A.N.: 9
Walsh, William: 203, 56, 122ff, 165, 175, 176, 182
War and Peace: 216, 154, 202, 216,
Warden, The: 200
Waste Land, The: 19, 42, 130, 186, 188,
Watson, George: 42, 82, 203, 206
Waugh, Evelyn: 38fn,
Way of the World, The: 195, 82
Webster, John: 21, 139, 190, 191, 197, 212, 216
Weldhen, Margaret: 34ff.
Wellek, Réné: 44
Wharton, Edith: 151
What Maisie Knew: 23, 159
Wheelwright's Shop, The: 202
Where Angels Fear to Tread: 202,
White Devil, The: 190
White Peacock, The: 85
Wilde Oscar: 200
Willey, Basil: 159fn., 180, 195, 198
Williams, Raymond: 47ff., 211, 214, 215
Wilson, Dover: 219
Winnicott, D.W.: 10-11
Winstanley: 195
Winter's Tale, A: 97, 197
Wisdom, John: 38fn.
Wives and Daughters: 200
Women Beware Women: 190, 216
Women in Love: 81
Women of Trachis: 130
Woodlanders, The: 200
Wordsworth, William: 37., 39, 41
Wuthering Heights: 56,, 159fn., 200
Wuthering Heights: A Drama of Being: 159fn
Wycherley, William: 195

Yalom, Irving D.: 15ff
Yeats.W.B.: 200, 208

Zangwill, Oliver: 18, 20